More Praise for *Negotiating at Work*

"Talent is the bedrock of every successful organization. As the workplace shifts from corporate ladder to corporate lattice principles, companies need to create environments where top talent can thrive. This book shows what individuals and organizations alike can do to make this happen now."

—**Cathy Benko, vice chairman and managing principal, Deloitte LLP**

"*Negotiating at Work* is for leaders and organizations looking to bridge the gap between wanting to improve the diversity of senior leadership and actually doing it. It is an invaluable guide to creating a culture that enables all of our most talented leaders to succeed. A very worthy read!"

—**David A. Thomas, PhD, dean, William R. Berkley Professor, McDonough School of Business, Georgetown University; coauthor, *Breaking Through: The Making of Minority Executives in Corporate America***

"If it were only about having the 'right' experience, we wouldn't have the lack of women in senior leadership we do today. There are still barriers—seen and unseen—that block women from the top. Learning how to negotiate these is a must for women and the organizations that need them to succeed. This book shows you how. I highly recommend it!"

—**Herminia Ibarra, the Cora Chaired Professor of Leadership and Learning, INSEAD**

"The fact is that the world is not a level playing field—especially for women. Deborah Kolb's latest book will challenge the status quo: it argues that negotiation is a litmus test for advancement. That we all overlook daily opportunities to turn small wins into much bigger gains. And that those bigger gains are powerful game-changers for us as individuals, and for our organizations that desperately need to help pave the way for a more diversified pool of leaders. Adopt Kolb's new approach and practices, and you will help create a better world in which progressive, modern leadership approaches pervade."

—**John Gerzema, chairman, CEO, WPP Group's BAV Consulting; *New York Times* best-selling author, including *The Athena Doctrine: How Women (and the Men Who Think Like Them) Will Rule the Future***

"Big change starts small. When we learn how to advocate and negotiate for the things that help us succeed at work, it can have a profoundly positive effect on others, in all parts of our lives. Deborah Kolb's contribution of bringing this idea into clear, practical focus is awesome!"

—**Stew Friedman, author, *Leading the Life You Want* and *Total Leadership***

"Tremendously resonant for women everywhere—across cultures, professions, or career stage. Deborah Kolb helps women see they can choose this *and* that instead of this *or* that in a way that brings meaningful change for them and those that follow."

—**Vicki Wilde, founder, former director, African Women in Agricultural Research and Development (AWARD)**

"My daughter Allison is a VP of Intuit, and I've told her that *Negotiating at Work* is a must-read for every woman executive. Building on Kolb's earlier seminal work, this book provides practical advice for executives whose critical negotiations typically take place within organizations and in the context of ongoing relationships. By providing a conceptual framework for thinking about how negotiations play out in organizations, the book suggests how 'small wins' can be used to change an organization's culture and accumulate to big gains."

—**Robert H. Mnookin, Williston Professor of Law; director of the Harvard Negotiation Research Project; chair, Program on Negotiation, Harvard Law School**

"There is nobody better placed than Deborah Kolb to write the book on negotiating positive change for women in the workplace. From decades of advising some of the country's most successful women, Dr. Kolb shares her knowledge on how to frame and negotiate issues that can impede a woman's career—steps that can have a profoundly positive effect on others and on the organization as a whole. Simply a must-read!"

—**Robin Ely, Diane Doerge Wilson Professor of Business Administration, Senior Associate Dean for Culture and Community, Harvard Business School**

"Are you trying to hammer out agreements on budgets, hiring lines, priority for your projects, or buy-in from senior management? Let Deborah Kolb's new book be your trustworthy guide to solving these and the host of other tricky negotiations every leader faces at the office. Research-based, easy-to-read, and actionable, *Negotiating at Work* will show you how to get great deals even as you enhance your organizational credibility."

—**G. Richard Shell, author, *Bargaining for Advantage*; director, Wharton School's Executive Negotiation Workshop**

"This is a must-read for all women negotiating at work—and for those who are supporting their careers. It goes beyond the common perceptions and the academic research to advocate, but provides proven and highly practical negotiating strategies and tactics. Debbie Kolb has made another essential and insightful contribution to winning in the workplace—for yourself and your organization."

—**Sheila Penrose, chairman, JLL; cochairman, Corporate Leadership Center**

"Debbie Kolb has the unique ability to integrate respected research and personal stories of accomplished executives into lessons we can all benefit from as we negotiate for career success. *Negotiating at Work* captures her years of experience working with executives generally, and women in particular, to provide examples that anyone can adapt to change the game within their organization. The big lesson is that by negotiating on our own behalf, we can improve the odds of success for others and for the organization as a whole. *Negotiating at Work* is a compelling read because each of us can put its practical advice to work, at work and at home, as soon as we put the book down."

—**Cheryl A. Francis, cochairman, Corporate Leadership Center**

"*Negotiating at Work* provides vital new insights that strengthen our understanding of negotiation as a tool for individual gain, while expanding its potential for organizational change. Deborah Kolb and Jessica Porter reveal how negotiations occur in organizational contexts, which in turn shape what is legitimate to negotiate and how negotiations are received. By focusing on negotiations around everyday issues in the workplace, such as work schedules and resources to do one's job, the authors broaden our conception of what can be negotiated and how individual negotiations can both lead to small wins for the individual and change organizational practices for the betterment of others. This framework illuminates how challenging the status quo can create opportunities to examine assumptions, norms, and practices that may be holding individuals and organizations back."

—**Shelley J. Correll, professor of sociology, the Barbara D. Finberg Director of the Clayman Institute for Gender Research, Stanford University**

"Deborah Kolb, one of the foremost experts in women and leadership, has created an extraordinary guide. It presents the best research, compelling and instructive case studies, and the most practical solutions you will find anywhere to help women—and men—negotiate small wins that create big gains for themselves *and* their organizations. A not-to-be-missed book!"

—**Ellen Galinsky, president, Families and Work Institute**

"This deeply researched and case study–driven book does an exceptional job of laying out the subtle, yet very real, challenges women face in the workplace that can derail careers and offers the precise strategies and tools needed to negotiate them well. This book will drive immediate change for women and the organizations that need them."

—**Linda Babcock, James M. Walton Professor of Economics, Carnegie Mellon University; coauthor, *Women Don't Ask***

"Every man and woman concerned with increasing the success of his or her career and organization should read this book. Kolb and Porter frame negotiation in three startling new ways: as a means for awakening us all to the assumptions, biases, and arrangements that constrain our opportunities and effectiveness at work; as a technique for members of marginalized groups to change the conversation and thrive at work; and as a potential tipping-point event leading to the kinds of reforms and re-visioning of our places of work that can make us proud and prosperous. Read it."

—**Peter Coleman, professor, psychology and education; director, International Center for Cooperation and Conflict Resolution, Columbia University**

"I love this book. It is filled with ideas about how women can negotiate for changes that benefit themselves, but which can also help the company as a whole. These ideas will help women at all levels of an organization, but the insights also apply more broadly. I wish I had read it years ago."

—**Dr. Paul D. McKinnon, Harvard Business School; former head of HR, Dell and Citigroup**

"*Negotiating at Work* will walk you through what does and what does not work in day-to-day negotiations at organizations, covering a wide range of topics such as how to deal with resistance, identify problems, recognize negotiating opportunities, offer creative solutions, build bridges with your negotiation partners, and claim your value. If you want to successfully negotiate for yourself and your organization, this is a must-read book, full of practical research-based ideas, insightful for the just emerging to the most senior professionals."

—**Boris Groysberg, professor, Harvard Business School; author, *Chasing Stars: The Myth of Talent and the Portability of Performance***

"The unnerving reality is that most organizations still struggle to ensure that the best minds get to the top. Women, especially, must take full advantage of every available skill, tool, and opportunity to advance. Deborah Kolb makes a fresh argument in her latest and best book yet, *Negotiating at Work*, as she shows how we all can better capitalize on every day's 'small wins' for greater gains—for ourselves, for the women around and behind us, and for our organizations. I recommend this book wholeheartedly because in these times, when women win, we all win. Buy a copy for yourself—and send one to someone you mentor—today."

—**Mary Davis Holt, partner, Flynn Heath Holt; *New York Times* best-selling author, *Break Your Own Rules***

"I recommend *Negotiating at Work* to everyone who believes in their greater potential. Regardless of your level, you'll gain strategies and skills that have the power to reshape assignments, advancement, and even lives for the benefit of you, those around you, and those who follow you. This book is also for those in positions to eliminate institutional biases that get in the way of many talented leaders."

—**Farah Pandith, key architect, Women in Public Service Project; consultant, author, and speaker**

NEGOTIATING AT WORK

TURN SMALL WINS INTO BIG GAINS

Deborah M. Kolb
with Jessica L. Porter

A Wiley Brand

Published by Jossey-Bass
A Wiley Brand
One Montgomery Street, Suite 1200, San Francisco, CA 94104-4594—www.josseybass.com

Jossey-Bass books and products are available through most bookstores. To contact Jossey-Bass directly call our Customer Care Department within the U.S. at 800-956-7739, outside the U.S. at 317-572-3986, or fax 317-572-4002.

Wiley publishes in a variety of print and electronic formats and by print-on-demand. Some material included with standard print versions of this book may not be included in e-books or in print-on-demand. If this book refers to media such as a CD or DVD that is not included in the version you purchased, you may download this material at http://booksupport.wiley.com. For more information about Wiley products, visit www.wiley.com.

Library of Congress Cataloging-in-Publication Data

Kolb, Deborah M.
  Negotiating at work : turn small wins into big gains / Deborah M. Kolb, with Jessica L. Porter.—First edition.
    pages cm
  Includes bibliographical references and index.
  ISBN 978-1-118-35241-0 (hardback)
  1. Negotiation in business. 2. Negotiation. I. Porter, Jessica L., 1969– II. Title.
  HD58.6.K664 2015
  658.4'052–dc23

                                                    2014032141

Printed in the United States of America
FIRST EDITION
HB Printing 10 9 8 7 6 5 4 3 2 1

CONTENTS

PREFACE

You might say that this book came about as a result of a negotiation. Several years ago a group of editors informed me that my book *Everyday Negotiation* would go out of print unless I revised it. I remember thinking this seemed not so much like a reality but like a bluff—a standard ploy in negotiation. But it got me thinking about what I wanted to write now, ten years later, in a book on negotiation and gender. When Judith Williams and I wrote *The Shadow Negotiation* in 2000 and then revised it for *Everyday Negotiation* in 2003, we were responding to dominant themes in the popular and scholarly fields about the negotiation process and how women fare in it.

The dominant discourse at the time was that women negotiate differently from men, and that compared to men, they come out deficient. In our interviews for those books, we set out to dig deeper and find out more about women's actual experiences when they negotiate. In so doing, we identified two nested challenges that women (and men) face: to be effective advocates for themselves at the same time that they try to establish collaboration and connection with other parties. By exploring these challenges—we called them the hidden agendas of bargaining—as well as how successful women (and then men) dealt with them, we identified what we called the *shadow* negotiation. The idea was that in our efforts to tell people how to get to yes and make good deals, we had not paid enough attention to the hidden challenges parties face to get themselves into a good position to negotiate and establish a good working relationship with the other person. Although *The Shadow Negotiation* began with a study of women, it was clear that what we described had implications for everybody who negotiates. Indeed, when the book was named by the *Harvard Business Review* as one of the ten best books of 2000, its general application to all negotiators was identified as one of its major strengths. We think this is true for *Negotiating at Work* as well.

Despite the initial overture from the editors, I knew I wasn't interested in revising *Everyday Negotiation*, for a number of reasons. The most obvious one is that *Everyday Negotiation* was already a revision; going back to it was like going back a decade in my own thinking and revising the book at its margins. I had no energy for that. What I wanted was to integrate the work I'd been doing on gender, leadership, and change into a practical book on negotiation for all leaders, but especially women. Trouble was, I didn't know how to do it.

Over the past fifteen years while I was the Deloitte Ellen Gabriel Professor for Women and Leadership at Simmons College School of Management and after retirement, I've been involved in both leading and participating in Women's Leadership Development Programs (WLPs). In them, I always teach a negotiation module that asks participants to focus on issues they want to negotiate at work. This is a departure from the negotiations we considered in *Everyday Negotiation*, where we covered a wide spectrum of bargaining situations. Those included the many places in which people negotiate: buying cars, dealing with office space, rallying community boards, convincing loan officers to lend, engaging faculty colleagues, seeking refunds on travel, and other such topics.

What distinguished the negotiation topics in the WLPs were that the women were negotiating for *themselves*—as principals, not as agents. At first, I used the frameworks from the *Shadow Negotiation* in these programs, programs that I ran in corporations and in nongovernmental organizations in the United States and abroad. Over time, as I listened to the stories of these participants, I began to see new facets of negotiation that I hadn't noticed before. I started to appreciate nuances in how these women (and some men) handled tricky situations in their organizations. Over time, I began to capture their stories. These stories became the data for this book.

Several examples are especially salient for understanding the trajectory of this book and how it differs from the previous ones. Leading Women Executives, a Chicago-based program for senior-level women from different companies who attend a multisession program, has been an important site of learning for me. As academic advisor as well as an instructor, I develop a strong working relationship with the participants. That relationship gives us multiple occasions to discuss their negotiation experiences. At the conclusion of one of the programs, a graduate saying good-bye to me whispered in my ear that I had changed her life. *Wow,* I thought. *What is that story?* It is a fascinating one—and it appears in this book. That led me to become more deliberate about capturing the stories about how these women and others used the negotiation module to get something they previously thought was not achievable.

The second incident occurred in another program where we taped women negotiating their own everyday negotiation, and we did the role play twice. The first time was after the negotiation module; the second time was after colleagues Robin Ely and Carole Levy did a session on leading with purpose. Two insights came from that experience: first, that one has to create occasions to negotiate at work—they are not always obvious—and, second, that focusing on the link between what is good for you *and for your organization* seems to work better at engaging the other party. We discovered this in the videos of the role play, as well as in the results the women reported. This experience led me to consider the various ways that people situate their negotiations in the context of ongoing relationships. It also helped me see that those who can connect their interests to their organizations are empowered to advocate more forcefully for what they want.

A third experience comes from a story that a very senior leader told in one of the programs. She wanted to negotiate a complicated office arrangement with her CEO. They had a good working relationship, but she expected this to be a difficult negotiation. In her story, she described how she let him know of her accomplishments to remind him of her value. But she also let him know of the other choices she had—in a way that was appreciative and nonconfrontational. Although we'd written about making one's value visible in *Everyday Negotiation*, this story made me look deeper into the ways that experienced executives do so. Where we had talked about raising the costs of the status quo in the earlier book, I was never confident about how one could do that and not raise the other party's ire. I had dropped it from my teaching. But from this story, I could see how a seasoned executive could do this smoothly, and that led me to collect other stories that led to developing the ideas about an "iron fist in a velvet glove."

A fourth experience led me to consider the limits of some of the strategies in the earlier books. This was particularly true in the context of "moves and turns." The idea behind "moves" is that other negotiators can say things that can make you feel defensive. "Turns" are actions that enable you to respond. *Moves and turns* is something that people associate with the earlier books. I've written more about them, and the papers and chapter have been reproduced in a number of publications. (We consider moves and turns in chapter 6 in this book.) However, in my experiences, especially in Africa and Asia but also Europe, I came to see the limits of some of the turns one might recommend. I remember vividly being called out by a dean at a university in East Africa who said to me, "I could never use that turn." So in this book, we are both more detailed in describing moves and turns and more circumspect in what we recommend.

Negotiating at Work is informed in another way from my teaching with executives. Over the past decade, and even before that, I've been involved in two different types of projects that touch on gender and change. The first was a series of research and intervention projects that focused on understanding the ways in which an organization's policies and practices that appeared gender neutral could have unintended but differential impacts on different groups of men and women. We later came to call these types of policies and practices *second-generation gender bias*. With funding from the Ford Foundation and under the banner of the Center for Gender in Organizations at Simmons College School of Management, I worked with a group of colleagues, including Lotte Bailyn, Robin Ely, Joyce Fletcher, Deborah Merrill-Sands, Debra Meyerson, and Rhona Rapoport, to uncover these types of practices within organizations. Then in collaboration with organizations, among them the Body Shop, and several international nongovernmental organizations, we tried to identify some small wins. We thought of these as experiments, pilot projects: many of them had to do with expectations about time at work, as well as how unexamined role requirements contributed to gender inequities in these organizations.

The second project is tied more directly to my teaching. I have incorporated this perspective—identifying workplace policies and practices that may have unintended consequences for women leaders—into many of the WLPs that I lead. We call the session *strategizing leadership dilemmas*. In it, cohorts from the same organization, a company or a division, spend a session identifying these second-generation biases, develop some practical ideas about potential small wins, and then craft strategies to make the small wins a reality. In truth, some succeed more than others. But what I have found in hearing the stories is that when cohorts have been successful in getting small wins started, many started with an individual negotiating some change in her own working conditions or status. These negotiation experiences led her to take more leadership in spreading the word about her situation or directly initiating other changes. We report some of these small wins throughout the book and suggest in chapter 8 ways that they may have broader impact.

Negotiating at Work has been a few years in the writing but many more years in the evolution of its ideas. Some I have already mentioned, such as my colleagues on the Ford Foundation–funded research projects where together we learned about ways to think and talk about gender in organizational contexts. Kathleen McGinn and I brought that perspective to negotiations first at a conference at the Kennedy School of Government in 2008 and then in a paper in 2009. When I turned to writing chapter 6 in this book, I was happy to rediscover that Kathleen and I had developed a coding sheet for moves and turns that proved very helpful to the writing. But it was really in the context of the WLPs that the ideas for this book came together.

Cheryl Francis, Sheila Penrose, and Diane Sakach of the Corporate Leadership Center in Chicago run an amazing program for women leaders, Leading Women Executives, that I have been associated with since 2009. Collaborating with them has given me an incomparable platform to develop the ideas set out in this book. Their commitment to advancing women leaders sets a culture for learning and experimentation that one finds only rarely in a leadership program. It was Debra Meyerson, my good colleague, who initially brought me into that program, and I am always grateful to her for what we've learned together over the years. I've been able to involve great colleagues in this program as well—Debra Noumair, Robin Ely, Stacy Blake-Beard, Sue Ashford, and Melissa Thomas-Hunt—and together we've learned about creating WLPs that make a difference in women's lives and especially in the organizations in which they work.

When the leaders at Leading Women Executives wanted to increase their leverage with organizations, their first step was to survey the literature on gender and leadership and turn this study into a usable model for organizations. That is when Jessica Porter joined the project. She had already been working with us on other WLPs, but now she would become our team's expert on gender and leadership. It became clear to me that her knowledge and expertise would enhance this book considerably. We agreed that as junior author, she would take responsibility for bringing her knowledge about gender and negotiation (and later more generally negotiation) into creating extensive notes that would make the book a valued resource to people who want to use the book in classrooms and for research. I have also worked with Herminia Ibarra, Carole Levy, Amy Anuk, Vera Vitels, and Kristin Normandin in other WLPs, and each has contributed to the ways I teach and do this work. Debra Noumair at Columbia Teachers College has been my partner in crime in developing our version of WLPs. She also brought me into her Executive Masters Program in Change Leadership, where I've tested these ideas with both men and women. Lotte Bailyn has been my mentor for more years than I choose to remember, and it is at our breakfasts that I get feedback on my ideas. So too in my regular meals with Jean Bartunek, Robin Ely, Joyce Fletcher, Kathy Kram, Hannah Bowles, Kathleen McGinn, and Karen Golden-Biddle. I leave each of these sessions nourished and ready to go back to work with a way out of the puzzles I present to them. Linda Putnam has been a wonderful partner and coauthor in developing many of the ideas about interdependence that now figure so prominently in this book. It was Carol Frohlinger in our teaching collaboration who came up with the idea of n-negotiation as differentiated from formal deal making, which is the way we describe negotiating at work. Mike Wheeler, Larry Susskind, Robert Mnookin, Jim Sebenius, and Bill Ury of the Program on Negotiation at Harvard Law School have always cheered my work, even though it is quite different from theirs.

Kathe Sweeney, formerly of Jossey-Bass, has been an editor and friend over the course of three books. For this one, she had to endure my continual excuses for missed deadlines. Rob Brandt then stepped aboard and has kept a steady hand on the helm, even when the seas sometimes get a bit rough. Christine Moore amazed us with her insightful editing of the book.

How can I express enough gratitude to Tim Murphy, our stalwart editor of this book? First, he had to figure out how to work with a person, me, who was clearly not writing the book, and then had to ramp up when things speeded up. His way with words—well, you can see.

I look to my children, Sam and Elizabeth, and their spouses, Karin and Greg, to learn how the younger generation deals with workplace negotiations. They should not be surprised to recognize some of their stories, well disguised, in this book. Their children, Jacob, Alexandra, Isaac, and Eli, are my diversions. My husband, Jonathan, is the patient listener and sounding board. Our dinner conversations are peppered with negotiation stories, where we continually find connections between my stories and what he hears in his work, a broader reality test for the ideas. He has been as always a great support even though nonfiction is not his favorite genre.

Finally, two notes about pronouns in the text. Because this is a book about—among other things—hidden gender bias, we've struggled with that famous flaw in the English language: what to do with the generic third-person singular. For obvious reasons, we can't simply accept the masculine "he" or "him." To use "they" or "their" as a singular justifiably erodes credibility with some readers. Such tricks as "he/she" or "s/he" come off as cheap gimmicks, and repetition of "he or she" and "him and her" is plain clunky. So our solution is to keep the singular pronoun and alternate between the genders—and may no man or woman feel excluded in the bargain. In sections about teaching or seminars, you'll sometimes see the first-person singular. That's me, Deborah Kolb. Plural first-person pronouns refer to me and Jessica Porter, and sometimes my other teaching colleagues.

November 2014   Deborah M. Kolb

A number of people influenced and supported me while writing this book. I thank all of the women I've met at Women's Leadership Development Programs who have shared their stories and experiences, as well as the friends and acquaintances who discussed their own negotiations with me. I'm grateful to Debra Noumair, Kathleen McGinn, and of course Deborah Kolb for helping me push my thinking and expand my areas of expertise. My friend Bob tirelessly brainstormed book title ideas, as did my patient spouse and true partner, Matthew. My teenage children, Emma and Jackson, have

The Seattle Public Library

Central Library

Visit us on the Web: www.spl.org

Checked Out Items 11/15/2019 16:17
XXXXXXXXX7501

Item Title	Due Date
0010089626468	12/6/2019
Negotiating at work : turn small wins into big gains	

# of Items: 1

Balance Due: $6.50

Renewals: 206-386-4190
TeleCirc: 206-386-9015 / 24 hours a day
Online: myaccount.spl.org

Pay your fines/fees online at pay.spl.org

provided me with the ongoing opportunity to practice negotiating with worthy counterparts. My parents, Tom and Judy, raised me in a dual-career family where work was a common topic of conversation. It was a great foundation for understanding the importance of negotiating for oneself at work, particularly for women.

November 2014   Jessica L. Porter

INTRODUCTION

Negotiating in the Shadow of Organizations

In the executive leadership programs that I teach, frequently to women leaders, I ask participants to come prepared to negotiate about something that matters to them. In addition to negotiations occurring in communities and families, I am particularly interested in those that take place in organizations. People often want to negotiate for more responsibility or a change in title, the goal of more than 60 percent of participants in one recent program. Yet the negotiations can vary widely. Some had a change agenda they wanted to pursue. Some were looking for financing for a new venture, others just more resources for an ongoing project. Others wanted more exposure for their work. Some wanted to achieve better integration between their work and personal lives; they were seeking a decreased workload or more assistance to make that possible. Some wanted to take on expanded roles in community or business associations.

These negotiation issues, and the contexts in which they occur, differ from programs that focus more on structured negotiations where parties typically act as agents for their respective organizations. Yet usually when we think of negotiation, it is those more formal situations that come to mind: mergers, legal settlements, salary, partnerships, purchasing agreements, and structured deals.

Merriam-Webster even defines *negotiation* this way: as "a formal discussion between people who are trying to reach an agreement."[1]

A great deal of study and expertise has been devoted to these formal negotiations—the kinds that take place between countries over borders or between companies over mergers and acquisitions, over sales and purchasing agreements, and between buyers and sellers generally. Best practices have been catalogued by many well-known scholars and practitioners in the field for these kinds of negotiations.[2]

Hundreds of studies, conducted primarily in research laboratories, have contributed to the public's understanding of what it takes to realize joint gains in a negotiation: the ability to make deals that create value for all parties, as well as the barriers to making this happen.[3] This work has been invaluable, helping negotiators in many settings manage the bargaining process so they can design deals that create value for the parties involved.[4]

WHY THIS BOOK? AND WHY NOW?

For all the value this work has brought to formal negotiations, it still misses some of the crucial dynamics that occur when people negotiate for themselves in organizations over issues that matter to them.

In order to work with those dynamics, we begin by identifying two distinct kinds of negotiation. In chapter 1, we fully distinguish *N-negotiations*, formal bargaining over contacts and agreements, from *n-negotiations*, which are unstructured and more personal. The lowercase variety is trickier: it's the kind in which you find yourself advocating for something you want in an organization. Think, for a minute, about what Madeleine Albright, Condoleezza Rice, and Hillary Clinton experienced when they negotiated with foreign governments. Despite any setbacks they had, they negotiated as representatives of the United States with all of the authority and formality that connotes. Now think about Lilly Ledbetter, who successfully sued Goodyear Tire and Rubber for pay discrimination after she retired. During her career at Goodyear, we can imagine the kinds of n-negotiations Ledbetter engaged in—attempting to get her contributions recognized, to get promoted, and to be compensated equitably for her work. As Lilly Ledbetter found, in n-negotiations setbacks are more consequential for our careers and well-being.

This book focuses primarily on those n-negotiations we all have at work. Along the way, we aim to:

- Demonstrate that n-negotiations have some features that draw on more classic N-negotiations. Yet they also present fundamentally different kinds of challenges. In n-negotiations, these are *our* issues, and it is up to us to raise the subjects of the negotiation and the process by which we will conduct it. No preexisting structures for negotiation—formal diplomatic meetings—exist. We create the structure and process as we initiate the dialogue.
- Reveal some of the ways in which organizations are anything but a level playing field on which to negotiate. You can bet that, like Lilly Ledbetter, you'll meet resistance when introducing certain topics and issues. We discuss tactics for meeting that resistance.
- Provide practical tools for your own n-negotiations no matter what your gender, ethnicity, or place in the hierarchy might be. These tools help you prepare and position yourself to get the n-negotiations off the ground and give you practical advice for how to keep a difficult negotiation on track.
- Convince you that the n-negotiations you successfully bring to the table can improve not just your own life at work, but also the life of your whole organization.

Let's start with a brief summary of what distinguishes these everyday n-negotiations and then connect them to the broader issue of gender and negotiation.

The Negotiated Order

In his 1978 book, *Negotiations*, Anselm Strauss criticized the negotiation field for its tendency to treat all negotiations as the same and so minimize the ways they're shaped by the organizational situations in which they occur and the problems they address.[5] As our students report, negotiations at work occur around a range of everyday activities. In addition to the usual topics of compensation and employment, we constantly negotiate about what kind of work we do, what jobs we have, what resources we need, our goals and objectives, our work schedules, the work itself, and our roles, resources, and goals.

Organizations shape negotiable topics. If these are the subjects of negotiation, it's also important to recognize that these issues are negotiated in organizational contexts that shape which issues are considered legitimate topics for negotiation and how they're treated. Strauss calls this the *negotiated order*—which suggests that an organization's structure, policies, and practices are the results of previous negotiations. Negotiations describe the activities involved in designing jobs, doing work, avoiding work, achieving status, and establishing boundaries of authority and responsibility, among a host of other potential issues. When we teach negotiation workshops, the issues people want to negotiate reflect their desire to negotiate about some aspect of the negotiated order in their organization.

Who is a negotiator? A second feature of negotiated orders is what it means to be a party in a negotiation. Traditional negotiating contexts conjure up images of buyers and sellers. But in n-negotiations, the parties are employees (bosses, peers, subordinates) who work in corporations, government, nonprofit and profit-making institutions, and universities. What matters to them, the options they develop, and the choices they make are influenced by their status and roles, as well as by their individual dispositions and interests. Certain people or groups may—because of their position, gender, or other attributes—have power in a negotiation to define what is negotiable.[6] To negotiate with a senior leader when one is considerably junior is not something people undertake lightly, especially when one is raising an issue that a more senior person might not recognize as one worthy of negotiation.

Problems and opportunities: Many potential negotiations aren't obvious. Third, because potentially negotiable issues are part of organizational routines, they are not as readily obvious or identifiable as having potential for negotiation, the way something like a contract or a formal dispute might be. They are created out of people's everyday experiences of potential disagreement and discontent.[7] These issues, basically the need to negotiate a problem, can result from disadvantage or perceived lack of fairness. Let's say that in your organization, leaders are expected to spend time in an overseas assignment in order to progress to senior ranks. Yet you are not asked to do so because it is assumed that your family situation means you're not available for such an assignment. This is a problem, and it's up to you to find the right occasion to negotiate about it.

Negotiations can also come about because somebody wants to change something—that is, negotiate an opportunity. The range of problems professional women negotiated about, according to a recent study, included a lack of recognition, being passed over for promotion, and organizational politics. The range of opportunities included leadership roles, promotions, mobilizing resources, and advancing new ideas.[8]

Each negotiation adds to the negotiated order. The fourth feature of a negotiated order is that organizational structure, practices, and policies are products of previous negotiations. Negotiating history provides the ongoing context within which a particular negotiation takes place. And a person's experience and reputation will also influence a current negotiation. This means that individuals have the potential to change the negotiated order—what becomes negotiable can change, and the very practices that are the subject of negotiations are potentially altered as well.

We continually shape the negotiated order. This feature is especially important when we consider how gender intersects with negotiated orders and the implications for different groups to negotiate issues that are important to them. Over time, efforts toward change may be successful, and others can feel empowered to raise issues that were not previously part of an organization's policies and practices. One way to understand the emergence of flexible work and family policies, for example, is as the result of individuals who first negotiated individual arrangements. These requests (negotiations) accumulate until leaders take the initiative to institutionalize flexible work policies and programs. Negotiating a leave or flexible schedule is different if you are the first ever to do so, since you're challenging a negotiated order; it's easier when others have already done so. And it's still more different if there is an organizational policy in place. When the executives in our seminars step up to negotiate about some aspect of their work, they are altering the negotiated order in small ways. These informal negotiations in organizations are n-negotiations and thus different from the N-negotiations that people typically think of.

GENDER AND THE NEGOTIATED ORDER

To consider n-negotiations gives us a different way to understand gender in negotiation. The topic of gender in organizations has been the subject of considerable research over the past forty years. In 1977, Rosabeth Moss Kanter performed the first major examination of women's roles in organizations, bringing attention to many of the phenomena we still see today: tokenism, for example, and leaders hiring in their own image.[9] In the years since, researchers from every discipline—economics, sociology, psychology, organization behavior, law, political science, education—have explored the impact of gender on individuals and at a collective level in institutions and organizations. More recently, dialogue about gender and leadership has become a more frequent topic in the mainstream, sparked in part by public conversations around books such as Sheryl Sandberg's *Lean In*, which offers advice for women to embrace professional achievement and take on larger leadership roles.[10]

Despite forty years of research to understand gender bias in organizations, women continue to be underrepresented at the highest ranks. Though women constitute nearly 50 percent of the labor force and graduate from college in greater numbers than men, they are still not anywhere near parity in the senior positions of corporations, professional services partnerships, governments, and large-scale international organizations.[11] Among S&P 100 companies, women make up only 19 percent of board of director positions, and the representation is even more disconcerting at the senior executive level: only 8 percent of the highest-paid S&P 100 executives are women.[12] Less than 10 percent of heads of state and heads of government worldwide are women.[13] At the current rate of change, it's unlikely that women will reach parity in any of these spheres soon.[14]

In *Lean In*, Sandberg presents the chicken-and-egg dilemma of gender inequality: Do women need to first address inequality on an individual level, overcoming their internal barriers (the chicken) to demand more responsibility and leadership roles? Or do we—as individuals and in organizations—need to address the external barriers (the egg) to women's parity by addressing the systemic and organizational issues that make it harder for women to move up?[15] Sandberg focuses on the chicken in her book, with tips for addressing those internal barriers, including those at home, which keep women from putting themselves forward.

We too believe that negotiation is a critical skill for women who want to "lean in." The ability and confidence to ask for opportunities—resources, new projects, buy-in, and promotion—is critical for any person who wants to be successful. This is even more important for people who don't look like our typical leaders: women and minorities. These groups are less likely to be asked, so they need to do the asking themselves.

When individuals negotiate within the context of the negotiated order, they address more than just their own circumstances. In fact, negotiating allows us to have an impact on the order and address systemic issues as well, much like Sandberg's egg. The example of flexible work applies here, since this is usually a case when policies are established after individuals negotiate agreements for themselves. Another example is that of performance metrics: by negotiating for clear criteria for promotion, we not only help ourselves in our own career, we also encourage objective standards for performance that will be important to everyone in the organization, particularly those who are more likely to be judged subjectively. It is this potential for individual small wins to lead to bigger gains that makes negotiation such a powerful tool for both women and men in organizations, a theme we revisit throughout this book.

Gender Issues in Negotiation

The major approaches to understanding how gender plays out in negotiation extend beyond individual behavior. Gender is embedded in organizational policies and practices, largely due to the fact that organizations, many of which at least begin as male-dominant institutions, build formal structure and informal norms around gendered notions of work and behavior. These create a gendered negotiated order that forms the context for the strategies and tactics outlined in the book.

There has been an explosion of research on the topic of gender within the field of negotiation.[16] Much of this work has been motivated by concerns about the gender gap in wages and achievement—the glass-ceiling effect—that causes women in organizations to plateau before they reach top leadership positions.[17] Furthermore, women are estimated to earn up to 40 percent less than men over the course of their careers.[18] This compensation gap has been growing recently, particularly among women of color.[19] While there are many societal and organizational explanations for these phenomena,[20] women can take actions to remedy these situations. One of them is to negotiate more proactively and effectively for wages and opportunity. It is in this spirit that much of this more recent work has been undertaken.

Are women deficient negotiators? Studies that examine individual differences between male and female negotiators often highlight women's general deficiencies as negotiators. Women are less likely than men to ask,[21] to initiate negotiations,[22] to be positively disposed toward negotiation;[23] they are less confident;[24] and they are more likely to set lower goals.[25] When it comes to compensation, the focus of most of the research, women expect to receive less in compensation than men expect,[26] feel less entitlement to higher salaries than men do,[27] or place less value on pay than on other aspects of their jobs.[28] These feelings translate into behavior that affects outcomes. Women demand and accept less in salary negotiations than men do,[29] are less confident and less satisfied with their negotiation performances,[30] and feel lower self-efficacy about their bargaining abilities.[31]

A Laboratory Is Not the Real World

This line of research consistently compares women negatively to men, who typically approach a negotiation on the offensive: seeing themselves entitled to and therefore not hesitant to request a higher salary. Thus, when men outperform women in salary negotiations, the reasons for these differences are often attributed to "problems" that women have.[32]

More recently, scholars have identified problematic aspects of this line of research.[33] Much of the research was conducted in laboratory situations, in which distributive negotiations, especially over pay, were the topics. Yet distributive negotiations, sometimes called win-lose negotiations, offer no opportunity for creative options. Furthermore, those artificial conditions often reproduce assumptions around gender and so fail to recognize the importance of context in real-life negotiations.[34] Each of us has multiple social identities (gender, race, education, and so on) making a focus on individual gender differences a problem because it ignores the interplay of different aspects of identity—our race, our age, our profession—as they play out in different situations.[35]

Negotiating for yourself: The backlash. More recently, the interest in comparing what men and women negotiators do has given way to considering what happens when women actually negotiate. And the fact is that women can face a backlash when they negotiate for themselves. This "social cost of asking" suggests that gender-linked stereotypes make it harmful for a woman to advocate freely for herself.[36] Women who act assertively in compensation negotiations are less likely to be hired and deemed good colleagues.[37] They are also less likely to be trusted and appointed to important roles and can pay a price in terms of how well they are liked and admired by colleagues.[38] Women often are expected to demonstrate a high degree of concern for others and may suffer when they do *not* do so. In addition, these expectations may be greater for women of color.[39] Indeed, women may risk censure and backlash when they fail to act assertively enough on behalf of others, as agents, and advocate for their team.[40]

Second-generation gender bias. A third way to consider challenges that women may face in negotiation is to consider the context, or negotiated order, within which negotiation takes place. Research on gender in organizations—in particular, work that seeks to explain women's persistent underrepresentation in leadership positions—has shifted away from a focus on actors' intentional, discriminatory efforts to exclude women to consideration of what we and others have called second-generation forms of gender bias.[41] These are the powerful yet often invisible barriers to women's advancement that arise from cultural beliefs about gender, as well as workplace structures, practices, and patterns of interaction that inadvertently favor men.

Visible and invisible structures. Let's use architecture as a metaphor for organizational and workplace culture. The US Capitol Building, like most workplace, was built when there were few women working, particularly in leadership positions. Therefore, there was no reason in the early 1800s for architects to consider including space for women's washrooms off the Senate and House floors: women wouldn't even be granted the right to vote in the United States until 1920, never mind run for office. As the Capitol Building was expanded and renovated over time, the structure continued to represent the majority of its users: (white) men. By the early 1960s there were seventeen women in the House of Representatives, who all shared a single bathroom that was far from the House Chamber. It was not until 1962 that congresswomen were given the "Congressional Ladies Retiring Room," which included a larger bathroom, though it was still some distance from the Chamber.[42] In the early 1990s, Senators Barbara Mikulski and Nancy Kassebaum were forced to share with visiting tourists the women's restroom downstairs from the Senate Chamber.[43]

The processes, values, and norms of organizations—like the physical structure of the buildings that house them—continue to reflect their original bias long after women become represented in greater and greater numbers. It's not that architects or male congressional leaders actively plotted to make the Capitol difficult for women to navigate; the building simply reflected the needs and experience of the dominant group. Yet that structure made it more difficult for women to navigate and obstructed their ability to do their jobs. When women were represented in larger numbers, it still took time to change the building's structure.

Change comes slowly to organizations as well. Systems, culture, and practices reflect the organization's history and cater to the dominant group, making the organization more difficult for minority members to navigate. Even when the need for change becomes obvious, it's hard to achieve and often done piecemeal. In 2011, a four-stall women's bathroom was built near the House Chamber,[44] and in 2013 the women's room near the Senate floor was expanded to accommodate a record-setting twenty female senators.[45]

Organizations are not gender neutral. Second-generation gender practices often appear neutral and natural on their face. But they can result in different experiences for, and treatment of, women and men, and they can vary for different groups of women. From this perspective, organizations are not gender neutral, and so their structures, practices, and policies are the negotiated order within which women and men negotiate. Understanding how second-generation issues are enacted in organizations helps us navigate organizations more effectively—and negotiate more successfully.

SECOND-GENERATION GENDER ISSUES

These second-generation issues can take a variety of forms that can be the bases for negotiations. The issues raised here are not merely about bargaining for a certain job and the accompanying compensation: they concern a much tougher issue of redefining norms and expectations. These may be norms around what is seen as an appropriate "fit," about expectations around people's family lives, around what skills are needed to succeed in a given job or at a given level in an organization, and around who is implicitly trusted versus who has to prove themselves.

Who Fits, and Who Doesn't

Jobs and opportunities can be gendered in the sense that certain people are seen to "fit" a job while others are not, and matters like race, class, and ethnicity can complicate these issues of fit. Leaders generally do not consciously dismiss women as a bad fit for some roles; rather, most of us—women as well as men—hold an unconscious association linking various roles to a certain gender. These implicit biases often lead us to connect men more often with leadership and career and women more often with family and caretaking.[46]

It's no wonder we make these implicit connections: those roles are reinforced everywhere we look. Men are far more likely to be quoted in the news media than women, and news bylines are more likely to be male.[47] One study found that only 25 percent of guests on US Sunday television news shows were women.[48] Women are also underrepresented and often stereotyped within the entertainment industry; of the top one hundred grossing films in 2011, only one-third of the characters depicted were women.[49]

The images we conjure of an investment banker, a prison guard, or a shop-floor supervisor tend to be men. In a complementary way, certain roles are seen as a more natural fit for women—staff roles like human resources and communication. Men are channeled into operational ones. In our executive programs, we frequently meet women who want to move to more operational roles, as these are the positions that carry more influence. Their challenge is to negotiate for opportunities when they are not automatically seen as the right fit.

Expectations around personal life. The issue of combining work and personal life is ripe for negotiation. Our notions of the "ideal worker" have changed a great deal in the age of 24/7 connectivity. Economist and founding CEO of the Center for Talent Innovation Sylvia Ann Hewlett calls this "extreme work": the belief that professional success requires heroic dedication, long hours, and global relocations.[50] Yet this construct tends to be gendered and fits only certain workers in the populations. Extreme jobs are a difficult fit for people who carry significant responsibilities at home, which despite changing norms continue to fall disproportionately on women.[51] We know that women *do* ask when these issues are on the table.[52] Yet because women are often subject to a "motherhood penalty," they must negotiate about pay and other work issues knowing they are likely to be penalized for asking.[53] Negotiating about these issues helps men and women by changing the negotiated order and challenging assumptions of what constitutes an "ideal worker."

Claiming value for invisible work. The kinds of work that are valued may similarly favor men, making their bids for leadership seem more valid. Research suggests that even when women are rated as more skilled in leadership, it is visible, heroic work—more often the purview of men—that is recognized and rewarded. Organizations tend to overlook equally vital but behind-the-scenes work that's considered to be more characteristic of women, such as building a team or avoiding crises.[54] We find this to be a common theme for women leaders in our programs. While they are held accountable for reaching specific milestones, they do not receive credit for the large amount of undefined work they do: building connections across silos, developing their staff, mentoring other women, or strengthening processes and practice. Claiming value for this invisible work is an important topic in workplace negotiations, as are negotiations around saying no to undervalued tasks.

Networks and sponsors. Access to networks is another way that second-generation gender bias can manifest itself. Social networks can give people access to information and support,[55] help them secure positions,[56] and enable them to negotiate compensation and other rewards more confidently.[57] Both white women and women of color cite a lack of access to influential colleagues with whom to network for their inability to advance.[58] Men tend to support and channel career development opportunities to male subordinates, whom they judge more likely than women to succeed. They're more likely to take risks on men, especially those they know well, and provide more informal help than either white or black women's mentors. Thus, women's networks yield fewer leadership opportunities, provide less visibility for their leadership claims, and generate less recognition and endorsement. Negotiating for sponsorship and support is another topic of everyday negotiations in the workplace.

Recognizing negotiable topics. To negotiate about these kinds of issues is tricky. First, these issues are not the usual negotiation fare, such as compensation or budget allocations. They are embedded in work practices that seem natural and neutral to many people. So the first step is to recognize that these *are* situations potentially ripe for negotiation, something that many people do not recognize is even possible. Furthermore, not all parties would recognize the negotiating potential. If we have social status based on our gender or race, we are often oblivious to the many ways that this status gives us privileges and advantages that other groups might lack.[59] Not only are we less likely to notice information that might challenge those beliefs; we may resist dealing with them. But people who resist usually aren't intentionally holding others back; they just don't realize that the environment favors them.

Even when not addressing gender issues directly, these negotiations often require raising awareness of and pushing back on potentially gendered structures and work practices. For example, negotiating a flexible work arrangement potentially reveals how an organization's practices make it difficult for mothers or other caretakers to succeed; negotiating for a leadership role can call attention to the fact that women have been overlooked in the past; and claiming value for invisible work can show how bias operates in performance reviews and compensation. Thus, before one can get down to the business of negotiating, even when proposing options for mutual gain, a negotiator has to think and prepare carefully for how she will raise an issue.

As we build the ideas in this book, we'll introduce people who are encountering negotiation problems of their own, and we'll explore the ways they might generate promising outcomes. For now, let's introduce Alicia's situation in order to outline the chapters in this book. She and others will return as the ideas in the book advance.

Alicia's Ambition: Navigating the Negotiated Order

Alicia is divisional vice president (DVP) for a sales region in one of the largest divisions of a leading technology company. She has learned that the regional VP is being considered for another job in the company, and she wants his job. She has an upcoming meeting with the vice chairman, Bob Barrett, to talk about what has been going on her division. She has heard that Barrett has somebody else in mind, Frank Lorenzo, whose relationship with Bob goes back a long time. Frank is probably not the best person for the role: he's generally known as a salesman's salesman, never really demonstrating the kind of leadership that this role will demand.

Alicia has a lot going for her: she's brought her team to a high level, had exposure to strategic initiatives at the company,

(Continued)

> and maintained a strong track record. Of course, her résumé isn't perfect; she's been in the DVP role for only four years. Although that wouldn't necessarily be a problem, people in Alicia's firm seem to think the women need more seasoning. Although Alicia has a good relationship with the customers in her area, she does not spend as much time entertaining customers in the evenings and weekends as her colleagues do, since that is generally her family time.

NEGOTIATING AT WORK: A CHAPTER OVERVIEW

Alicia will need to negotiate with Bob, though he is likely not expecting to. The chapters in part 1 describe the kind of preparation that Alicia needs to undertake. Because her negotiation involves some challenge to the status quo, this will entail not only figuring out what to ask for but also making herself feel confident to do the asking. The four chapters in part 1 focus on how to prepare for the n-negotiations that so often occur in organizations.

Chapter 1 is about preparing to negotiate, and begins with a problem that negotiators have in organizations: it is difficult to figure out what one wants. The chapter describes how you can recognize negotiating possibilities. It then delves into the importance of information gathering as a way to help the negotiator feel that what she is asking for is defensible. Alicia needs to figure out what she wants. Her goal is the regional VP job, but she is obviously not recognized as a contender for it, so she will need more information—not just about the role but also about Bob, the person with whom she needs to negotiate.

Chapter 2 begins by considering how negotiators can undermine themselves and describes the importance of positioning yourself to negotiate. This requires understanding your value to the other party and finding ways to make that value visible as well as considering possibilities outside the negotiation. Bob does not know Alicia, so she'll need to figure out his reasons for negotiating with her: what value she contributes to the company. It can be a challenge to get people of higher rank to negotiate with you. Since Bob is not expecting to negotiate with Alicia about the opportunity, he will likely not be "at the table" at the outset.

Chapter 3 begins by observing that when one negotiates in organizations, the choices are often perceived as yes or no. Preparing to problem-solve walks through the well-accepted steps of mutual-gains negotiations, which vary when the issues are located in organizations. But the preparation is especially important given the types of issues likely to be raised; in this kind of situation, the other person might perceive you as a problem. This is why it's critical to have creative options to propose. Alicia will need to figure out where her interests and Bob's align in order to come up with some creative options. She wants the job, but she may want to have ideas beyond just getting the promotion or not getting it. She will also need to be mindful about the constraints Bob faces.

Chapter 4 lays out some ways that Alicia can get Bob to the table to negotiate with her. She is trying to build interdependence with him, so she'll want to find ways to make her value visible to him in a currency that matters to him. She might also want to find ways to make him rethink Frank as an option. That can be tricky to do, so having some allies might help her with this.

Part 2, chapters 5 through 7, focuses on putting n-negotiations into practice.

Chapter 5 describes the importance of openings in understanding what unfolds in the negotiation. What happens in the first few minutes of a negotiation can often predict the eventual outcome. Openings set the context for the interaction, providing opportunities to position yourself in the negotiation and creating a space for the other to work with you. Good openings help engage the other person and frame the issues for them. Because Alicia does not know Bob very well, she will need to find ways to make a connection with him and also to open up their conversations to some of the concerns and interests Bob may have.

Chapter 6 details a "moves and turns" framework that helps negotiators deal with challenges. Moves and turns are a way of understanding what is happening in a negotiation as the parties deal with their issues. *Moves* are actions negotiators take to position themselves (and others) in the negotiation process, and *turns* are responses to the others' moves. Alicia will need to anticipate Bob's objections in order to determine how she will deal with or "turn" them as he raises them, and how she will do so in ways that further both his and her interests.

Chapter 7 describes the actions a negotiator can take to bring the other party along. Alicia will need to engage Bob in her thinking. In order to do so, she will need to remain curious and figure out how she can get him to support the concept of her promotion so that they can work out the particulars. He will have to justify this to important constituents, and she will need to help him do so. Despite the best planning and preparation, a negotiator will face challenges about her ideas and proposals. It is possible that both parties get stuck—and so we will explore what Alicia can do to keep the negotiations moving ahead in a productive way.

WHAT'S GOOD FOR ALICIA IS GOOD FOR THE COMPANY

Alicia's situation introduces some of the concepts that we discuss and describe in the following chapters. But it is important to make another observation about what happens when Alicia negotiates about this role. To the degree that she defines the success criteria for the role, she at least puts herself in the running. Alicia will have made subtle progress in making appointments more transparent and enlarging the pool of candidates considered. That's beneficial to both Alicia and the company. And you would be surprised how merely thinking about negotiation in this way is empowering for women executives—and for the men whom I've taught as well.

But something else has happened as well. Simply by opening up the conversation, she has, on a small scale, interrupted one form of second-generation bias in her company—giving senior roles to those in your network—and she has enlarged the slate and made it more diverse. In this way, what might be considered a small win for Alicia can lead to increased opportunities for others in the organization as promotion practices evolve. We explore the implications of these actions and others organizations can take in chapter 8.

Women are like the canary in the coal mine; looking at their experience gives us insights about what is working and not working for everyone in organizations. It is not just women who suffer as a result of second-generation gender issues; men are affected as well. For example, consider the concept of the ideal worker we mentioned above. When employees are rewarded for "total commitment" and 24/7 responsiveness, men who violate these norms by spending time with their families or care for aging parents face promotion penalties in much the same way as women do.

Furthermore, much has been written about how organizations that encourage diverse leadership have superior performance.[60] More and more organizations are looking to decrease barriers to women attaining leadership positions. We focus largely on helping individuals negotiate on behalf of themselves, with the conviction that doing so will likely help them contribute more effectively to their organization as well. Yet we shift this focus in chapter 8 to the organizational level and discuss how small wins from individual negotiations can be leveraged into bigger gains that address second-generation bias for the entire enterprise.

Throughout this book, we include research and insights about gender in organizations. We also examine the cases of several women to provide a view of how real-life negotiations take place in organizations. We end chapters 1 through 7 with "Putting Principles to Work," summarizing the strategies from each of those chapters. These principles are relevant for men *and* for women, at all types of organizations—from large corporations to small partnerships, and in the for-profit, nonprofit, and public sector.

ABOUT THE AUTHORS

Deborah M. Kolb is Deloitte Ellen Gabriel Professor for Women and Leadership (Emerita) and the founder of the Center for Gender in Organizations at the Simmons College School of Management. From 1991 to 1994, she was executive director of the Program on Negotiation at Harvard Law School. She is currently a senior fellow at the program, where she codirects Negotiations in the Workplace. Kolb is an adjunct professor at the INSEAD business school in Fontainebleau, France.

Kolb is an authority on gender issues in negotiation and leadership. In addition to the many articles she has written on the topic, she has coauthored *The Shadow Negotiation*, named by *Harvard Business Review* as one of the ten best business books of 2000; *Everyday Negotiation: Navigating the Hidden Agendas of Bargaining*; and *Her Place at the Table: A Women's Guide to Negotiating the Five Challenges of Leadership Success*. In addition to her research, Kolb organizes and leads executive development programs for senior women and serves as a consultant to organizations interested in retaining and advancing their best women. In 2008, Kolb received the Outstanding Achievement Award for her contributions to women's leadership issues by the Equality Commission of the Massachusetts Bar Association, the

Boston Bar Association, and the Massachusetts Women's Bar Association.

Kolb received her PhD from MIT's Sloan School of Management, where her dissertation won the Zannetos Prize for outstanding doctoral scholarship. She has a BA from Vassar College and an MBA from the University of Colorado.

Jessica L. Porter is a writer, researcher, and consultant with extensive experience advising organizations across sectors and across geographies to create change. As an architect of women's leadership development programs, she leverages academic research to produce a wide variety of learning solutions that advance women in organizations. In the United States, she works with Fortune 500 companies to design and deliver global programs for women. In Africa, she consults to nongovernmental organizations to create sustainable opportunities for women. In every arena, her work reflects her expertise in connecting research and practice with her knowledge of gender, diversity, and leadership development.

While a research project manager at Harvard Business School, she was the lead researcher for *Sleeping with Your Smartphone: How to Break the 24/7 Habit and Change the Way You Work*, by Leslie Perlow. It documents the longitudinal study in which small interventions with project teams at the Boston Consulting Group evolved into a firmwide change initiative.

She has a BA from Clark University and an MBA from Simmons School of Management.

NEGOTIATING AT WORK

PART ONE

PREPARING FOR
n-NEGOTIATIONS

You Can't Get What You Want If You Don't Know What You Want

Several years ago, I was teaching a negotiation program for women in Addis Ababa, Ethiopia. The women in the program, scientists from all over the world, worked for large international development organizations, universities, and local nongovernmental organizations (NGOs), all in the field of agriculture. Our curriculum focused on how the women could better advocate for what they wanted and needed in their careers during negotiations at work. Their issues ranged from securing the resources to attend international conferences to working out disagreements between different groups of scientists over grants, to negotiating for promotions, to securing more resources for a project.

One evening, some of the local women invited me to shop with them for tablecloths at the local market. In this environment, my African escorts were pros at negotiating the price with cloth vendors. They had a keen eye for the value and quality of the embroidered fabrics and knew just what they wanted. They knew which vendor was likely to make the best deal, and they were well informed. Their experiences negotiating in African markets, N-negotiations, made them confident in ways I admired.

Back in our classroom the next day, the situation changed. It was our final session, and the women had to plan an n-negotiation that they would have at work, at home, or in the community about something that mattered to them. While many were highly successful in their fields, they had really not thought about negotiating to get what they wanted in these contexts.

One participant whom I'll call Beatrice colorfully and metaphorically described how her boss continually changed his expectations of her and her work in her institute: "He asks me to get water, and when I bring it in a glass, he says he wants it in a mug. When I bring water in a mug, he says, 'Why did you get the water in the first place?'" Again and again she tried to figure out what he wanted; finally, she decided her situation had become untenable but had no idea what to do about it. She knew she wanted to negotiate, but for what? She knew she was dissatisfied with the situation, but did she want to leave? Did she want to seek a different position in the organization? Her husband suggested a sabbatical, but this was something that had never been done in her NGO.

Fortunately Beatrice had an extensive network of other women scientists, many of whom worked in local universities. She gathered ideas from them on how a sabbatical might be structured. And because she knew her boss very well, she was able to construct a proposal and be prepared to counter his objections in such a way that he was more likely to agree. To her surprise, he ultimately granted her a sabbatical.

TWO STEPS TO PREP FOR NEGOTIATING

This chapter focuses on the first steps in preparing for a negotiation: figuring out what you want and learning what you need to know in order to advocate for it. It's pretty obvious that you can't get what you want if you don't know what you want. And figuring out what you want can be particularly complicated when negotiating in an organization. It's one thing to be clear about the topic of negotiation if, for example, you want a salary increase. The challenge there is to learn enough to set high but realistic aspirations that can guide your negotiating strategy. Gathering that kind of information is not always easy, but it makes the issues to be negotiated relatively clear. However, things become more complicated when one is trying, as Beatrice is, to figure out what exactly to negotiate about in order to make her situation better. Like the women in the Ethiopian marketplace,

Beatrice needs good information about the organizational equivalents of tablecloth prices: what people who negotiate in similar situations get, what it is reasonable to ask for, and more knowledge about the people she is dealing with.

CHALLENGES IN FIGURING OUT WHAT YOU WANT

As Beatrice knew, it is not always easy to figure out what you want or what a reasonable goal might be for a particular negotiation. Some of the challenges are individual and become evident especially when somebody is negotiating for oneself; others derive from the ways that negotiations unfold in the workplace. In their book *Ask for It*, authors Linda Babcock and Sara Laschever suggest that figuring out what you want can be complicated, especially for a woman.[1] The challenge can come from confused messages that she received as she was growing up, making it difficult for her to distinguish what she wants from what others expect of her. This was certainly true for some of the scientists in the African negotiation program and was likely compounded by cultural issues, particularly the role of family and community that many African women face. The scientists explained that women in these settings must always be cognizant of family obligations when negotiating at work. But when the focus is on changing something about your work—for example, a new title or position or garnering support for a new project or a change in workload—figuring out what you want can present an additional hurdle for both women and men.

Several challenges add to the difficulty.

Challenge 1: Negotiating for Yourself, Not as an Agent

First is the challenge of negotiating not as an agent of your organization but for yourself. When I work with executives, both women and men, I typically begin by asking them about their experiences negotiating with clients and customers. They generally describe what they

think makes them successful in what we have called capital
N-negotiations.

N-negotiations are the familiar kind. These are formal exchanges
where both parties recognize that they are in a negotiation over a
contract or a deal of some sort with internal and external clients and
customers. Participants in these situations credit their acknowledged
success to such attributes as an ability to listen well, learn about what
the other party wants, gather good information to support what they
want, develop flexibility to create options that meet mutual needs,
and marshal the support of their organizations to back them up.[2]

But n-negotiations are different in kind. I then shift the conversation to what we call lowercase *n-negotiations*: those exchanges in
which we're negotiating mostly for ourselves. I ask what difference it
makes to negotiate for oneself as a principal versus negotiating as an
agent for an organization—and people never hesitate to describe
these differences. When negotiating for themselves, they say, it's
difficult to be objective: they feel less secure; the negotiations feel
more personal, making it easy to become emotional. There are also
power dynamics involved. Will those in authority see it as legitimate
for me to negotiate? Will negotiating affect how others see me? This
holds especially true when the negotiation is with a boss. How will
she respond? Will she see the negotiation as necessary? Will she challenge me for even bringing up this issue? How will the negotiation
affect our working relationship going forward?[3]

Negotiating for resources at budget time is an N-negotiation.
There is a formal process and a routine for how and what you ask for.
You put together your case, connecting your requests to goals you will
commit to achieving. You schedule a meeting, and you and your boss
both expect there will be some sort of negotiation over budget,
resources, and priorities.

But other situations in which you need to negotiate with your boss
differ greatly. For example, imagine you have accepted a new role and
made a commitment to implement a new program. Once into the

role, you discover that the resources you requested (or were just assigned to you) are not sufficient. Now you have to launch a negotiation that nobody expected to have—and asking for more resources may raise questions about you and your ability to do the job. In the former case, negotiation is expected, and as part of a particular *negotiated order*, there is likely to be an associated routine, probably of some back-and-forth. But there is no expectation of negotiation in the second situation. In fact, raising it at all may invite resistance, because your ask might put the other person in a difficult situation.

Gender may heighten these concerns. People tend to ask women more frequently than men for favors or help, such as picking up extra responsibilities, taking up certain support roles, helping a colleague, and mentoring other women.[4] And for a number of reasons, women are more likely than men to say yes to these requests. They might want the person who asks for help to like them,[5] or they might be more concerned about the welfare of others.[6] Adding to the pressure to say yes to these types of extra tasks is a gendered expectation that women are helpers, more collaborative than men, and therefore likely to say yes.[7]

And just as there might be a social cost to asking, there can be costs to declining such requests.[8] William Ury in *The Power of a Positive No* catalogues some of the reasons people fear saying no: they don't want to jeopardize a relationship, they feel guilty, or they may feel their job is on the line. Women can be particularly conscious of the costs of saying no, since they are more likely to decide whether to perform a favor based on a fear of negative consequences, whereas men are more likely to base their decisions to accept or decline a favor for instrumental reasons, such as the status level of the person making the request.[9]

Gender-status beliefs. It is also just as likely that women may raise issues that others might not recognize as problems. As we discussed in the Introduction, second-generation gender issues appear neutral and are often taken for granted. That means that not everybody will have the same experience or recognize a problem of inequity. Gender-status beliefs that presume men to be more deserving of rewards can make it more challenging for a woman to raise issues of fair treatment or to question whether she has been overlooked for an opportunity.[10] Likewise, when women negotiate about issues such as flexibility, they might be drawing attention to gendered expectations of work hours and what it means to be "committed," particularly in the context of what is required for promotion.[11]

Challenge 2: Your Own Negotiation History

The second challenge comes from your experience. Maybe you have rarely or never negotiated for yourself about a work situation before. Some of the research suggests that women, more so than men, fail to recognize negotiation as a possibility.[12] If they are offered a new role or opportunity, many women take it without any discussion. I've been surprised to find how seldom even the senior women I work with negotiate anything about a new role, its contours, and some-times even its compensation. Some fail to negotiate even when it's a role they don't want to accept!

We train each other in what to expect and not expect in each interaction. If you have never previously negotiated in your work-place, then you've essentially trained people to expect that you will not do so. This may present a challenge when you do choose to negotiate: the surprise of the people with whom you're negotiating since they expect you to do one thing, but then you do another. You must therefore use what you know about the other party when prepar-ing to negotiate. If others are likely to be caught off guard by even the fact of your negotiating, your preparation should address their surprise and consider how they will react to the content of your negotiation.

Challenge 3: The Negotiation Culture around You

A third challenge is cultural. It comes from uncertainty about whether it is even deemed legitimate to negotiate about the issue. In American culture, as distinct from that of my students in Africa, it's not typical to negotiate the purchase price of goods at a store or even your local produce market. While it's possible—I frequently assign my students to do just that, and they are often successful—we don't usually consider these situations to be negotiable.

It's not always obvious that negotiation is a possibility. This barrier may be even higher in organizations where hierarchical relationships are a factor. Some issues are more likely to be seen as negotiable—salaries and budgets—although not by everybody, as research on gender and salary negotiations have shown.[13]

Adding your organization to the mix. The situation is even murkier when you're dealing with organizational issues. Sometimes you may be warned that negotiation is not an option and that this is a take-it-or-leave-it matter. But organizational considerations can also make you reluctant to raise an issue. You might worry that negotiating a flexible schedule will lead others to see you as uncommitted. Negotiating for more resources for a project might cause you to be labeled as a slacker, or less than a team player, or unwilling to step up. Without good information about what gets negotiated, you may think that there is no possibility for changing the status quo. To the degree that certain groups are not well networked to have this kind of information, they may be at a loss to see their way to negotiating the change they are seeking in their workplace situation.

Challenge 4: Your Organization's Negotiated Order

Your organization's own codes. There's a fourth challenge when it comes to framing negotiation as a possibility: understanding your organization's negotiated order. Every organization has its informal codes about which issues are and are not open to negotiation. Part of the routines of work or family life that everyone takes for granted, the negotiated order challenges you to bracket what a potential negotiable issue might be—whether you're negotiating for yourself or for others.

Identifying the contours of the organization's negotiated order is not trivial. Not only do you have to figure out which issues are negotiable; it is not always clear, as in Beatrice's situation, what you want to negotiate for. For example, if you and your team are working very long hours, you might just stick to the status quo and continue to do so; or you might decide that the situation is ripe for negotiation. Once you recognize that possibility, there are a number of ways to frame the issue. Perhaps you decide that it is time to renegotiate the scope of the project, the team's responsibility, or the possibility for others to pick up some tasks. Maybe you negotiate for an extended time line on deliverables to spread the work out. Or maybe you decide it's time to negotiate for more resources and expand your team's size. Deciding which of these avenues to pursue depends both on what you think might alleviate the pressure on your team and what you're most likely to achieve. It might also depend on what information you have.

Getting good information from within your negotiated order. Having good information extends beyond knowing the range on a clearly demarcated issue such as price or potential salary. It requires a broader understanding of what others, both inside and outside the organization, are getting and doing. Good information that might come from benchmarking comparable data on salary and compensation packages can be enormously helpful in negotiations. But while these data are important, the kind of information we're talking about is broader: it includes learning about what others negotiated for as well as what they got. What did they ask for when they were offered a new role? How did they garner resources for a new project in a down economy? How did they get the support they needed for a new and perhaps risky initiative? This information provides insights about an organization's culture, norms, and politics that influence how any proposal will be heard.

LEARN ALL YOU CAN ABOUT THE WHAT AND THE WHO

Information is critical to helping you clarify what you want from a negotiation, to set your aspirations high enough, and most critically to make you feel more confident in your asks. Two types of information are important. The first is benchmarking—learning about what others have negotiated for in comparable situations. The second is more contextual—the insights you gain about the style and preferences of the person with whom you will be negotiating. If the first type of information set is about the *what* that is possible, the second is about the *who*. Collating information about the person with whom you will be negotiating—what you already know and what you can learn from others—helps you feel more confident and prepared to initiate a negotiation. But you also need to pay attention to the *how*. In the second part of this chapter, we discuss the role of networks as the critical source of intelligence.

When I teach a workshop, I often use a cartoon in which Dilbert asks for a raise and threatens to quit if he doesn't get it. The Pointy-Haired Boss responds, "Good-bye," whereupon Dilbert says, "Noo," then promises to work every weekend for nothing. I use this as an example of what some have called aspirational collapse. Often attributed to women, aspirational collapse occurs when a person is primed to negotiate and knows what she will ask for—yet simply accepts that and says "okay" when the other person refuses.[14] There are many ways to avoid this trap; one critical approach is to be sure that you have facts to support what you ask for. It is an axiom of negotiation theory that information is power: the more you know, the more confident you can feel about asking for what you want.

The What of Negotiation: Benchmarking

My students bargaining in the marketplace in Addis Ababa exemplify the axiom that information is power. They knew about the quality of the products and their likely worth. They knew the price ranges for the tablecloths they were bargaining over. They knew which sellers offered the best products and which ones were most likely to give them the best deal. And they knew enough about the sellers' likely behavior to plan and carry out their price negotiation strategy. As a result, they felt great about their purchases at the end of the day; they got good deals. In these kinds of marketplace negotiations, where there is a single issue—in this case, price—knowing the possible bargaining range for the negotiation enables a negotiator to set realistic yet high aspirations.

This is important. We know that if you spend some effort gathering information, you are likely to set higher aspirations than if you do not.[15] We also know that aspirations become self-fulfilling: aspire low, and you'll likely realize lower returns on your efforts; aspire high, and you'll more likely stay in the negotiations in a way that makes you more likely to achieve your aims.[16]

Benchmarking means comparing. We use the term *benchmarking* to capture this dimension of information gathering. It is a shorthand term that means evaluating or checking something by comparison with a standard. We know that having good information makes a big difference in job negotiations. In their study of MBA graduates, Hannah Bowles and her colleagues show that in industries where information about compensation packages is widely known, such as consulting and investment banking, men and women graduates receive identical packages, controlling for experience.[17] However, salary discrepancies are high in more ambiguous situations with few consistent standards and where good information is less readily available.

Benchmarking makes what you are negotiating for feel defensible. People are understandably very curious about negotiating their pay and are very likely to search out benchmarks for their compensation packages.[18] Having these benchmarks gives you confidence in what you are asking for—the knowledge that what you're asking for is defensible. In other words, you feel legitimate asking.[19]

The same way of thinking applies in n-negotiations, where many dimensions of a job are subjects for bargaining. The first question to ask yourself is, "What do I need to succeed in a new role?" To begin to answer this question, ask another: "What do other people negotiate for in this role?" Discovering what other people have negotiated for fulfills a similar function to compensation benchmarking. Asking this question, and finding people to pose it to, can also lead you to uncover issues you'd never thought about before.

Benchmarking: Two Cases

Consider the role that benchmarking plays in the negotiations of
Claudia and Marisa. Both are negotiating new opportunities, but
under two different circumstances. Claudia, a director at a large
international bank, wishes to relocate from Chicago to London.
However, the London office's leaders seem to put up a number of
obstacles that make her feel powerless in the negotiation. Marisa is
being recruited for a job she does not particularly want but feels she
has to take. Having good information will help in both situations—
and both women need to use their networks to learn more about what
they can legitimately ask for.

Claudia's Case: Getting Good Facts

Claudia is a highly successful managing director in sales for a
large international bank, where she has worked for fifteen years.
She's based in Chicago, but her husband recently took a job in
London. For the past year, they've managed a very tiring commuting relationship, and she's anxious to relocate. Her current
boss recommended her to the head of the London branch for a
position that would be basically a lateral move for her. Giles
James, a vice president for sales in the London office, contacted
her about a potential job. It was a difficult conversation. James
seemed not at all enthusiastic about having Claudia in the
group, despite her reputation as a star performer in Chicago.
He presented her with a client list that seemed to her composed
of discards from others in the group, then brusquely told her he
needed an answer in two days because he had several other
promising candidates.

James's approach threw Claudia. Her track record in Chicago
had led her to believe that the London group would be eager
to have her join them, so she was unprepared for his dismissive
attitude. Furthermore, she had other issues that were important

(Continued)

to her in the move. Although she was an individual contributor, she always had support staff to cover the trading floor when she was away. With no administrative support in her current role, handling the details of the move—visas, health care coverage, renting her condo, shipping—seemed overwhelming. She'd heard that people who relocated overseas could avail themselves of an ex-pat package. However, she had no information, and James had not mentioned anything about it. Claudia was stumped. She really wanted this job and was tempted to say yes, even though she was not at all sure it would work for her. She had never negotiated about a position before and was unsure about what to do.

Because she had no further information, Claudia was ready to accept the terms James offered. Her low aspirations were about to become a self-fulfilling prophecy. But then she stepped back and called a friend outside the bank to help her think more clearly about what she needed to do. Her friend told her to gather some information; without it, she was undermining herself in the negotiation. Her friend suggested that Claudia contact her human resource person to find out about the company's ex-pat package because that seemed to be a major concern for her. Claudia, however, was reluctant to contact people in her Chicago office. She worried that if she did, word would leak out that she was considering a move, and she knew from experience that this could reverberate badly.

When she got off the phone, she sat for a while trying to go through her "mental Rolodex" to see whom she could contact to get the information that would help her. She needed to know more about James and to get a clearer picture of his situation. Did he truly have other candidates he was ready to hire, as he'd claimed? What was the client pool he offered like—and was that really going to be the pool? She wanted to know how the London office handled support in the group: Could she expect an assistant? Finally, the most important issue was the ex-pat package. She didn't see how she'd be able to manage without support, and she had no idea what the packages were and whether she would be eligible for them.

At first she was stuck. Although she knew other managing directors at the bank from a leadership program she had attended, only one or two would have useful information related to her function. But she kept at it and finally identified two people in London she could contact. The first was Helen, a woman from human resources whom she'd been introduced to in London. She called Helen and learned quickly about the ex-pat packages: what they were and what she could expect.

Having this information totally changed how she felt about the negotiation. "Without the facts," Claudia explained, "you have no confidence. With the facts, I had a totally different approach."

We'll discuss more about Claudia's approach later when we relate what she learned about James and how that changed her strategy to the conversation.

Marisa was in a different situation, being asked to take on a new role in her professional services firm that she did not seek or even particularly want. Marisa's situation is similar to that of many of the other women in this book. They are asked to do something—take on a new role, pick up extra work, help somebody out—and see their choices as yes or no.[20] Often the women I teach say what they want to do is learn to say no more often. But we think the challenge is to take these occasions—when you are asked—and turn them into a negotiation.

To do that, you have to think in terms of "Yes, and…" "Yes, I will take the role. And here is what I need in order to do so." That was Marisa's challenge.

Marisa's Case: Taking a "Yes, and..." Approach

Marisa, a tax partner in a large professional services firm, led the tax practice in the Santa Fe area. The practice handled mostly medium-sized accounts, and Marisa's role, primarily an internal one, made her directly responsible for the tax department's profitability—hiring and deploying staff and managers, as well as evaluating and developing them. Happy in her situation, Marisa's career goal was to play a regional or national role in the tax function; she anticipated that her next step would be to assume a leadership role in a larger city or region.

But that's not what happened. Instead, Marisa got a call from Alice Parker, regional managing partner in the Southeast. She wanted Marisa to consider taking on a totally different role in the company: to become a marketplace leader in Miami. In Marisa's firm, the role of a marketplace leader is wholly different from a functional leader position. In this external role, Marisa would be responsible for developing and implementing a business development strategy to land new clients, increase revenues quickly, and extend service lines.

Marisa had a number of concerns. First, she loved being a leader in the tax function and couldn't see why she just shouldn't hold out for a more visible tax position. Second, she loved Santa Fe. Having grown up there, she had family and friends who helped and supported her. Miami would be far more expensive and a long way from family. She was also aware of the Miami office's reputation of being a place where the partners couldn't or didn't work well together. While it was true that the market had been challenging in all the regions, the Miami office was among the poorest performers.

Marisa also knew there would be questions about her. After all, she'd never held a marketplace position. She was also concerned about whether she'd have the appropriate resources to do the job. The firm had recently undergone a round of layoffs and had cut back on support for marketing. To meet the goals set for the Miami office, funds would need to be expended, but if she took the job, she'd have to wait for a while to get the necessary funding. Nothing new here: it was typical to ask people to do more with less.

Although certain aspects of the role intrigued her, she was inclined to say no and wait for the kind of role she wanted in tax. But then she got a call from a senior leader in the firm who told her she just had to take the job because it would be such a great opportunity for her. He also told her that he knew it was a challenge and that if it didn't work out, the firm would find another place for her. After hanging up, she decided that given his support, she had no choice but to say yes.

New Opportunities: The Best Time to Negotiate

When someone is offered an opportunity, like Marisa, or is seeking one, like Claudia, it is often the best time to negotiate—for two reasons. First, there is often the expectation that one will negotiate. Second, it is also the time when the other party is likely most willing to negotiate. Once you've taken a role under the conditions offered, it's more difficult to change these conditions—not impossible, but more difficult. Assuming that the other person really wants you for a role, as in Marisa's case, or because the other party has put a partial offer on the table, as in Claudia's case, they are likely to be more open to the conditions it would take to get you. This is the time to find out what people in the organization negotiate about when they take on a new role.

Pointers from your network. Like Claudia, Marisa contacted women she knew in her network. But she had an advantage over Claudia. There were many women partners in her firm, and she knew some of them from a leadership development program she'd attended the previous year. She contacted Katherine Jones, a regional leader in the tax function whom she knew well. Jones's less-than-easy experience led her to advise Marisa to make sure to negotiate the resources and support she'd need in the new role. That included funds to use in the marketplace for charitable events and other client interactions. Jones also suggested that Marisa establish an agreement about the kind of support Parker would give her. After all, Marisa was heading into a difficult office situation that would challenge her experiences. That included how Parker would present her to the partners and support her if she had problems dealing with partners who might not be willing to accept her.[21] Jones also suggested that Marisa at least start a discussion with Parker about what positions would come next, given what the senior leader had told her. Although there was a possibility that this experience would put her on a new trajectory, she felt her heart was still in tax and would want some assurances that she would support her next move. Jones mentioned some other women partners in consulting and audit who had negotiated their next move as part of the discussions about the current offer.

Marisa also had concerns about how a disruptive move would affect her family. She knew two women who had recently relocated and learned from them what kind of relocation package she could expect. One had gotten help not only with financing the move but also with getting her children settled in school. Marisa wondered whether, given the firm's move to more remote forms of work using recent technology, she could structure a long-distance role. She knew a partner in the advisory services of the business who had done that, but she learned that the nature of that work lent itself to a commuting structure. Marisa was not sure she could make it work but decided she might give it a try. As a result of her benchmarking and her reaching out to other women partners in the firm, she developed a pretty good idea of what the "and" to her yes would be.

Putting the "Yes, and…" approach into action. When you negotiate in n-negotiations, it helps if you think of your initial response as "Yes, and…" when asked to do something. It's easy to fall into the trap of thinking that there are only two answers to a request: yes or no. But when you say yes, there is no possibility of negotiation. And if you say no, you've also cut off the possibility of negotiating for things that might otherwise have led you to say yes. When you consider the options for "Yes, and…," you open the way for creative thinking. But you'll need to do some research to figure out what that "and" is.

The power of benchmarking. Information you glean from benchmarking increases your control over a negotiation. The more you know ahead of time, the more realistic you can be in setting your goals and the easier it is to figure out what steps you need to take to get what you want. The interesting twist here is that you are much more likely to make an effort to gather information if you set your aspirations high. Claudia started her negotiations aspiring low and made no attempt to gather the benchmarking information that would increase her aspirations. After she sought counsel from a friend, she discovered information that raised her aspirations—which led her to both work harder to get a good agreement and be more patient in getting there.[22]

Benchmarking makes you feel your ask is "defensible." Benchmarking is an antidote to that aspirational collapse we discussed earlier. Knowing that others have asked for and received similar things makes us feel more comfortable asking. In our minds, we can defend it. Even if the other person hesitates or says no, we can stay in the conversation because we feel legitimate asking. We have confidence when we know that someone else has achieved what we are attempting to achieve.

Don't confuse your aspirations with your bottom line. Aspirations are what you hope you can achieve; your bottom line is what you can live with. When you aspire high, you are more likely to search out information that would help you figure out what you should ask for and that makes you more confident asking for these things. You don't use your benchmarking directly—saying, for example, that Jane got this deal and so that's what you want. It's simply that the knowledge that Jane got X when she took on a new project arms you to stay in the negotiation. It also means that you are less likely to suffer from the winner's curse, the situation that occurs when you ask for something that is quickly granted.[23] There is nothing like the sinking feeling of having your opening offer accepted immediately and realizing that you likely could have asked for more than you did. Then you know that there were more possibilities than you had considered.

The Who of Negotiation: Knowing Your Counterpart

Knowing what you know about the person you are negotiating with is another vital source of information. This is the all-important "who" factor. The importance of this element became especially clear during a conversation with a CEO of a professional services firm who told us that he never negotiated salaries because the offers he gave were, he said, "fair." Obviously if you knew this about him, negotiating over salary would not be a good idea. He would find an insinuation that his offer wasn't fair to be insulting. But then he told us a story about a time when he did negotiate over salary. He had given a promising partner, Joan, an opportunity to develop a new area of business for the firm. She told the CEO that in order to succeed in developing this new area, she would be hiring specialized talent whose market-place value meant that she would have to pay them more than she was getting. Having subordinates who made more than she did could jeopardize her credibility and make it harder for her to be successful, she pointed out. The CEO told us that she had made a good case, and he increased her salary.

Using what you know about your counterpart. There are two interesting parts of this story. One is what Joan knew about the CEO. She could not base her ask on the going comparable salaries for people in her position because that would have challenged his sense of himself as a fair CEO. So what she did was connect what was good for her (increased compensation) to what was good for the organization (hiring the right talent for the task).

Gathering this kind of information about the other party helps you think about how to phrase what you are asking for. Does the other party like to cut right to the chase and hear your proposals?

Does he want to explore the data and come up with a plan together?

Maureen was a senior executive in talent at her bank who needed the resources for the extended groups she managed on a yearly basis. Her CEO generally accepted her budget proposals and was interested in negotiating over only a few issues—something like 10 percent of her budget. Recently a new CEO was hired—the kind of leader who likes to take a "deep dive" into the data. He wants to jointly negotiate the budget with Maureen. Maureen has had to change her approach to these yearly budget talks, and she now comes prepared to explain each issue and get the CEO's buy-in on her programs.

Let's return to Claudia, who wanted to relocate to London, and Marisa, who had been offered a new position in Miami.

What Claudia's case teaches us. Claudia didn't know Giles James at all when they first spoke. She interpreted his actions as hostile and diminishing of her. However, she realized she knew another woman who had recently relocated to the London office. Claudia reached out to her and learned that James was being pressured somewhat to consider Claudia by the global head of sales. Claudia also learned that James found Americans rather "pushy." Her contact urged her to take a collaborative stance and seek to engage James in a discussion about ways they could make her transition easier.

How Claudia used what she knew about her counterpart. Claudia followed this advice in a few ways. First, the information she'd learned about the ex-pat packages gave her more confidence, so she could focus on engaging James. She decided to signal her collaboration right from the start by beginning the negotiation with issues that would appeal to James. When they spoke again, Claudia began by talking about how excited she was about the possible role (more on this in chapter 5). She then turned to the disappointing client list. She introduced the issue by saying she wanted to make the group successful and wanted to make sure that the client list had potential to do that. She linked what was good for her to what was good for the organization. James responded immediately; he told her that the client list was fluid and that they would work it out when she arrived. She addressed the other two issues that concerned her—support staff and the ex-pat package—by asking questions. On the support staff, she had ideas about what she could do about that when she arrived. Perhaps, she suggested, she and others could share resources.

When Claudia asked about the ex-pat package, James said he didn't know about it but would investigate. If he'd said that in their first conversation, she would have been suspicious. But because she knew about the types of packages available and what she was likely to get, she felt confident enough to let it go and trust him to investigate and get back to her. He did get back to her, and with a package that she expected.

For Claudia, networking to get the information she needed, especially on the ex-pat package, gave her a different outlook on the negotiation. And learning more about the situation that James was in, his impressions of Americans, and how he liked to negotiate gave her the approach to take.

What Marisa's case teaches us. Marisa already knew Alice Parker, who wanted her to take a new role in their firm, from many interactions they'd had as partners over the years. Of the issues she planned to negotiate, she knew that the ones directly related to the business would be easiest for Alice to say yes to. These included having the resources to build market share in Miami. Alice agreed, although she was cutting back on those resources in other city offices in the region. The other business issue was what regional leader Katherine Jones had recommended: that she made sure that Alice would give her the necessary support and backing to position her in the new role. Marisa and Alice were open with each other about the issues she might confront. There were several partners in the office whom Alice thought might pose a problem. In conversations with the head of the firm, Alice had already worked on getting at least two of them to consider retirement. She easily agreed to give whatever support Marisa thought she might need. At Marisa's request, she planned to attend a strategy meeting for the office to help Marisa get the other partners on board. She suggested that Marisa get a coach and then helped her find one.

Marisa also had two financial issues to raise, which were a bit more complicated because they meant asking Alice to agree to something that violated precedent. Marisa had known Alice for eight years and knew she had worked hard to get to the regional role; in fact, she was the first woman to do so. She also knew that her salary and relocation requests might be difficult for Alice to agree to. So in contrast to the other issues, Marisa planned to go easy on these issues and not push too hard. The first was salary. The role Marisa was taking was more senior than her functional role in Santa Fe, and she thought she deserved an increase. However, Marisa had recently had a bump in salary grade, and Alice thought she would not be able to get her an increase immediately. But she agreed to try.

The final issue was more complicated: her idea about how to do the job remotely. Marisa had done her homework and knew the dollar value of the relocation package. She also knew that Alice would expect her to relocate; after all, that is what Alice had always done. So Marisa approached dealing with this idea in a more collaborative mode. She discussed that she had a child in high school whom she was reluctant to move and a husband who had a job working for the City of Santa Fe. While she knew the firm would help with schools and finding her husband a job in Miami, she wondered with Alice whether they might experiment with a commuting role. At first, Alice did not see how she could do the role with all its challenges if she were not there full time, so Marisa proposed a plan: she would spend a certain number of days per month in Miami—a significant number, especially in the early months of the new role—and manage the rest of the time remotely. The firm had been moving in this direction anyway.

Alice couldn't agree to the second issue. Although there were many roles that could be done remotely, a marketplace leader job demanded being in that market. Marisa reluctantly agreed to relocate but in return asked Alice to commit to helping her move into a more senior role in tax once she had done her time in Miami.

Marisa and Claudia's stories are great examples of how important it is to have a network for gathering information. To figure out what you want, it's incredibly helpful to have examples about what is possible from others.[24] Research shows that people who are well networked tend to receive higher salaries even than people who are advantaged for other reasons in a salary negotiation.[25] But the same holds true for other aspects of a package. People's informal networks provide many important supports in negotiation. They help channel the flow of information and referrals; supply emotional support, feedback, political advice, and protection; and increase the likelihood and speed of promotion.[26] In settings where men predominate in positions of power, as in Claudia's bank, women have a smaller pool of high-status, same-gender contacts on which to draw—which was part of the challenge Claudia faced.[27] Luckily, Marisa had a much broader pool of women to draw on. Both women recognized the importance of their networks to gain information. They found people in their network willing to share their knowledge and expertise.

SECOND-GENERATION ISSUES AND SMALL WINS

We noted in the Introduction that when people in organizations negotiate for themselves, they can change the organization's negotiated order and can thus have an impact on more widespread change. While people often think of organizational change as being grand, intentional, and top-down, we adhere to another model of organizational change—that of small wins. These are simple actions that people throughout the hierarchy can take and that accumulate to create substantive change. The power of small wins is that they are achievable. It's daunting to think of changing an entire organization, but creating a pilot program or experimenting with a new hiring process on your own team is not as far-fetched.[28]

The act of negotiating can create small wins—particularly when we negotiate in a way that alters the negotiated order. There are countless other opportunities for small wins, some as a result of negotiating, that can accumulate to change organizations. We can see in the stories of Marisa and Claudia that networks play an incredibly important role in gathering information needed in order to be successful. When I teach negotiation and leadership development programs, I emphasize the importance of this function of networks, particularly when people ask about compensation.

Discussing compensation is often taboo, since we frequently assume members of our networks won't share that kind of information. It feels awkward to ask a colleague, acquaintance, or even friend about her compensation, or whether she negotiated for a promotion or was just granted one. Yet this taboo is something we can each chip away at by being responsible, active network members. By talking openly about our own experiences and outcomes, we can expand the possibilities for others. If Claudia makes a point of telling other women about the ex-pat packages and possibilities for overseas transfers, more women will consider those possibilities for themselves. By enlisting the human resource person in London, she signals that it is important that people understand these packages, making it more likely others will get this information in the future. And by sharing this information, she contributes to a more open culture around information. If Marisa shares what she has learned about negotiating for the next move to advance in the organization, that information will help every partner faced with a request she feels she can't refuse. Marisa has also set a precedent by negotiating the possibility of doing a leadership job remotely.

For this and other materials, visit www.deborahmkolb.com.

Putting *Information* to Work

Remember: Information Is Power
- The more information you have entering a negotiation, the more confidence and power you bring to the table:

(*Continued*)

- Set high aspirations. This helps expand your search for information, increasing the likelihood that you will find information you can use to your benefit. In addition, searching out good information will prompt you to raise your aspirations.
- Remember "Yes, and..." By keeping the *and* in mind, you stay open to creative possibilities. Ask yourself, "What would allow me to say yes?"

Benchmarking: The What
- Collect data. Gather information from websites, news articles, and other sources.
- Leverage your network, inside and outside your organization:
  - Learn what types of issues are negotiable in your organization.
  - Understand the range of possible outcomes—from salary to support staff, scope, resources, or, like Claudia, ex-pat packages.

Understanding Your Counterpart: The Who
- Reflect on your own experiences with your counterpart (if applicable):
  - What is his communication style?
  - What approaches have you found successful in the past?
  - Gather data from others in your network.
- What is her negotiating style? What are her priorities, pressures, biases, and assumptions that could play into your negotiations?
  - How does he like to hear things? As problems? Solutions? Choices?

Recognizing Opportunities and Positioning to Negotiate

Several years ago at our regular Tuesday morning game, my tennis partner arrived close to tears. It was obvious that we had to spend some time talking about what was troubling her before we got on the court. As her colleague, I knew she was going through a challenging time. She'd recently put into motion a plan to adopt a child from South America. In fact, she had just received notification that all had been arranged for her to travel to Paraguay the following month to pick up an eighteen-month-old girl. Her maternity leave had already been set. Anticipating her new role as a single mother, she'd prepared for the challenges she foresaw.

On the day before we met, she was shocked when the most senior member of her department visited her office and announced that the department had decided she should become the next department chair when she returned from maternity leave. "No way," she told him. She was already afraid she'd be overwhelmed just keeping up with her normal teaching, research, and service roles. Still, her senior colleague persisted: it was her turn to take the role, he said; other members of the department had taken their turn. Again, she told him no. After some back and forth where he persisted and she resisted, he told her that she was not being a team player in the department. It was that insult that put her over the edge. When she arrived at our tennis match, she told me she was going to quit the university. I observed that this was a precipitous move, given that she had tenure!

It was clear to me that she had not seen this request as an opportunity to negotiate.

OPPORTUNITIES TO NEGOTIATE

It's often difficult to identify negotiating opportunities during occasions like these. Whether such exchanges look like a request or more like an order, they are embedded in ongoing structures and relationships within the organization—what we call the *negotiated order*.

Consider some examples from situations where people are asked to do something:

- A dean asks a female colleague to teach an extra session of an oversubscribed course that they need her to do because of high student demand. Already very busy, she says no. The dean then asks her male colleague and he says sure—as long as he doesn't have to teach it again for the next three years!
- A partner in a professional services firm is promoted to lead her office. Firm leaders believe she's the right person to lead a turnaround in the practice, and she excitedly says yes. After eighteen months, she brings the group to breakeven but is then taken out of the role. She'd never thought to negotiate what the expectations for a turnaround would be.

As we saw in chapter 1, even very senior women often fail to negotiate anything about the role, its contours, even its compensation when offered a new role—even when it's a role they don't want. They assume that turning down an opportunity might mean it will never come again, so they feel they have to say yes. Too few recognize the ways they could negotiate to make the role fit the person they are and what they want to accomplish.

It's not just requests that go unnoticed when it comes to potential negotiating possibilities. One of my colleagues incurred the wrath of those around her when she took a rigid stance about an administrative issue. Absolutely convinced that she was "right," she kept arming herself with legal arguments about her position.[1] Since then, she's suffered the consequences of her actions: an erosion of once-cordial relationships with her colleagues and the administration. What she failed to appreciate was that she could hold her interest in the merits of her position yet still leave room for the possibility of a negotiated outcome.

These examples could easily lead us to subscribe to the notion that "women don't ask."[2] But the issues are a bit more complicated—because they have to do with different negotiating contexts.

GETTING IN YOUR OWN WAY

We discussed the difference between n-negotiations and N-negotiations in chapter 1. One thing this distinction helps us to recognize is that negotiators can get in their own way as they prepare to negotiate for themselves—in a number of ways. There are also a number of steps you can take to overcome these tendencies.

Don't Miss Opportunities to Negotiate

Since the problems are embedded in organizational routines, it can take effort merely to see a new situation as potentially negotiable. When asked to take on extra responsibilities, people can feel their only options are black and white: yes or no. I am struck in the programs I teach by the number of people whose goal is to learn to say no more often, a position that eradicates any further possibilities. Instead, I encourage people to think about these situations as ripe for negotiation.

Some of the research suggests that men may be more likely to recognize situations as negotiable—at least if we believe what they report in online surveys. Such research establishes that men are likely to have negotiated more recently than women.[3] But while gender difference is the attributed reason,[4] there may be more at play.

One element of this is that it's quite possible that women and men have varying ability to access the kinds of information that would help them recognize negotiation as a possibility. A colleague of mine observes that male faculty members are more likely than women to negotiate. She doesn't attribute this to a deficiency in the women; rather, she realizes that male colleagues have role models and supporters who coach them and demonstrate how it is done. It is likely that men within organizations have networks that grant them more and better access to information about the negotiated order itself—around what types of issues are negotiable and possible outcomes.[5]

Don't Bargain Yourself Down

There are other ways that people can get in their own way. If they feel as though they're on less secure ground, they may tend to focus on their own weaknesses and bargain themselves down. When pricing contracts, a colleague of mine routinely estimates the number of days she will need to prepare and then subtracts a day. She has made the first concession in her head: she rationally figures out what should be a legitimate opening offer, then discounts it. Sadly, this is all too common. Either we cannot imagine achieving something, or we worry that the other party will see it as unrealistic or too aggressive. Indeed, some research suggests that women may be more likely to drop their opening offer from what they originally intended.[6] And if we are to believe, as Henry Kissinger suggests, that one's opening offer is as good as it will get, then making a first concession in one's head can be a real handicap![7]

Setting lower goals isn't the only way we bargain ourselves down. We often focus so much on negotiating about one issue that we decide not to bring up other things that are important to us and necessary—to do our jobs effectively. For example, women can sometimes be so grateful about the flexible work options they've already negotiated that they fail to ask about other issues.[8] The fact that you've arranged to work remotely one day a week shouldn't keep you from asking to serve on the new task force that reports to the chief information officer. The challenge is to feel empowered by past negotiations—not let them hinder you from asking for more.

Don't Let Expectations Limit Your Options

There's a third way that potential negotiators can undermine themselves in negotiation: letting projections and expectations limit their options. For example, there is frequently the cultural expectation that a woman will be collaborative when negotiating on her own behalf by putting others' interests before her own. Such an expectation can create a dilemma or double bind for her. In other words, she is expected to be communal, when it is agency that determines successful negotiation outcomes.

Acting communally versus acting with agency. This expectation has several implications. First, it forces a woman to choose between efficacy as a negotiator (having agency) and fulfilling gender stereotypes of niceness and accommodation (being communal). These kinds of double binds occur when women are faced with acting in accordance with ideas of femininity—when others judge them as less competent—or acting in accordance with ideas of masculinity, whether others see them as aggressive and unlikable. (We discuss double binds more thoroughly in chapter 4.)

This dichotomizing of style choices evokes a private-sphere ethic of care: because women are associated with caregiving, they are expected to put others' needs before their own.[9] In the context of negotiation, this can mean that a woman is expected to make accommodations or feel responsibility for ensuring that all parties are satisfied with a deal. When she "owns" that responsibility, she may put others' interests before her own and make concessions that fail to benefit her. Indeed, they might actually result in suboptimal deals for everyone involved.

Owning the responsibility that everyone leave satisfied. In her work on relational practice, our colleague Joyce Fletcher has described this tendency to feel responsible for ensuring that all parties are satisfied at the end of a negotiation. As Fletcher demonstrates, this is not a positive approach to relationships or to the task of getting work done. Indeed, she labels this behavior relational malpractice: it's possible for women to focus so much on what others want that they lose their authority and fail to make use of their expertise.[10] They may be focused on being liked or trying to create a caring environment at the expense of completing the task at hand. Fletcher suggests that whatever stance one takes needs to be connected to what is necessary for the task at hand. Thus, when a negotiator focuses on what is likely to be best for all parties—herself included—she is less likely to sacrifice her own interests for those of others. She can take up her own agency in the service of community and accomplish the dual tasks of doing well for herself and for others.

These observations about potential pitfalls of negotiating for oneself require us to think about preparation in a somewhat different way. We have discussed the importance of gathering good information so that you can feel that what you ask for is defensible. But more is involved in getting you to feel more secure in asking, especially when issues of legitimacy may be involved. You must have the tools to be an effective advocate for yourself in order to create interdependence with the other party—which you need to get negotiations going and to keep them going.

POSITIONING TO NEGOTIATE

In N-negotiations, we generally consider that parties are positioned to negotiate.[11] There's an assumed structure to the negotiation; the parties have roles—say, buyer and seller—and they are theoretically engaged in trying to make a deal. Obviously there are many slips twixt this coming together and the actual deal; every year, an entire industry publishes books on this very subject. While getting to yes is obviously a challenge, there is a shared understanding in the N-negotiations that the parties are engaged in some form of bargaining—whether it succeeds or not.

"Constructing" n-Negotiations

Organizational n-negotiations are less clear-cut.[12] Roles may be murky: you or the other person might not even know you're involved in a negotiation. Furthermore, buyers and sellers implicitly understand their interdependence in a way that n-negotiators may not. These n-negotiations often have to be "constructed," in the sense that someone needs to take some actions in order to get them started.

Let's say that you want to negotiate for a promotion or a new project, but your boss is oblivious to the issue. Or you're assigned a project with no discussion expected and no clear objective. Or you want to create a flexible work schedule. In all of these situations, it is not sufficient merely to have ideas to propose once the negotiations are under way. You have to get them started, which requires two different processes. First, you have to get yourself into a position to negotiate—that is, establish yourself in the role of negotiator. Second, you have to prepare to position yourself in relation to the other party to get the negotiations off the ground.

Both steps are captured in the concept of positioning.

Positioning: Your Role as Negotiator

When experts speak about getting ready to negotiate, they typically focus on helping the person figure out what she wants, her interests in the negotiation, her aspirations, her walkaway, and her walkaway alternatives.[13] Then she's advised to think similarly about what these are on other side. But the notion of positioning to negotiate is somewhat different. Drawing from a tradition that's different from the psychological and decision sciences most popular in negotiation theory, positioning has its roots in communication and discourse analysis; it refers to the ways that negotiators seek to construct legitimate social roles and identities for themselves, subject to the expectations and constraints of the social structures in which they operate.[14] The idea is that we do not play a static role during a negotiation; it is not something totally up to the individual or set by the other's expectations. This role is negotiated just as much as the issues to be discussed are.[15] And a significant part of that negotiation is creating interdependence between you and the other person.

Positioning: The Other Person's Role

The late Jeff Rubin once observed that negotiation is the quintessential illustration of interdependence. Just as clapping requires two hands working in synchrony, so negotiation requires two parties moving to a common center.[16]

We can think of interdependence in two primary ways. The first concerns your relationship with the person with whom you plan to negotiate and the value that person sees in you. People negotiate with you because you have something they want. So a first task in preparing is to assess that value.

The second approach to analyzing interdependence, the more common in the negotiation field, is to consider alternatives outside the negotiation. The idea is captured by using the acronym BATNA: the Best Alternative to a Negotiated Agreement.[17] Positioning yourself in a negotiation requires that you prepare to take stock of your value and assess the relative BATNAs for yourself and the other person; then you figure out how you'll use that information in the negotiation. We discuss the details of BATNA later in the chapter; for now, let's look at Charlotte's situation.

Charlotte's Chance

For the past five years, Charlotte has been the director of client relations at a medium-sized consulting firm. In that role, she's been responsible for managing and servicing current clients, as well as identifying opportunities to expand accounts. She has earned a solid reputation as a personable, innovative leader who manages well, sells well, and does whatever it takes to make the organization successful. Her colleagues see her as somebody who will jump in and contribute whenever she is needed.

Four months ago, Charlotte's boss, William Donovan, the vice president of client advisory services, left the company. As VP, Bill managed large consulting engagements, bringing in new business and assigning consulting teams based on clients' needs. Since Bill left, Charlotte has been unofficially filling in for him in addition to performing her own director responsibilities—putting in more than eighty hours per week as a result. While Charlotte is great at negotiating with colleagues and clients, she has trouble negotiating for herself. She's overworked and underpaid, and yet she still hesitates to use her additional workload to justify more money and the title that goes with it. She knows that others with less responsibility are paid more than she is, and that eats at her.

Charlotte's history at the firm has not prepared her for the challenge she now faces. She was hired as an analyst out of business school. It was a great opportunity, so she jumped at the chance and never bargained over salary or benefits, and did not even question what her opportunities would be. Successful at each of her assignments, she adapted well to the competitive fast-paced environment at the firm, developing a good reputation for her client service skills. But she said yes to each assignment she was offered and never questioned the title, salary, support, or working conditions that went along with it. She just took what came along and did not think much about it. With Bill's departure things have changed.

This past month, Charlotte landed a major new client, which will likely result in an increase in revenues of at least 10 percent for the firm over the previous year's earnings. Charlotte has decided that since she has essentially been doing her boss's old VP job, she wants it to be official. She has always been on good terms with the head of the firm, helping him out on special projects when he needed it.

Deciding the time is right, Charlotte plans to meet with the CEO to negotiate her promotion to the VP position with an increase in pay that the job merits. She needs to position herself for what she expects will be a challenging negotiation.

TAKING STOCK OF YOUR VALUE

Participants in my workshops often ask me about how they can become more confident negotiating. It is a concern that many have when they enter into n-negotiations. I always tell them that it is not a matter of just looking in the mirror and saying, "I'm self-confident." That doesn't work. Rather, you need to take stock of your value. It often helps to have people who can work through some of the issues with you. There are many ways to assess your value in a negotiation—for one thing, the skills and competence you bring to the job. Then there are the experiences you've had: building a well-functioning team, the successful projects you've participated on and maybe led. There is the hard work and commitment you give to your team, to your colleagues, to your clients and customers. There are innovations you might have introduced. All of these accomplishments help you take stock. But they do not necessarily get you to the place where you are working toward establishing the kind of interdependence that would get negotiations off the ground.

Set Your Value in a Currency That the Other Party Values

To fully take stock of your value, you need to think about what the other party values. You can start with some general observations. If you want to negotiate with the chief financial officer, highlighting your team-building accomplishments will not be especially persuasive; your revenue or cost-cutting innovations are what matter most to her. So the first step is to consider what about your performance is most important for the other person to know. What is your value proposition to her?

Next, you need to think about your value proposition in a more finely grained way—that is, what is it now? I have often observed that people think the person with whom they're negotiating appreciates their value and is aware of their accomplishments. A more useful rule is to assume that your performance doesn't speak for itself. If you've been doing a good job, it is not clear that the person with whom you want to negotiate knows about it. So you really need to do two things here: figure out what your value proposition is and find ways to make it visible.[18]

Of course, this doesn't always come naturally. Sometimes we shy away from opportunities to demonstrate our value to the organization. Sheryl Sandberg recounts an 'aha' moment after attending the Fortune Most Powerful Women Summit. She'd been self-conscious about the title of the event and opted to change the title on the web calendar she and her Google colleagues shared.[19] Afterward, she was chided by a *Fortune* editor for not owning her power now that she was listed along the ranks of Meg Whitman, Carly Fiorina, and Oprah Winfrey.[20]

If Sheryl Sandberg can be reflexively self-conscious about owning her power, it's not surprising that this is something many find difficult. Still, there are several simple actions you can take to document your value. As in Sandberg's case, you can make your calendar public so colleagues can see whom you meet with or present to. You can keep a record of positive feedback that you receive in case there are opportunities to share it with your team or boss. On a more routine basis, you can celebrate the achievements of your peers, teams, and direct reports to demonstrate the effectiveness of your leadership. When someone praises you or your team, you could even ask them to mention how well you did to your boss or other colleagues.[21] We discuss this further in chapter 4.

Challenge 1: Figure Out What Your Value Proposition Is

This can be tricky. A leader once told me that somebody who wants an opportunity should be forthright and boldly ask for it—advice he gave to both men and women without reflecting on whether it would be heard differently. Yet we know that sometimes women face a double bind in which acting assertively can challenge traditional stereotypes about women. As a result, they can experience a social cost to assertively putting themselves forward and risk being perceived of as pushy, demanding, or overly self-promoting.[22] We need to take these considerations into account when finding ways to make our own value visible.

Identify your challenges. Taking stock of your value also requires that you consider the less-stellar parts of your performance and discern where you are vulnerable. Thinking honestly about your weaknesses means considering what the other party might identify as counterpoints to the claims you make. Maybe your team didn't meet your target this year. While you might have good reasons to explain the shortfall, it may still be seen as a point against you. That would particularly be the case if you think the other party is likely to resist what you're asking for. Think about Alicia's example from the Introduction; though she had been in her role for four years, she was still considered unseasoned in her company, so she will need to think about how to position this when she negotiates for the promotion.

Challenges can have a gendered dimension. A woman's career track can present a challenge when certain experiences—say, overseas assignments—are deemed a requirement.[23] We know that while not a weakness per se, motherhood is sometimes used as a reason for excluding women from certain roles.[24] This is why being aware of your potential vulnerabilities in a situation is an important step in positioning yourself for a negotiation. This will prepare you to deal with these issues if the other person brings them up during a negotiation—which they likely will, particularly if you're negotiating about something that the other party finds difficult. Being prepared to deal with challenges means having an account or story that you can tell which explains possible shortcomings.

Let's consider Charlotte's challenge. First, it looks as though Charlotte does not have much of a track record of negotiating for herself. We know that she failed to negotiate anything about the role each time she got a new assignment or promotion—which might mean that she's trained people, including the CEO, to expect that she is not likely to negotiate. Indeed, when she picked up Bill's work, it was probably the best time to negotiate. This pattern can be hard to break out of; the longer you go without negotiating, the greater the expectation is that you won't do so and the harder it is to feel confident speaking up.

This situation is complicated by different perspectives on the issue. Charlotte may feel she is being overlooked, whereas the CEO is unlikely to see it that way. In fact, the CEO likely hasn't had the experience of being overlooked, so it might be hard for him to identify with her. Gender may be playing a subtle role; maybe women don't come to mind when vice president roles open up. All of this means that Charlotte needs to be prepared for a surprised reaction from the CEO. He may even deny that there is an issue.

It is clear that Charlotte wants the VP role formerly held by her previous boss. But it is not at all clear that the CEO sees her as the incumbent for this role, even though she's been doing it in an acting capacity for some time. So Charlotte needs to take stock and ask herself why he should give her that role. What does she bring to the table? She has a consistent track record of performance. In this negotiation, her value proposition seems quite compelling. She clearly has good relationships with clients and has demonstrated that she's willing to jump in when work needs doing. Witness her taking on Bill's role, even though it added considerably to her workload. Her immediate value proposition is that she has already been doing the role—and quite successfully: she landed a new client with the promise of substantial revenues.

Challenge 2: Plan to Make Your Value Visible

Charlotte will have to think hard about how she makes that value proposition visible to the CEO, since he might not know precisely the role she played in landing the client. There are a number of ways she might make this value visible to him. Perhaps there are some communications from the client to Charlotte that she can pass on to the CEO or bring to their meeting. Maybe there are others from her firm on the sales team who might be able to let the CEO know the role Charlotte played. Charlotte herself can be prepared to do this, perhaps before the meeting with the CEO or at its start. Maybe she could transmit some messages from the client or have other members of the firm vouch for her.

The role of allies in making the case can be particularly important for those who worry about the reaction of claiming too much credit for themselves. Many suggest that when women do claim this credit, they are best advised to do so by emphasizing their own role but giving credit to a team as well.[25] As Charlotte considers ways to position herself and make her value visible, knowing more about the CEO and how he responds to different types of overtures, a topic we discussed in chapter 1, would help her prepare.

Putting challenges in a positive light. Charlotte also needs to work through how she will deal with possible perceptions of her shortcomings—and she has several. We know that she has no track record in negotiating and might have missed her best chance when her boss left the position vacant. Of course, it is possible to see this as a potential strength, as her time filling in gave her a chance to prove herself. Indeed, potentially this is her major vulnerability: it is not clear she has the range of skills or the depth of experience to be appointed vice president. So how can she deal with this potential vulnerability?

Since we can expect her vulnerabilities to come up in the negotiation, she needs to develop a narrative that puts them in a positive light so she's ready when the CEO raises the topic of her inexperience as a barrier to her taking the role. Her response will need to demonstrate that she has the experience, demonstrated by her picking up the VP responsibility. But she also needs to be realistic; she is obviously not as experienced as someone who has been a vice president of client advisory services for more than a few months. So she'll want to go in with ideas about how she might compensate for this—ideas about people who could mentor her, for example.

Because of her relative lack of experience, it is quite possible that the CEO has other candidates in mind. Therefore, Charlotte needs a way to discuss her relative strengths compared to, say, someone who comes to the firm from the outside. All her years working at the firm in different capacities have given her firm-specific human capital that can give her an advantage in pulling together and leading engagement teams.[26] If the CEO questions her experience, Charlotte can point not only to what she has accomplished in the role, but also to how she plans to get the help she needs to grow. If the CEO brings up a plan to hire from the outside, she can talk about how her experience in the firm makes her a better candidate.

Recognizing vulnerabilities, advocating for yourself. By working through your vulnerable areas, you are better prepared when challenges come up. Being ready with these kinds of stories or accounts positions you to advocate for yourself. It will also help to have some clear ideas about how to implement the role in a way that makes it easy for the CEO to say yes—which we discuss in more detail in a later chapter.

BATNA: POSITIONING YOURSELF IN LIGHT OF ALTERNATIVES TO AGREEMENT

The concept of BATNA—the Best Alternative to a Negotiated Agreement—was introduced with the publication of *Getting to Yes* in 1980 and refers to the choices you would have to accept if you cannot reach an agreement. BATNA, in other words, sets the bounds for the range of acceptable outcomes in negotiation. As BATNA is generally introduced in work on negotiation, it is used to help negotiators figure out their bottom line or reservation price. In other words, it helps calculate the point at which you would walk away from a potential deal.[27]

While the notion of a deal and alternatives outside it become more complicated in n-negotiations, they're still quite relevant. The assessment of the BATNAs between parties gives us one way to analyze relative bargaining power.

BATNA in the Context of n-Negotiations

In most books on negotiation, the concept of BATNA is introduced very close to the beginning, since the clearest and most obvious way to discuss BATNA is in terms of distributive or single-issue negotiation. If you are going to negotiate about price, the strategic way to think about making a good deal is to consider your other choices.

Recall my Ethiopian students bargaining over tablecloths in chapter 1. Having compared prices of comparable cloths, they were ready to set an upper limit on the price they would pay. This is what we call their reservation price: that price either above which (as buyer) or below which (as seller) they would walk away.[28] My students knew what they would pay, and they had the alternative of ending negotiations with one vendor and going to a new one if the bargaining wasn't fruitful. This makes it clear that having a well-defined BATNA is important: it lessens the chance that you will overpay for something or undervalue what you are selling. That's why most negotiation books will tell you that the first step is to figure out your BATNA—even better, to have multiple BATNAs.

Next, you would want to know as much as you can about the other party's BATNA, because knowing both your own and theirs brings clarity to the range of possible deals you could make. My students could evaluate several factors to consider the various vendors' BATNAs in the Ethiopian market; for instance, bad weather or low crowds would suggest the vendors had fewer customers, and the number of vendors selling tablecloths would give a sense of how much competition they have.

BATNAs are clear in some contexts. Figuring out your BATNA is naturally clearer in some situations than others. Compensation negotiation is one. When negotiating for a new job, it helps to have another offer. That second offer is a BATNA, and it is likely not as good as the one you are negotiating about. If it were, you'd take it. Almost by definition, your BATNA is never as good as the deal you hope to make.

Improving your BATNA can improve your agreement. If you don't have a good BATNA, try to improve it. It is time well spent to, say, get another offer or find another buyer: doing so helps you assess offers and counteroffers more confidently and probably more rationally. In this regard, the axiom that "a bird in the hand is worth two in the bush" applies. Wishing you have a BATNA does not make it so.[29]

It's important to be creative in how you conceptualize BATNA. I often use the example of Almaz, who runs a small textile company in the outskirts of a major African city. She has responded to changes in the economy by shifting production from high-end decorative sweaters to simpler garments that will sell for a lower price. As a result, she no longer needs the high-end stitching machine she acquired several years ago. A European designer offers to buy the machine for a fraction of what Almaz paid several years ago. She knows what it would cost to buy a new machine—considerably more than she is being offered—but she doesn't know what price to accept for her used machine. Although Almaz does not have another buyer, which would give her a clear BATNA, she investigates other options: what it would cost to haul the machine away, the charitable tax advantage she might get by donating it to a nongovernmental organization that works with women to develop handmade goods, and the benefit of the status quo: keeping the machine but selling high-end sweaters only to the tourist market. Considering each of these alternatives helps her figure out a realistic reservation price. When she knows her alternatives, she can then determine whether to negotiate with the designer and at what price she would walk away.

BATNAs are less clear in n-negotiations. Consider the negotiation (or lack thereof) I introduced at the start of the chapter. My tennis partner said at the outset of our conversation that she was prepared to quit—a BATNA—rather than take on the extra responsibilities of the department chair. "A bit precipitous," I responded, since she had tenure.

Let's say you want to negotiate a flexible work arrangement. What will you do if you don't get it? Sure, you could quit. Again, it's hardly desirable, but perhaps a necessary option. Or you could stick with your full-time role, which would be the status quo. Although it is quite easy to talk glibly about developing your BATNA in negotiations at work, it can be a challenge. And what does that mean as a practical matter in the negotiation? This brings us to a discussion of bargaining power.

Analyzing the parties' interdependence. Power in negotiation is typically defined by considering the nature of the interdependence of the parties.[30] One who is more dependent on a deal is presumed to have less bargaining power; the reverse is true for those less dependent. Dependence, independence, and interdependence can all be analyzed through the parties' relative BATNAs. Thus, negotiators with good BATNAs are presumably in more powerful positions in negotiation: they're more independent and less dependent on a deal. Obviously other dimensions of power are also relevant: access to resources, hierarchical position, and access to influential others, to name a few.

In organizational negotiations, BATNA is an important counterweight to most people's initial presumptions that bargaining power is correlated with position in the hierarchy. We tend to assume that bosses will have more power in a negotiation than do those who report to them.[31] This is often the case; however, a subordinate with a great BATNA might enter a negotiation in a more powerful position than a boss with weak alternatives or a high level of dependence on her subordinate.

A negotiator who seems to have few viable alternatives to an agreement may be negotiating with someone who is in a similar situation. We might glibly say that a negotiator has a BATNA of quitting, which is generally not a great alternative. But we don't want to minimize the costs of that option when we consider the other party's BATNA. If our negotiator does quit, her boss faces hiring and training costs, lost time, and the personal cost of having to get someone new up to speed. It's important to keep in mind that even if your alternatives aren't great, your counterpart's might not be either.

In a workshop I've taught with women scientists, I use a case study in which a boss asks a young woman to work on a project that doesn't interest her. When we discuss BATNA, people agree that she is unlikely to have good alternatives. But interestingly they almost universally believe that her boss does have good alternatives; for example, he could ask somebody else to do it. While that is certainly his possible BATNA, it assumes that he asked her because she was the first person he saw when he emerged from his office that morning! We have to recognize that his BATNA might not be that good; he likely asked her because she has the skill set he needs for the project. This means she then has some leverage in the negotiation to craft an arrangement that works.

What Charlotte's Case Teaches Us

Analyzing Charlotte's BATNA. Let's return to Charlotte. She has several potential BATNAs. She could go to work for the new client. In order for that to be a viable alternative, she would need to explore this seriously. That is something she could pursue prior to her negotiations with the CEO. She has other alternatives; she could dial back and just continue to focus on her role as a director, which would have obvious implications for both her and the firm. After having been exposed to the challenge of the VP role she has been doing, she is likely to find the director role less challenging. This might make it more likely that she would then explore other external job possibilities. And of course, one BATNA that is always a possibility is the status quo—she can keep doing her job and that of the VP who just left. Clearly Charlotte has alternatives. They probably don't excite her, but that is the nature of BATNAs: if they were just as good, she'd be doing them. Still, having clear BATNAs gives her leverage in the negotiation. She is not totally dependent on a deal with the CEO.

Analyzing the other party's BATNA. The CEO has alternatives too. He could hire a vice president from the outside. Indeed, he may be preparing to do this. However, there are clear drawbacks to hiring someone from outside the organization. It takes a new person time to get up to speed, to learn about the organization and its culture. The CEO might have others in the organization besides Charlotte whom he can promote. In this case, the costs might be less than hiring an outsider. But the fact that he has not already done so sug-gests that he's content to have Charlotte continue in the dual roles she's been playing. As an aside, it would help Charlotte position herself if she had this contextual information (see chapter 1) about the CEO's plans for the role. And of course, it is always possible that the CEO might still be unwilling to negotiate—even recogniz-ing that Charlotte has alternatives and that his might not be that attractive. But it is clear that in this situation, the CEO has a pretty sweet deal: Charlotte is doing two jobs, presumably well, given that she landed the new client, and he is paying her for just one—the lesser-status one at that. The CEO might prefer the status quo, although she would likely not.

Both Charlotte and the CEO have alternatives outside the negotiation—but who has the better ones? That would help us answer the question of who is more dependent on the deal.

This is a difficult question to answer. And that's the point. While each has alternatives, it looks as if they—and the firm as a whole—would be better off if they could negotiate an agreement that works for Charlotte and the firm. Establishing interdependence (not think-ing solely of dependence and independence) creates the conditions for a more fruitful negotiation. While analyzing and developing alter-natives is critical to positioning oneself, fostering interdependence is something that happens once bargaining commences. This is a topic we return to in chapter 7.

SECOND-GENERATION ISSUES AND SMALL WINS

Gendered opportunity structures—that is, situations where certain jobs are seen to be more appropriate for men and others for women—are the undercurrent in Charlotte's situation. Despite the fact that she's been doing the job of VP, the CEO does not automatically see her in this role. To the degree that Charlotte negotiates with the CEO about her role, it may be a moment of learning for the CEO. He would have to consider what criteria he uses to judge a candidate's suitability. Charlotte has been in an acting role. In what ways is that developmental ground for the VP role? Might that be a way to groom people in the firm? If the firm is challenged by not having women in senior leadership roles, maybe Charlotte's negotiation will start a new practice.

By negotiating for the role she has been doing, she is also forcing the firm to think more clearly about criteria for leadership roles. Charlotte compels the CEO to clarify the skills and experiences required for the VP role. Often women are highly rated on their performance but yet not seen as having the potential for more senior roles. This situation forces the CEO to be clear with Charlotte about why she does not have what it takes. That kind of clarity and transparency makes it much more likely that people will have a better road map for their own development.

For this and other materials, visit www.deborahmkolb.com.

 Putting *Positioning* to Work

Avoid Getting in Your Own Way
- Remember to look for n-negotiating opportunities.
- Don't bargain yourself down; don't make the first concession in your head.
- Don't let your options be limited by others' unreasonable expectations.

Position Yourself to Negotiate
- Take stock of your value.
- Express your value in a currency the other party recognizes.
- Identify your vulnerabilities, and be prepared to address them in a positive light.
- Be prepared to make your value visible to the other party.

(Continued)

Identify Your BATNA
- Assess your BATNA in the context of an n-negotiation.
- Look for ways to improve your BATNA.
- Assess the other person's BATNA relative to yours.
- Analyze the interdependence between you and your counterpart.

Anchoring, Mindfulness, and Preparing for Problem Solving

Mutual-gains problem solving, a topic that's been the subject of many important and practical books, goes by various descriptions: interest-based as opposed to positional bargaining; the creation of value as opposed to the claiming of it; integrative as opposed to distributive negotiation; win-win as opposed to win-lose.[1] When the idea of mutual gains is introduced, it is typically in contrast to its opposite. And that certainly makes sense in many discussions of negotiations where parties are negotiating a deal over prices of real estate, business deals, and contracts[2]—the capital N-negotiations we've referenced in previous chapters.[3] This distinction may also make sense when discussing budgets and compensation.

But the distinction takes on a somewhat different cast when we consider it in the context of n-negotiations. Preparing for mutual-gains problem solving at work is the subject of this chapter.

MUTUAL-GAINS PROBLEM SOLVING IN n-NEGOTIATIONS

At work, n-negotiations often originate as problems or opportunities rather than as traditional occasions for deal making. These may start out as requests that one party assumes invite only one option: a yes-or-no choice. When Marisa was offered an opportunity she really did not want in chapter 1, she thought her only choice was to accept it. In chapter 2, we saw how Charlotte, trying to position herself for the leadership role she'd already been doing, wanted to press her boss to say yes. These are the kinds of examples to which we must compare mutual-gains problem solving. The probability of a good outcome becomes even more likely when we take both parties' interests and concerns into account.

Mutual-gains negotiation in organizations is a way of thinking about choices as more than saying yes to something or rejecting it outright. We discussed in the previous chapter how people tend to overlook opportunities to negotiate because they think their choices are to do something or not do it, This chapter covers the ways you can prepare to open up the conversation and consider more options. To do that, we begin with some basic tenets of problem-solving negotiation preparation and elaborate the ways they play out in n-negotiations.

To push the ideas further and come up with creative options requires a deeper understanding of each party's context. Preparing to negotiate in a problem-solving way means also preparing yourself to be open, to be mindful—to listen in a manner that helps you *jointly* create options.

These two forms of preparation can create a tension—one that we address later in the chapter. For now, let's look at the three possible resolutions to conflict put forth by a 1920s pioneer.

DOMINATION, COMPROMISE, INTEGRATION: IT ALL STARTED WITH A WOMAN

Much has been written about the process of problem-solving negotiation, including Getting to Yes, probably the most influential book on the topic in decades.[4] In it, negotiators are advised to do two things in order to create options for mutual gains: separate the person from the problem and focus on interests, not positions. In the book's first edition, the authors credit some of its central ideas to Mary Parker Follett, a management consultant who worked with industry and labor in the 1920s. In "Constructive Conflict," a 1925 paper she delivered to the Bureau of Personnel Administration, Follett explains three ways of dealing with conflict: domination, compromise, and integration. The first two of these, she suggested, end with less than satisfactory results.

Follett defined *domination* as the victory of one side over another. Although it's often the easiest way to deal with conflict, at least in the short term, domination seldom ends successfully. Writing in the mid-1920s, she cited fallout from World War I as a contemporary example that was clearly shaping up to be less than satisfactory for all parties.

Follett described the second option, compromise, as the most typical resolution to a conflict: each side gives a little in order to get back as quickly as possible to the activity that caused the conflict. She used contemporary trade union negotiations as an example. The trouble with compromise, she asserted, was that each side starts by asking for more than they think they can get, and in the end no one understands what the other really wanted in the first place. The longer-term problem with compromise, she said, is that the conflict solved through this method is likely to arise again and again.

Compared to domination and compromise, Follett recognized a better method:

> The third way is integration... When two desires are integrated, that means that a solution has been found in which both desires have found a place that neither has had to sacrifice anything... In the Harvard Library one day, in one of the smaller rooms, someone wanted the window open, I wanted it shut. We opened the window in the next room, where no one was sitting. This was not a compromise because there was no curtailing of desire; we both got what we really wanted. For I did not want a closed room, I simply did not want the north wind to blow directly on me; likewise the other occupant did not want that particular window open, he merely wanted more air in the room.[5]

Integrating Interests: Yours and the Other Person's

From this perspective, problem solving refers to integrating divergent interests. Preparing to problem-solve means becoming clear about your own interests, as well as setting the priority among them. It also means gauging the other party's interests and priorities as well as you can, a planning exercise that can yield creative options for both people involved. While this approach is typically described in the context of more formal N-negotiations, it has some interesting applications when we look at what happens in organizational n-negotiations. Preparation involves working to understand these different interests before you begin a negotiation.

Understand the different interests, but beware of the trap. While this kind of preparation is certainly important, it does present a potential trap: sometimes it can lock us into our way of thinking, causing us to adhere to our ways of understanding interests and think only of the options that we invented prior to the meetings. In so doing, we can fail to hear other ideas.

The circular response and the linear response. In her 1924 book, *Creative Experience*, Follett takes a different approach. In it she developed the idea of the circular response and contrasted it with a linear response, where people's interests are more or less fixed. The challenge with a linear response comes in figuring out ways to integrate the interests as in the library example. In a circular response, our interests are refined in interactions with the other party: "I never react to you but to you-plus-me; or to be more accurate, it is I-plus-you reacting to you-plus-me."[6] Follett suggests that a person cannot really assess his own interests apart from the interaction with the other: "We do not stop to examine a desire until another is disputing the right of way with it."[7]

Charlotte's negotiation with the CEO for a promotion to vice president, a role she was already doing (chapter 2), provides a good example of how considering our own issues in isolation is insufficient. When her negotiation starts, she believes the CEO will share her interest in enlarging the client base and find it compelling that she has brought in a new client. However, he tells Charlotte she was merely closing a deal the former VP already had in the pipeline; it was not her accomplishment. Charlotte then realizes he has a misconception of what she has accomplished and that one of the reasons he has not made her acting role official is that he undervalues her contribution. This gives Charlotte a new understanding of the issues. Now she needs to revise her justification for the promotion and use the negotiation to alter his misperceptions. Before hearing the CEO's response, she had thought that merely acting in the role was sufficient.

Follett's observations suggest that there are two steps to preparing to solve the problem. The first is figuring out your own interests and the trade-off you might be willing to make, then trying to gauge how the other person is likely to see and hear these ideas. Of course, the second part is more complex: it means thinking in a more expansive way about another's motivations. And to do that, you need to prepare yourself to be open and listen to the other person in mindful ways.

These two ideas—planning for linear problem solving and planning for the circular response—are the focus of this chapter.

CREATIVE OPTIONS AND THE ANCHORING EFFECT

We typically apply the concept of anchoring to the effects of opening offers in distributive or win/lose negotiations. In situations of uncertainty, an initial offer tends to serve as an anchor around which subsequent offers revolve. In other words, our minds tend to fix on initial impressions and data, which influence our subsequent judgment and decisions.[8] If you make an opening offer, assuming you have the right information to do so, that offer becomes a reference point, an anchor, that shapes the negotiations.[9]

The Anchoring Function at Work

Anchoring functions somewhat differently in the kinds of workplace negotiations we are interested in here. Raising a second-generation issue brings up a problem that likely hasn't been recognized as such.

This approach runs the risk that the other party will anchor on that problem, and likely link you to that problem in his mind. In his mind, *you* become the problem. That's why it's important to frame n-negotiations with options and solutions. By offering options from the beginning, the negotiation becomes anchored on solutions and problem solving.

Anchoring in the context of our cases. Let's think about how anchoring applies to the cases we've discussed so far. In the Introduction, Alicia puts Bob in a difficult position by stepping forward for a role for which she was not being considered. After all, if he has somebody else in mind, why open up the conversation? But if she has ideas about how to deal with the situation—options to propose— she can shift the focus from problem to solution. Likewise, Marisa (chapter 1) has many concerns about the role, but presenting them as problems without solutions could make the managing partner rethink the offer. If Claudia (chapter 1) just rejects the client list she is offered, she becomes a problem even before she has started in the new job. In contrast, if Charlotte (chapter 2) has ideas for how to transition to the vice president role, including some suggestions for who might take over her director responsibilities, she is more likely to have the CEO start a negotiation with her rather than just see her ask for the promotion as a problem.

Be the person who brings the solutions. Developing and bringing forth ideas about how to deal with each of the issues in advance can lead to more productive negotiations. I've learned over the years of teaching leaders that they often assume the other person will have ideas about these complex issues. But that's usually an unrealistic expectation. You raise an issue; they focus on the problem. If you are the one with ideas, you can frame the negotiations in ways that will help make the negotiations more productive.

Beyond the Zero Sum

Since 1980 or so, the field of negotiation has grown exponentially. Consequently, our thinking about how to create value in negotiations has become increasingly more sophisticated. But a basic premise still holds: if you negotiate over a single issue, you are by definition in a distributive, or win-lose, situation. This means that the outcome of this one issue—whether it's the price you will pay or the hours you will work—will be some form of compromise between the two positions of the parties. In other words, the size of the pie is fixed. This holds true no matter how nice you are. Converting a distributive or win-lose game to one where you can create value means acting with two simple principles: one is to focus on interests (what each party wants); the other is to enlarge the conversation so that more issues become the ingredients for an agreement.

Expanding the range of trades. Noted negotiation researcher Dean Pruitt outlines several ways to expand the range of issues to make possible trade-offs—simple trades, trading time now for time later, payment in other "currencies," making contingent agreements, and trying to find bridging solutions.[10]

Trading on time. Trades can be made based on time: agreeing to do something in the current time period in exchange for something later. You find that you cannot reach agreement on funding for a project: you want more; your boss thinks it should be done for less. You can reach agreement to start the program this year and phase the rest in later over the course of the year. In chapter 1 Marisa agreed to take a role in the southeast region and negotiated, among other things, support for another career move at the end of three years in the new role.

Paying in another currency. You can also make trades by paying in a "currency" other than the one initially being negotiated. When you can't reach agreement on the issue under discussion, you include another issue that might have very little to do with the initial issue but enables you to make a trade. The classic example of this is adding vacation days and bonus structure to discussions of compensation rather than focusing solely on salary. When we can't reach an agreement on compensation, paying in another currency might mean a move to a better office, a new development opportunity, a better title, or an extra staff member. The principle in these examples is that you transform what could be a stalemate into an opportunity to come to an agreement through trades. Think back to Alicia's case in the Introduction: to address the CEO's concern that Alicia was too green, she might suggest that she would attend a leadership development program to help her prepare for a future role.

Contingent agreements. Another ingredient for shifting a negotiation from a single issue is to include contingent agreements, that is, basing the agreement on something happening (or not happening) in the future.[11] Let's say you think your project will exceed goals set for it, but your boss is unsure. The contingent agreement could be that you carry out the project. If you are correct, your budget for the next year increases; if not, it might decrease. You are willing to make the deal because you're convinced that you're right. Your boss is willing because if your project produces according to your estimates, there will likely be more revenue to share.

Charlotte from chapter 2 can use a contingent agreement in her negotiations with the CEO. She believes she's ready for the vice president's role, since she's done the work for the past few months. The CEO is unsure. Charlotte could propose that she be appointed acting vice president for three months, with clear metrics to assess her performance. In this way, Charlotte attains her aim to be appointed vice president, and the CEO commits to the permanency of the role only when Charlotte has clearly proven herself.

Bridging solutions. A strategy to avoid negotiating on a single issue can be to bring in other parties in the form of bridging agreements. Let's revisit the example of trading on time: you find that you cannot reach agreement on funding for a project. You want more time; your boss thinks it should be done for less. An alternative to trading on time would be to look for funding partners. Perhaps other departments would benefit from the project and could use their budgets to help. In chapter 1, Claudia used a bridging solution when negotiating with Giles James about support staff. This was an issue that was important to her, but rather than push for her staff, she proposed sharing support staff with other directors. Bridging solutions shift the negotiation from being about a single issue—will we or won't we support this project—to thinking creatively about multiple issues.

The possibilities for bridging and contingent agreements, as well as other ingredients for making trades, make mutual-gains agreements more likely even around some thorny issues. Consider the case of Cheryl, a senior leader who felt trapped between the job she'd coveted and the family she was committed to.

Cheryl's Commute

Cheryl is a vice president and CFO for a major division— Global Supply Chain Solutions—at Laminate Systems Inc. (LSI), a large heavy-equipment manufacturing firm with headquarters in Texas. When she took the job two years ago, a promotion she'd been working toward for many years, one of the requirements was that she move to headquarters. At first, this made sense. A big part of her job was to connect with the heads of sales, marketing, and operations in the division. Although reluctant, Cheryl and her husband and two children moved to Texas outside of San Antonio. The family was not happy there. Recently her husband, supported by their teenage children, announced that they wanted to move back to Pennsylvania, where they had lived prior to the move. "We're moving back," he said, "with or without you."

Cheryl understood their feelings. She too missed the family and community connections in their hometown in Pennsylvania. But she also loved her job, and negotiating an arrangement with her boss would be a challenge. First, there was no precedent for negotiating a flexible work or telecommuting arrangement, where she would do her job off-site. And this was

(Continued)

complicated by the fact that a condition for taking the job, a promotion in the company, was that she would move to Texas. She knew that no one at the company had ever been required to move to a location for a promotion and then been given approval to move back to his original location. Second, her boss, José Garcia, had a reputation for being somewhat risk averse, typically unwilling to try anything new in the business or in personnel matters. And although he was theoretically supportive of work-life balance, he expected his staff to be fully committed and available. For all these reasons, Cheryl doubted she could come up with a viable plan. And even if she did, it wasn't clear that her boss would agree.

During the fifteen years before taking the CFO job at LSI, Cheryl had a distinguished career in financial management, covering both international and financial reporting, deal strategy and structuring, and merger-and-acquisition valuations. Most of her experience had been with a number of heavy-equipment firms in the construction industry located primarily in the mid-Atlantic. Before joining LSI, Cheryl had been on the fast track in another company but found that its expectations of 24/7 commitment conflicted with the need to care for her young children. LSI offered potential long-range opportunity along with more reasonable expectations about commitment. After four years working in various capacities at LSI, where she established a stellar track record, Cheryl was invited to interview for the VP/CFO role. Of course, a condition of taking that role was that she move to corporate headquarters in Texas.

As VP/CFO for the Global Supply Chain, Cheryl is the financial lead for the $3 billion division with operations in the United States, Asia, and Latin America. Financial managers in each of the worldwide operational centers report to her.

When Cheryl was promoted to the VP/CFO position, she reported to the previous executive vice president. Now she's worked with Garcia for less than a year, and it has been an adjustment. But because her work is in the company's largest division, she has insights and relationships in the business that her boss does not have. She is José's lifeline to their business— only one of two officers associated with the worldwide supply chain system. The other, the VP of international operations, travels all the time, and the rest of the team is scattered over the world. In short, José has little visibility with the divisions, except what Cheryl provides to him.

PREPARING TO NEGOTIATE: FOCUSING ON CONCERNS

Figure Out Your Own Concerns

The basic principle behind a focus on concerns is the need to step back and ask yourself not only what you want, but also why you want it. Let's say you're seeking an 8 percent increase in salary. You could negotiate back and forth with your boss and come up with the compromise that Mary Parker Follett spoke about, in which each side gives a little but neither side leaves very satisfied. Or you could ask yourself why you're even looking for this in the first place. Do you think your performance merits it? Are there inequities between you and your peers? Have your child-care expenses increased? By focusing on the reasons behind what you want, you increase the possibilities for creative agreements. In other words, there are many ways to get compensated for performance—bonus payments, enhanced responsibilities (with perhaps an attendant increase in salary), or more support for the work you do. Inequities in compensation may signal a broader organizational issue, and you might receive more support for child care indirectly through a company benefits plan.

Cheryl's interests are clear: she wants to keep her job but do so in a way that enables her to live with her family in their hometown. At the same time, she has worked hard to get to this position, and she wants neither the negotiation process nor the agreement they reach to detract from perceptions about her performance and future potential.

Anticipate the Other Person's Concerns

Cheryl has outlined José's potential concerns. She expects some resistance on the central issue itself: her request, after all, would be a departure from the norm no matter what form it took. Because José prefers to avoid risk, he is not a leader who embraces departures from company policy. His major concern would be whether Cheryl could continue to perform her job in ways consistent with the results of the existing structure.

Cheryl's primary goal in preparing to negotiate is to propose options that clearly demonstrate that her performance would remain consistent and that there would be some criteria to evaluate the plan. Concerned about efficiencies, José would also want to contain the costs of any agreement. At the same time, Cheryl knew that her relationships to the field operations had made her crucial to his success. This would give him some incentive to negotiate with her if it meant that she would stay in the role. That insight was crucial as she prepared to negotiate with her boss.

Locate the Other Person's Incentive to Negotiate

At the beginning of her preparations, Cheryl could not see how she'd be able to convince José to agree to a flexible work arrangement outside the corporate office. And she knew that she would be raising an issue that he would rather avoid. However, once she recognized how crucial her field relationships were to his success, the two had the makings of a beneficial trade. She could propose some form of flexible work arrangement that worked for her and provide assurances to José that his relationships with the field would remain intact. Each of their BATNAs included the possibility that she would leave the company. While that was not a desirable alternative for Cheryl, her leaving was not a great BATNA for José either, since he would lose his connection to the field entirely. Thus, Cheryl realized, José did have some inducement to negotiate.

Generate Multiple Ideas, Based on Multiple Trades

Cheryl put together a proposal composed of multiple facets. First, rather than suggest telecommuting, she decided that framing the idea as a kind of tri-office arrangement would meet José's concern that she would not be located at corporate headquarters. Second, given his interest in controlling costs, she developed a clear plan for the incremental costs of the arrangement and how they would fit within her budget. Third, Cheryl developed an explicit plan for keeping José connected to the field. This was a form of "other compensation." In return for his agreeing to the tri-office arrangement, she would work with him to create more occasions for him to interact with leaders from the field. Finally, Cheryl developed a contingent agreement option. She proposed that the tri-office arrangement be a pilot for six months with benchmarks so that they could assess how it was working after that period.

Anchor on Solutions

The fact that Cheryl had options to propose that appeared to meet both her and José's concerns was critical and increased the likelihood that he would say yes. Cheryl knew that her desire for a flexible work arrangement was going to create problems for her boss. If he saw her request as a problem—just something else he had to deal with—he would be inclined to say no. With options to propose, Cheryl critically anchored the negotiation around solutions that would meet both their needs. Her anchoring on options shifted the focus from a problem to a discussion about how to make the different structure work.

The Other Person: Use What You Know

Cheryl was also prepared to use what she knew about José. As we discussed in chapter 1, this knowledge helps you frame any ask in a way that the other is more likely to hear. Cheryl knows José avoids risk and is attached to the way things had always been done. If your role as CFO of a division necessitated that you be present at

headquarters, then that is what it had to be. She also expected that
José could lose his temper if he felt backed into a corner. Cheryl used
these insights about her boss to frame what she was asking for as an
overture for him to work with her on figuring out the tri-office
arrangement.

Put "Yes, and..." to Work

In this case, Cheryl is the one raising the issue. But as we have
observed in other situations, such as Marisa's (chapter 1), sometimes
the other person is raising the issue and doing the asking. The ask in
Marisa's case was an interesting opportunity yet not without costs, so
she negotiated for support and other perquisites that would make the
role and the move it entailed more appealing. Marisa did so by using
the "Yes, and..." strategy for proposing creative options. For Cheryl,
having creative options to propose and options that she saw as being
responsive to José's likely concerns would, she hoped, forestall a no.
She wanted to make it easy for him to say yes—because she was
prepared to give him the "ands."

Let's turn to the case of Elena, whose CEO has asked her to lead
a new initiative. While the problem the initiative is meant to solve
is important within the firm and to Elena personally, it isn't the
sort of project that typically moves people up into the top leadership
roles.

Elena's Case: Converting an Ask into a Negotiation

Elena is a senior partner at a professional services firm whose
CEO is concerned about the fact that few women were making
it to partner. They were losing women at a much higher rate
than their male managers and associates. After careful study,
they learned that the women were not leaving the firm to
be home with their families, but to take jobs in organizations
that offered more opportunities and were more hospitable to
women.[12]

Committed to making change, the CEO asked Elena, a well-respected senior woman partner, to head the new initiative. He emphasized that the firm needed her help in this and that it would give her good exposure. She would interact with offices throughout the country and work closely with managing partners and directors. It would add value in a visible way, and people at the top, including the CEO, would appreciate her efforts.

Elena was tempted to accept the offer. She thought it was an important issue that, if handled poorly, could be quite costly for the firm. And she agreed with the CEO that she did have the skills to do it well. In addition, this was something she cared about. The problem was that a job like this rarely propelled people into senior leadership roles in the firm, which valued rainmaking and client service above all else. Accepting this assignment would take her out of the marketplace and therefore not contribute value in the way the firm traditionally measured and rewarded performance.

Elena was torn. Her decision was complicated by the norm in the firm never to say no to an opportunity. She asked the CEO to give her some time to think about it.

And think she did. She clearly wanted to say yes, but to do so might have negative consequences for her career. So Elena tried to come up with an "and" that would enable her to take on the role but with terms that would keep her in the running for leadership. She reasoned that rainmakers were rewarded by meeting revenue targets. Could she be similarly rewarded by cutting costs? Elena hypothesized that if the initiative were successful, the turnover among junior women would be reduced. Since the cost to the firm of losing a manager was estimated to be about 150 percent of their compensation, reducing turnover could have a significant impact on the firm's bottom line. Under these terms, the creative option she proposed worked both for her and for the CEO. And reduce turnover over the next several years she did.

Use "Yes, and..." to Turn an Ask into a Negotiation

People are often asked to take on extra assignments or projects—what we call invisible work—that compounds their workload. Sometimes they are asked to move into roles that, like Elena's, offer some benefits but considerable downsides. When responding to "requests" you are expected to accept—such as becoming an acting director, a chief of staff, or other roles that you might be ambivalent about—the "Yes, and..." tactic can be incredibly useful. Showing your willingness and interest is the *yes* part; the *and* part is figuring out how it will work for you. Akin to Cheryl's situation, where raising an issue can make you the problem if you say no when somebody expects a yes, you yourself can be seen as a problem. Like Cheryl's anchoring with options, "Yes, and..." is another way to use creative options.

Still, having these options to propose was only one part of Cheryl's and Elena's preparation.

PREPARING TO NEGOTIATE: BEING MINDFUL

Sometimes it is easy to get stuck when preparing to propose options. One may suffer from what Ellen Langer in her work on mindfulness calls *premature cognitive commitment*.[13] This occurs when we jump to conclusions based on our perceptions of the problem, our analysis of the other's interests, or our ideas about what options might work, any of which might differ from the other party's assessment. Furthermore, we often come to believe that the other parties' interests are more or less fixed as we prepare—that they will not, as Mary Parker Follett described, be influenced by the process of negotiation.[14] In many of the decision analytic treatments of integrative negotiations, preparation involves deciphering trades among fixed preferences that the parties have.[15] Indeed, when my colleagues and I teach negotiation using scorable games, figuring out trades becomes the main focus.

Tensions in the Circular Response

Preparation requires another dimension if we are to adopt Follett's concept of the circular response: believing that new understandings, hence better outcomes, can arise during the negotiation process. As we prepare, we need to hold a bit of a tension between three facets of preparation: preparing creative options and solutions, considering our counterpart's concerns, but also being prepared to learn and hear more. Advance preparation is most helpful when we make a concerted effort not to let it set our expectations in stone.[16] Acting mindfully allows us to be more open to solutions both in the process of preparation and during the negotiation itself.

Appreciate the process, not the outcome. To be mindful requires us to be situated in the moment and aware of the emotional context of what is happening.[17] Mindfulness is an enriched appreciation for the details of the situation—for the process rather than a preoccupation with the outcome. This can be particularly helpful for women, who are at risk of triggering a double bind if they come across as overly focused on outcomes over process. Women who act mindfully are more likely to be perceived as genuine and authentic, making them less prone to experiencing backlash when they act assertively by negotiating for themselves.[18] The challenge lies in preparing to be mindful.

Extend your understanding of concerns beyond substantive interests. There are two major steps to mindful preparation. The first is to expand and extend our understanding of concerns. Typically, when we think about the other party's concerns, we focus on those directly related to the issues under discussion—their substantive interests. So in a negotiation over compensation, we assume our boss's direct concerns involve costs and possibly equity. However, other dimensions of interests often come into play, such as organizational concerns: how they look to important constituencies, for example, or how any agreements made might affect their group, their function, and the broader organization. We care about how important constituencies will judge the agreements we make and whether we can justify them. Our boss would have to validate her agreement of increased compensation to her boss and perhaps to human resources—and she would need the ammunition to do so, which can come from you.

Another way to increase mindfulness is to consider the set of "good reasons" the other party would have to say no to you.

Appreciate the interest of face. Image is a major concern for all of us during negotiations. How we look to ourselves and others who matter to us often counts as much as the particulars of the deals we make; in fact, these are seldom separate. Face, a concept popularized in the West by sociologist Erving Goffman, captures what we value about ourselves and the qualities we want others to see in us.[19] Negotiators go to great lengths to preserve their face. They stick to their guns against poor odds simply to avoid losing face with those who are counting on them.

We also have relational interests. As buyers and sellers, we may not see the other party again in transactional negotiations; however, negotiations in the workplace are different because we want and need to maintain our relationships. Therefore, it's critical to ensure that the other party feels good enough about the agreement that it doesn't jeopardize our working relationship. At the same time, we also do not want to unilaterally sacrifice our interests for the good of the relationship. We need some reciprocity.

What Cheryl's Case Teaches Us

Putting the circular response to work. As Cheryl prepares for her negotiation, she has to be mindful of the need to think in a more complex way about José's concerns. He clearly would be concerned about how the organization would judge any action he took. Because he was still new to his role, it was asking a lot to make such a major change in company policies. She needs to think about how his colleagues would react to this kind of change and be ready to discuss this with José to see how they might frame whatever agreement they reached so he looks good to his senior leadership. Precedent might also be an issue for him: How would they portray the arrangement?

She knew her boss well enough to understand that bringing up any change would elicit an almost instinctive resistance. It was never easy to introduce an idea that contradicted his usual way of doing things. And when stressed, he tended to get angry. Therefore, Cheryl has to think about how she could introduce her proposal in a way that would get him to listen and not react negatively. At the same time, Cheryl recognizes that José has a strong interest in keeping a good relationship with her because of her well-developed relationships with people in the field.

The other party: More than a mere monolith. In addition to delving more deeply into another's concerns, you also need a more complex and nuanced appreciation for the other party's context. This is a key tenet of mindfulness as well—openness not just to new information but to multiple perspectives.[20]

We tried to capture this idea in *Everyday Negotiation* by using the metaphor of stories. Each of us has different stories we tell ourselves about what is occurring. Once into the negotiation, it is inevitable that we process whatever happens through that filter. A certain sense of mindlessness can set in that leads us to become fixed in our pre-conceptions rather than staying in the moment and reacting to what is happening. It puts you at a distinct advantage to approach a nego-tiation as a compilation of stories, since stories alert us to the chal-lenge we face in hearing the other person. Each story is told from a specific point of view and never includes every detail. We need to prepare to listen to and hear these stories.[21]

Consider the other person's good reasons for saying no. I've found a particularly effective exercise to prepare to hear the other side's perspective, his story: to delineate what would be his good reasons for saying no to the options you propose. To do this, it is important to recognize that his good reasons are those told from his perspective. Let's go back to Charlotte (chapter 2), who may think that the CEO just wants to avoid making a decision or hopes she will continue performing both roles because it saves the company money. But those reasons stem from Charlotte's story about what is happening. The CEO likely has his own story, one that compels him to see what he is doing as rational and reasonable. He may believe that she has not proven herself in the role, that she only closed a deal that was already done. Or he may believe that he needs a vice president with more experience.

As negotiators, we all see ourselves as operating based on good strategic reasons. Yet it's often difficult to give the same benefit to the other party. I describe how we see ourselves when I teach—as strategic, collaborative, and flexible—as opposed to how we see the other party: opportunistic, uncooperative, and rigid. Nobody looks in the mirror and sees these negative things about themselves; rather, we all see ourselves as operating from good and legitimate intentions. But mindfully preparing to problem-solve means trying to capture how others might see the situation. Thinking about their five good reasons for saying no to your proposal helps you prepare to hear them.

Analyzing "good reasons" in our previous cases. Marisa from chapter 1 may assume that Alice, the managing partner, might be very concerned about the precedent she's setting if she concedes to Marisa the commuting arrangement—and that it might become the norm in future negotiations. Similarly, if Claudia's boss in London agrees to her request for support staff, he can quite reasonably assume that others in the group will ask for similar treatment. These are good reasons from the other person's perspective.

In Charlotte's case, the CEO likely has some good strategic reasons to reject her proposal to become the vice president. He may think she is not ready; he may already have started a hiring process and have somebody else in mind; or he may be worried about who would fill Charlotte's shoes as director. Understanding these "good reasons" does not mean that she should abandon her proposal to become vice president; it just means that she'll be prepared to hear his objections and refine her proposal to account for these issues. It helps her think conditionally about how she will handle his objections to her ideas. The "good reasons" for saying no are what we have called the *hidden agenda* of the negotiation. They are the reasons you can expect a no to what you propose. We discuss in detail in chapter 5 how to put these "good reasons" to work.

Analyzing the "face" we present. Finally, we want others to see the face we present to the world as fair and evenhanded. One of the negotiators we most admire tells a story about how taking that stance helped her get what she wanted and at the same time give the president of her division a way to save face. She had recently been promoted to a senior role in her bank and learned that her compensation was not comparable to that of her peers. Rather than start a negotiation about it, she told him what she had discovered. And then she said, "I have just discovered that my salary is less than what my peers earn. I know now that you are aware, and that you will do the fair thing." She left it at that—and he did.

We gave this advice to a young woman who had just been promoted from a director in her company to vice president. She wanted to know what she should do about the salary. To her, the most important thing was to have the resources to hire a director to replace her. We asked whether she had any knowledge that the compensation package her boss was offering was out of line with that of other executives at her level. She wasn't sure but did not think so. So we advised her to start by saying that she was sure he was making her a fair offer. She did so and then went on to discuss the issue that was really important to her.

People like to think that they are fair and do the fair thing. By suggesting to them that you assume the same, you protect their face and have confidence that you think they will correct a problem if one exists.

Cheryl's case: Assessing the other person's good reasons. Cheryl knew she had to think more deeply about her boss's context and his good reasons for saying no to her, especially since her relationship with José was still developing. Although she saw his strengths as a leader, she also had some rather negative perceptions about him—his aversion to risk, rigidity in approaching work practices, and expectations about work commitment. All of these led Cheryl to consider José not very approachable and someone who tended to overreact when stressed. Still, she knew that her boss did not see himself in these terms.

With options to propose about the tri-office, Cheryl also went through an exercise of delineating José's good reasons for saying no to her. As part of her preparation, she recognized how her boss's lack of field exposure made her instrumental to his success. So in thinking about his good reasons for saying no—in addition to the analysis she did of his organizational, individual, and relational interests—she focused on this other dimension. What would be his good reasons for saying no if he feared that what she proposed would not work?

Cheryl's case: Five good reasons her boss could say no. Cheryl considered what she thought were José's five good reasons for saying no to her. The first was that with all the commuting, her performance would suffer. Second, the proposal was too costly—he had already paid for her move to Texas. Third, if she was not located in the Texas office, he would lose the informal interactions they had, which could jeopardize his connection to the field. Fourth, this would violate a precedent and in her experience, Jose was not one to champion any change. Finally, he could be worried that Cheryl would tire of the commute and leave.

A good part of Cheryl's preparation included how she would respond to these reasons. To respond to the possibility that she would tire of the commute, she outlined a calendar of her whereabouts for the year—when she would be in Pennsylvania, when in Texas, and when in the field. Second, she also planned to remind him that she had actually been in a dual-office arrangement in the six months before she moved to Texas and was prepared to propose that they agree in advance on a way to handle the problem if it arose. Finally, Cheryl anticipated that he would resist the incremental expenses associated with the tri-office. After all, she wasn't just proposing a tradition-breaking approach: he would have to justify these additional expenses. She came prepared with a spreadsheet of these expenses and was ready to negotiate about them. She also anticipated that he might balk at paying relocation expenses twice.

Because Cheryl had so thoroughly considered José's good reasons for saying no, she could enter the negotiation itself confident that she had a number of creative options to propose. But even more important, she considered his legitimate reasons for saying no. By doing this, she put herself in a mind-set to hear his concerns and to consider options that would work from both of their perspectives.

Good Positioning Sets Up for Mindfulness

In order to be mindful in a negotiation, it helps if you are well positioned to negotiate—which we described in chapter 2 as being in a state where the parties experience their interdependence. At first, Cheryl thought that she would be unable to get José to agree to any change in status because she didn't think he had any reason to do so. It was only when she began to consider the informal role her connections to the field played in José's success that she realized she could deal with his resistance, stay in the moment, and work through it with him.

Preparing to engage in mutual-gains negotiations at work involves a dual focus—creating possible options in anticipation of the negotiation yet not becoming so wedded to your approach that you close out new possibilities. Having options to propose is critical in negotiating over second-generation issues. Options focus the negotiations on solutions, which can be crucial in these potentially challenging interactions. Cheryl's negotiation requires her to challenge accepted policy and practice—not something easy to succeed at. Recognizing that, she needs to prepare herself to think deeply about how the other party will likely hear the options she proposes.

By preparing to be mindful in the negotiations, you enter them ready to hear objections and resistances—and as Cheryl did, you can come up with ways to deal with them as well. She was able to negotiate her tri-office relationship; after six months, she and José reviewed

the arrangement, and both agreed that Cheryl's performance continued to be exemplary.

Nothing needed to change.

SECOND-GENERATION ISSUES AND SMALL WINS

Cheryl's case provides a good example of how her negotiation trans-
lates into a potential small win. Leaders often relocate to take on
ever-increasing areas of responsibility and usually are asked to undertake these relocations with scant regard for the impact on the family.
Traditionally it was assumed that the family would follow along. This
unexamined assumption is often cited as a reason that women do not
accede to senior leadership roles at the same rate as their male colleagues. This is attributed to two reasons. First, because people frequently assume that a woman will not agree to relocate, no one
bothers asking her to do so. Second, a woman will occasionally turn
down the relocation if she feels it will have a negative effect on her
family. Marisa faced that consideration. Cheryl's negotiation and
her subsequent success with the tri-office arrangement demonstrates
to the company that it may be time to reexamine its policy of having
senior leaders relocate to the corporate office. This makes it a small
win not just for Cheryl but for future company leaders.

It is also a small win in another way: the motivation for Cheryl's
negotiation stems from her desire to have both a challenging work
life and rewarding home and community life. Initially Cheryl thought
she would have to choose: either the one or the other. Indeed, she
did have to make those choices earlier in her career. For too many
organizations, this assumption remains unexamined. The notion is
widespread that senior leadership jobs require all-in commitment
24/7. That is a second-generation assumption that fits some people's
lives but not all. Cheryl's negotiation demonstrates that it is possible
for organizations to enable their leaders to have both: a challenging
work life and a rewarding life outside work. Successfully negotiating
the tri-office arrangement can inspire others to come up with similarly creative ways to integrate work and family life.

For this and other materials, visit www.deborahmkolb.com.

Putting *Anchoring* and *Mindfulness* to Work

- Focus on people's concerns, not their positions.
- Develop a repertoire of creative options for problem solving:
    - Trade on time
    - Contingency agreements
    - Other currencies
    - Bridging solutions
- Anchor negotiations with options (solutions) to avoid a focus on the problem.
- Prepare to be mindful: open to new information and perspectives:
    - What organizational and relational interests matter beyond those directly related to the issue at hand?
    - What are the five good reasons he has for saying no to your proposal?
- Prepare options, but be open to new solutions.

Getting Negotiations off the Ground

Invariably when I give a talk about how to prepare to negotiate a lowercase n-negotiation, somebody in the audience will raise her hand and let me know that it's all well and good to talk about the importance of preparation, but how do you get the negotiations off the ground?[1] We are always told to prepare, prepare, prepare—get good information, position ourselves to negotiate, come up with creative options, and be mindful of the other person's situation. Yet despite all this preparation, getting people to the table to negotiate with you can still be a challenge. This is especially true at work where there are no clear-cut occasions to negotiate, with the possible exceptions of budgets and salaries. Getting negotiations off the ground is often a challenge in these contexts. Yet with a few exceptions, most treatments on negotiation begin with the parties already at the table.[2] The challenge, then, is to explore the determinants and obstacles to getting n-negotiations off the ground.

PRENEGOTIATION TECHNIQUES
DEPEND ON THE CONTEXT

The actions required to launch negotiations differ by context. In some situations, both parties enter primed to negotiate. If we find a car we like, we are ready to bargain. We see an antique vase in the marketplace and start the process with an offer. These are uppercase N-negotiations where buyers and sellers come together to see if they can reach a deal. In these situations, we generally assume that these negotiations actually get under way when one or the other party makes an opening offer.

In other contexts, the process of getting negotiations off the ground is more ambiguous.

Getting n-Negotiations off the Ground

International scholars describe a formal prenegotiation phase of defining the problem and developing a commitment to negotiate. As William Zartman defines it, prenegotiation begins when one or more parties consider negotiation a potential option and ends when there is either a formal commitment to negotiate or a decision not to negotiate.[3]

A range of contexts—from hostage taking to major deal making. It is more difficult in certain settings to separate the starting point from the process itself. For example, getting the negotiations off the ground in hostage-taking negotiations—in the sense of building the relationship—is a fundamental component.[4] Parties bargaining in the shadow of the law, in divorce or business relationships, might require time and estimates of what a court might decide to initiate negotiations. Serious labor negotiations often do not begin until a contract expiration looms, even if the parties are officially meeting.[5] Finally, we know from large-scale deal making that there may be a longer period of planning, even what often appears to be a seduction, to establish conditions for negotiators to start serious bargaining. *Star Wars* fans might have been surprised when they learned in October 2012 that Disney was the new owner of the franchise; what they didn't know is that the deal had been over a year in the making. Disney CEO Robert Iger and *Star Wars* creator George Lucas had been slowly building trust in each other since May 2011, when Iger first broached the acquisition with Lucas.[6]

Similarly, the 2013 merger between US Airways and American Airlines came only after US Airways CEO Doug Parker went to great lengths to get his counterpart at American, Tom Horton, to the table after originally being rebuffed. Horton refused to talk to Parker about a merger after American first declared bankruptcy. Parker went on to talk up the benefits of a merger on Wall Street and to court American's pilots and other unions. Once it was clear that so many of his stakeholders were in favor of the merger, Horton had no choice but to negotiate.[7] These are clear examples of how getting negotiations off the ground will differ from one scenario to the next.

In n-Negotiations: Asymmetrical Incentives to Negotiate

Getting n-negotiations off the ground presents special challenges. As we've already discussed, these negotiations are not as readily obvious or identifiable as a potential negotiation in the same way as buyer-seller or labor-management are. One party or the other will need to launch the process. Furthermore, the fact that n-negotiations often occur in organizations means that lower members of the hierarchy may be reluctant to raise issues.[8]

As we've discussed, power differentials and status expectations can discourage members of lower-status groups—women, people of color—from raising issues or for pressing the matter once they're raised.[9] Adding to the complexity of negotiating within a hierarchy, new research suggests that men and women negotiate differently depending on the issues being addressed.[10] Certainly there are situations in which women have been shown to negotiate more effectively than men, such as when negotiating on behalf of others.[11] Likewise, women are just as likely as men to initiate negotiation when they perceive injustice.[12] So it's important to remember that n-negotiations take place in a context of power differentials and that the issue being negotiated can make a difference.

Getting the other side to see negotiation as a possibility. This is a critical step in starting n-negotiations. Interest in negotiation is not likely to be symmetrical: one person may have a higher incentive to negotiate and appreciate the need for it, while the other may see no need whatsoever. While this type of situation can also characterize negotiation in other contexts, these dynamics are more likely to become obvious only once the negotiations have started.

No preexisting structure. What distinguishes n-negotiations is that there is no preexisting structure for the negotiation. One person sees the glimmer of an opportunity to negotiate about some facet of work, but the other party may be oblivious that anything is wrong or that it even requires negotiation to fix it. A boss asks you to take on a project, and she expects acquiescence, not negotiation. A manager asks for your advice about who could take on a new overseas role: he has assumed that family responsibilities prevent you from wanting the job but you do want the position. So you initiate a negotiation for an opportunity that your manager had not expected. Or, like Marisa in chapter 1, you're offered what a leader assumes is a great nonnegotiable opportunity.

These are the kinds of roles that can fall to women by default— the fixer, the party planner, the mediator. As one senior leader we interviewed said, "I'm one of the few women at my level, so I'm asked to do everything. I'm on four different diversity task forces, and it takes a lot of my time." It's challenging to initiate negotiation on these issues. Even though you recognize the problem to be negotiated, your counterpart is often oblivious to it.

Initiating n-negotiations in an organizational hierarchy. It's not just that the other party might be surprised that you're raising issues she hadn't considered; it might also be that bosses and others more senior in an organization may feel no special need to negotiate at all. Their position in the hierarchy can make it difficult for them to see issues from different perspectives and make them less empathetic toward others.[13] After all, as our examples suggest, the subjects of the negotiation will likely involve changes to the status quo—one with which they are likely quite comfortable.

Prenegotiation Challenges

Challenges to get negotiations off the ground can also take subtle forms:

- *Challenge: The other party refuses to negotiate, likely in an understated way.* You request a meeting to discuss a project or want to ask for something that implies a negotiation, and your boss says no to the meeting. Outright rejection to meet, however, is less common than a more typical indirect approach. Although she is trying to appear collaborative, the other party can evince interest but put up excuses. "Of course," she might say, "I want to discuss the project or the resources you need; it's just that the timing is wrong. Wait until the busy season ends."

- *Challenge: The agenda is hijacked.* The person agrees to meet, but before you can start the negotiation, you find that he is calling the shots and directing the conversation to where he wants it to go. That's what happened to Fran, a partner in a professional services firm. After she had attended a leadership development program, Fran planned to negotiate with her managing partner for her next role. She knew exactly how she was going to discuss the opportunity she sought and how her current responsibilities would be covered. After a greeting and a query about the program she had attended, her boss immediately shifted the discussion to problems with certain clients that had arisen in her absence. Despite her efforts, Fran could not get the negotiation going. Then the phone rang and her boss took the call, ending the meeting.

- *Challenge: You are stonewalled.* That's initially what happened when Charlotte from chapter 2 tried to start the negotiation with her boss over her promotion and bonus. When she pointed out that she deserved a bonus for bringing in new business, her boss diminished her contribution and told her that she had merely closed a deal that was already in the pipeline. When she tried to negotiate about the promotion, her boss told her he could easily hire a more experienced person from the outside. In order to launch these negotiations, Charlotte had to neutralize these claims and make it worth her boss's while to actually negotiate. His comments suggest that he sees no need at the moment.

Before we talk about strategies for kicking off negotiations, it's important to recognize that getting started is obviously not the end of the story. As we've noted, much of the research and writing on negotiations start with parties already at the table—yet still challenged to find ways to come to good agreements. But a perspective and discussion on getting negotiations off the ground makes it clear that already being at the table does not mean that negotiation has actually commenced or that any opening offer has been made.

TWO WAYS TO GET NEGOTIATIONS STARTED

There are two major ways to begin negotiations—much like the carrot and the stick. The first is to make it appealing for the other person to negotiate by showing her that it is worth her while to negotiate with you (the carrot), which you can do by making your value visible. A second approach, raising the costs of the status quo, shifts the focus from the value you contribute to the consequences of not coming to an agreement with you (the stick).[14]

Both of these strategic moves involve taking the information you've gathered as part of your preparation—figuring out your value and assessing relative BATNAs—and making it real to the other person. But whichever approach you choose, having allies to help you make the case is invaluable in getting negotiations off the ground.

Isobel's Inducements

Isobel is a regional manager for communications for a large southwestern manufacturing company, responsible for seven states in the Southwest. Recently a leader in government operations asked her to help out in a crisis relating to problems with potential audits of a state contract. Ordinarily government contracts were not in her area of responsibility. But in this case, problems with the contract and the attendant media attention were seen as potential threats to the work itself, the revenues from the project, and the company's reputation in the state.

Isobel saw this as an opportunity to demonstrate her capacity to deal with complex regulatory issues and help her firm in a crisis. She put in long hours and helped the company prepare both a response and a strategy to protect their contract and the revenues from it, as well as avoid any bad publicity that could harm the company's reputation and bottom line. Her outstanding work, outside of her functional area, gave her visibility to the senior leadership of the company, and she was thrilled.

But as often happens in these situations, she did such an outstanding job that the operations group kept asking her to repeat her success in other states where they were having similar problems: "Isobel, you were so helpful in the last situation— we're having the same problem in another state and could really use your expertise." At first, Isobel was happy to help; she enjoyed the work and the thrill of working on high-stakes projects. She liked the visibility. But she was being stretched too thin, having to do her own job and the job of the person in governmental affairs who was supposed to be handling these projects (and who had the budget to do so). Though Isobel wanted to negotiate with her boss in order to get the resources to continue to do this work, she was not optimistic. For him to begin a negotiation with Isobel meant that he would have to confront the ways in which other parts of his organization were not functioning. Knowing that he was a conflict avoider, Isobel recognized that she would have a difficult time getting her boss to negotiate about a change in roles and responsibilities.

Making Your Value Visible

Part of preparation is recognizing the value you bring to your work and capturing it in a way that will have value to the person you are negotiating with. Making that value visible to the other person creates an incentive for him or her to negotiate with you.

Tailor the value message to its recipient. Claire, a senior executive at a major bank, described how she routinely lets her leadership know about her team's accomplishments instead of just discussing these matters when it's time for negotiation: "If they've done something great with one of our clients, I will send a message to the CEO; he really cares about the relationships we have with clients. My CFO, on the other hand, is really concerned about our expenses, so I let him know when we have had a success on this front. He could really care less about a new client relationship." Claire does two smart things here: she tailors her value proposition to different executives so that when the time comes to negotiate with them, they are likely to be willing to sit down with her, and she makes her—and her team's—value visible on an ongoing basis.

Relay value messages from other stakeholders. Gabriela is a senior manager at a global consulting firm who works with multiple clients. She got into the practice of printing out and posting in her office "thank-you" e-mails from clients. Promotions at the firm were largely based on one's ability to retain and recruit clients, and Gabriela saw the e-mails as a way to remind the partners that she had happy clients. This subtle approach worked well in Gabriela's firm, where there could be backlash for overt self-promotion.

Collect records of your achievements. It is important that you find ways, as Claire and Gabriela did, to make your value visible to potential negotiating partners on an ongoing basis. Keep records of your accomplishments. When you receive a compliment from people both inside and outside your organization, ask if you can share what they said. You can forward it on with a comment about what your client said about the work. Best-selling author Lois Frankel demonstrates that "nice girls" (the ones who don't get the corner office) don't do this enough. She suggests that you share your achievements, and to avoid the sense that you might be self-promoting, present them as a best practice that others might want to know about.[15] Television host Mika Brzezinski recommends documenting your achievements and all the ways you have exceeded expectations, focusing especially on the market value of your contributions.[16]

Strategic Moves to Make Your Value Visible

As the time nears for a negotiation, you can also employ some strategic moves to make your value visible. Think explicitly about what the person with whom you are going to negotiate values most. That's what Janice, a controller in a manufacturing plant, did when she was tasked with getting the sales group to work more closely with operations to ensure that delivery promises did not exceed the capacity of the operations group to deliver. Her first move was to speed up the cycle for expense reimbursements; she knew they'd appreciate not having to wait the traditional thirty days for their checks. This made her value apparent to them, raising the odds that they would sit down with her. When she shortened the reimbursement turnaround time to four days, they saw her value and were willing at least to sit down and talk about possibilities.

Anticipate the other person's power moves. Think too about what you can do in the moment—as the negotiation is actually happening. Consider the story of an evening news producer who was about to begin new contract negotiations with the station manager, who had a reputation for being a tough negotiator.[17] He always sought the advantage, including how he used the furniture in his office. You would come in and he would have you sit on a very soft couch where you would sink down, and he would tower over you from behind his desk. Our producer took this into account and began the negotiation by bringing in her own stool so that she could sit facing him eye-to-eye. She had also scheduled the meeting at a time in the day when she knew her staff would need her input for the evening news. So during her negotiation with the station manager, there were frequent knocks on the door as her staff came in to ask her questions. If the manager did not appreciate her value prior to the meeting, he certainly did after a few interruptions.

Lisa's Case

Lisa is a senior director in business development for a growing financial services firm. In a consequential negotiation with the CEO of her company, she put all these moves to work as she planned to negotiate a flexible schedule and get a raise at the same time. Any arrangement that Lisa negotiated would set a precedent—nobody had previously done so. Lisa also knew that the CEO really valued face time and would likely resist any suggestions that took her out of the office. Furthermore, he wouldn't be pleased that she was going to couple this request with one for more money. The situation was complicated by the fact that Lisa's immediate boss had recently left. She knew that the window for negotiating this arrangement was short; she needed to do so before a new boss was hired. Even more interesting was the fact that headhunters had begun to contact Lisa as word got out that her boss was leaving. This gave Lisa a good idea about her value on the market—an often invaluable asset.

Lisa's strategy to make her value visible during the negotiation had several components.

What Lisa's Case Teaches Us

Lisa's strategic moves. First, Lisa was careful to assure the CEO of her commitment to the firm. She began by mentioning that of course headhunters had been in touch with her, but she was not interested in making a move. This was important to get on the table. Second, Lisa outlined her performance and contributions she'd made during the past months: "I knew that Joe [the CEO] knew about my work and what I had accomplished, but I felt I really needed to remind him. So we went over my results over the past six months." And like Cheryl from chapter 3, Lisa also had a plan for how to manage her flexible schedule. She anchored on workable options: three days in the office and two working at home. She was convinced that this would work. Finally, she asked for a salary increase, mentioning that she had a good idea of her worth on the open market. She did not name a number but left it to the CEO to come back to her. Indeed, his offer was considerably more than she had anticipated.

Making Lisa's value visible. There are important insights about making one's value visible that we can glean from Lisa's case. First, she knew her value based on the headhunter's external offers—information that made it easier to ask for a raise. Second, she knew that she had to make her value explicitly visible. Although the CEO generally knew of her performance—she'd kept him informed along the way—she wanted to preface her requests with clear indications of her value to the company. And third, Lisa's effort to make her value visible was not just a one-time shot; it was more like a campaign. She had made the CEO aware of her contributions to creating new business over time. Lisa's approach reinforces the idea that making your value visible is an ongoing activity.

What Isobel's Case Teaches Us

Making Isobel's value visible. Isobel's goal in setting a conversation with her boss was to negotiate with him to restructure her role, and indirectly the department, so that she could more effectively deliver on her existing responsibilities but also incorporate the new demands that were being made on her time. She was not clear that her boss knew very much about the work she had been doing; she had failed to make this aspect of her work visible to him on an ongoing basis. So she pulled together a presentation that described her efforts with governmental operations and the extent of the extra work she had been doing. She also carefully delineated the results of her efforts— what she'd saved the company by her interventions—in the first case and in the ongoing work she had been doing. By focusing on the communication strategy she'd developed and how it had paid off, she tried to make her value visible in a currency that he valued.

She wanted, she told him, to discuss her role as it was evolving. He was enormously flattering, telling her what a good job she was doing. But, unfortunately, he said, the timing was not right for any change.

Making your value visible has the potential to create the incentives for the other person to negotiate with you, but in Isobel's case, it was not enough to get her boss to negotiate. She knew she had to take stronger measures—and raising the costs of the status quo is one way to do that.

Raising the Costs of the Status Quo

The CEO in Lisa's situation was not such a reluctant negotiator. He knew Lisa and knew her value and clearly wanted to keep her with the company. If the arrangement she proposed could work, he would be for it. But sometimes negotiators are more reluctant.

Raising the stakes with reluctant negotiators. Occasionally you successfully make your value visible, yet the other person sees no incentive to negotiate with you. That's when it's time to raise the stakes and put more pressure on the other party to negotiate with you seriously—which requires that you make the status quo appear less promising. In negotiation terms, that can mean making each party's relative BATNAs—Best Alternative to a Negotiated Agreement—more obvious. Here, we consider how BATNAs are related to both parties' relative bargaining power.

Formal power and informal power: An interdependent relationship. Because n-negotiations occur within organizations, it's often assumed that bargaining power follows hierarchical lines—that is, a boss has more power and control over negotiating outcomes than her employee. We assume this is the case because as subordinates, we are more dependent on a boss than she might be on us. However, dependence on others during negotiations also has to do with alternatives outside the agreement. A good alternative allows us to accrue bargaining power, while a poor one loses bargaining power.

We have seen the BATNAs of some of our heroines in previous chapters. For Marisa in chapter 1, it was to not take the new role. In chapter 2 Charlotte had several BATNAs: she could stop performing the vice president's role and just stick with her director role, she could explore an opportunity with the client she'd just recruited, or she could quit. However, quitting without another option is generally not a great alternative! Lisa's BATNA was to pursue the headhunters' leads or just stay with her existing working arrangement. Our heroines had relatively good alternatives in each of these situations; as a result, they felt they were in a powerful bargaining position. The challenge, then, is to make one's BATNA real to the other side: they should be able to recognize some dependence—or at least interdependence—on you. That recognition will compel them to negotiate with you.

Raising the cost: Isobel's case. Isobel's mentor advised her to raise the costs of the status quo. He pointed out that she was preserving the status quo by continuing to do the extra work; her boss lacked any incentive to negotiate about her role. That's when Isobel realized that her BATNA was to stop doing the extra work. The operations group's BATNA was to find some other way to get their campaigns handled. Her boss's BATNA was to maintain the status quo—in essence, turning a blind eye to the extra work Isobel was doing.

So the next time the client asked for help, claiming that they were really in a pinch, Isobel forced herself to say no. It was not easy to do. She liked the work and liked to see herself as a team player. She told them that she was sorry, but her current assignments left her no time to do the extra work. Once she stopped doing the work, the clients approached her boss and told him they really needed Isobel on these cases. That tipped the balance—and he was then ready to negotiate with her.

Risks in raising the cost. While making it real for the other party can bring a high payoff, it also entails risk, especially for women. Isobel had good reasons to stop doing the extra work: it could compromise her "real" job. Making the relative BATNAs visible gave her boss an incentive to negotiate with her. The negotiation resulted in a reorganization and promotion that made her side work official. That was the challenge that Isobel faced in getting her boss to negotiate about her role and staffing for it.

Raising the cost: Katherine's case. Katherine, a senior vice president at a large bank, took an even more direct approach. She had worked in and developed the custodial business considerably, and she knew she was ready for a new opportunity. But while the men at her bank tended to have others put them forward for promotions, it fell to the women to do so themselves.[18] So Katherine told her boss that she wanted another opportunity; he told her to be "patient." Katherine knew her boss and knew that patience could mean several years. So Katherine told him that she was going to interview with other banks. Her boss told her not to rush and came up with a plan for her to interview throughout the company. This shocked the human resource department, since this had apparently never been done out in the open. Katherine received several offers and was promoted to executive vice president within a year. Her "threat" to exercise a BATNA and look outside brought her boss to the table to negotiate with her.

Choosing the best move. There is a fine line between making your value visible and raising the costs of the status quo; the strategies can blend into each other. Lisa's disclosure that she was being recruited in some way raised the cost of the status quo. When Isobel stopped doing the extra work for the internal clients, she was surely raising the costs of the status quo, but that move also made her value visible. In my experience, people are more comfortable finding ways to make their value visible than they are raising the cost of the status quo. Charlotte (chapter 2) might make her value visible by talking about how she brought in a new client. Cheryl (chapter 3) made hers visible by explaining how she could ease her boss's relations with the field. There are times when making one's value visible is not enough—and that is where raising the costs of the status quo can become important. But there are caveats.

AN IRON FIST IN A VELVET GLOVE

Raising the costs of the status quo has two distinct but complementary requirements that I call using an "iron fist in a velvet glove."[19] The implication is that you must make these moves carefully. The first part is to strengthen your iron fist.

An Iron Fist: Prime Yourself to Feel Powerful

Some interesting research suggests useful tricks for "powering up" before using your iron fist. Psychologists have studied the impacts of priming—how exposing someone to a particular memory or stimulus can have an impact on his thoughts or actions. For instance, if I say the word *hat*, then ask you to mention a part of the body, you are likely to say *head* because you've been primed with the association between hat and head. Adam Galinsky, Deborah Gruenfeld, and their colleagues have explored how priming can influence one's psychological power and even influence their actions in negotiations. They've found that one can temporarily boost one's feeling of power by thinking about a situation or negotiation in which she has been powerful in the past.[20] This can be a helpful technique to use just prior to initiating a move to raise the status quo. Feeling more powerful can help orient you to action and make you more likely to be optimistic and confident about a negotiation, such that you recognize that initiating a negotiation has the possibility to result in a positive outcome.[21]

Use power poses to feel and act more confident. A second approach to empowering yourself is to use what social psychologist Amy Cuddy and her colleagues call power poses. It is relatively accepted that our body language can affect how others think and feel about us; some people seem more confident and powerful based on how they hold themselves. Cuddy and her colleagues have learned that body language can also influence our physiology and how we feel about ourselves. They found that holding certain poses—standing or sitting with open shoulders in a way that takes a lot of space—prompted individuals to increase the level of testosterone in their bodies. Increases in testosterone are associated with increased self-confidence and risk taking. Cuddy and her colleagues found that by holding a power pose for just two minutes before going into a negotiation or difficult situation, people feel more confident and are perceived as more confident and effective by others.[22] When it comes to initiating a negotiation with a reluctant counterpart, feeling more confident may make it easier for you to raise the costs of the status quo.

The power of a positive mood. Another crucial move is to reduce anxiety before going into the negotiation. Researchers have found that mood can have a substantial impact on a negotiation: being in a positive mood has been linked to finding creative options and cooperative problem solving, while being in a negative mood is linked to decreased joint gains and an increase in competitive strategies.[23] If you find yourself anxious before your negotiation, you can try listening to quiet music or breathing deeply to go into the negotiation in a more relaxed state.[24] Like power priming and power posing, anxiety reduction can help shore up the iron fist.[25]

The Velvet Glove

The velvet glove is important for everybody, and especially so for women. We know from the popular press and from research that being too direct can have negative consequences for females. You'll recall the double bind we discussed in chapter 1: if a woman acts too assertive, she's not liked because she's deemed "not feminine enough." If she acts too nice and feminine, her competence can be thrown into question.[26] This is particularly so for African American women, who risk being thought of as overly aggressive when they assert themselves on their own behalf.[27] In negotiating salaries, we know that women may face a social cost for asking if they too directly advocate for themselves. So raising the costs of the status quo, an assertive move, risks tripping the double bind. As we can see with Katherine and even Lisa, people might view their raising the issue as an implied threat to leave the company. And if they actually exercised their BATNA, that would be the case. Luckily, there are a number of velvet glove moves that can make tripping a double bind or encountering outright resistance less likely.

A velvet glove: Smooth out your BATNA. It's easy to read a mention of a BATNA as a threat. By smoothing it out, you still make it known but suggest that it isn't an option you want to pursue. You make the other person aware of the reality but act in a reassuring way. For example, Lisa coupled her mention of outside headhunters with assurances that she wanted to stay in her firm. Isobel focused on the time requirements it was taking her to do two jobs as the legitimate reason that she needed to focus on her "day job." You want to make these kinds of statements in reassuring ways. Author Anna Quindlen summed it up colorfully in describing Hillary Clinton and her ongoing double bind: "Hillary has soldiered on, damned if she does, damned if she doesn't, like most powerful women, expected to be tough as nails and warm as toast at the same time."[28]

One of our favorite stories about smoothing out BATNA is that of Emily, who was promoted to run a major segment of a large bank. It was widely known and part of the bank shorthand that all of the senior executives at this bank had offices on the sixth floor. Just going to a "meeting on the sixth" elevated one's status. After her promotion, the head of human resources called Emily to congratulate her on the new role and offer her a very nice office on the fifth floor. Emily responded that she thought it made sense to stay in her current office, on the third floor. She could have accepted the office on the fifth floor and been complicit in signaling that she wasn't as important as the rest of the senior execs. Or she could have told the HR director outright that she thought she deserved an office with the rest of her peers. Of course, if she'd done this, she might very well have triggered a double bind and been perceived as too demanding. Instead, by refusing the fifth-floor office she caused the HR director to realize that a fifth-floor office would be a problem for the same reason a third-floor office was. She found Emily an office on the sixth floor.

Make the consequences of no agreement obvious by asking questions. Rather than assert your intention to take an action—which others might read as a threat and an action that can trip a double bind—asking questions takes the directness out. William Ury suggests using BATNA as a means to educate, not threaten, and he recommends asking questions to serve that purpose. Ury describes this approach as "reality testing," with questions such as, "What do you think will happen if we don't agree?" "What do you think I will do?" "And what will you do?"[29]

When Faith, a partner in a major consulting company, wanted to arrange a reliable schedule, she worked with her managing partner to pare her portfolio of clients in order to keep her hours in bounds. The partner was outwardly supportive but kept postponing her final approval. Faith needed to get closure, so she decided to use what she called "indirect threats," which were really questions she felt comfortable proposing. She asked the managing partner how she would cover Faith's clients when Faith's new schedule went into effect and what she would do if she were in Faith's situation and a decision had yet to be made. These kinds of questions raise the possibility of exercising a BATNA—but do not do so directly.

Link your action to the good of the company. If you can connect your issue to a larger organizational one, your fellow negotiator is less likely to perceive it as a threat and more as a concern you have about your company's well-being. Research by Hannah Bowles and Linda Babcock suggests framing an ask in terms that account for organizational relationships in order to avoid tripping a double bind.[30] By linking your issue to the good of the organization, you are not only advocating for yourself—you are advocating for others as well, which is less likely to provoke a backlash.[31] Robin Ely and Deborah Rhode suggest that focusing on purpose and collective goals—what is good for your group or your organization—allows women to escape the double bind.[32] When asked about navigating the double bind that women in politics face, Massachusetts Senator Elizabeth Warren explained that she actively battles it by ignoring it and focusing on a larger purpose. "You try to get to…the issues that matter to you, to make sure that your voice gets heard on behalf of the people who sent you to Washington to work for them."[33]

Our case heroines have carefully navigated these strategies as well. When Isobel stopped doing the extra work, she framed it as a situation where she had no choice: her real work was suffering, and the existing structure did not support the important government work that needed to be done. She knew that was not something her boss would support. And, of course, in trying to move her boss to reorganize, it would mean better results for her group, as well as the operations group. Katherine framed her intent in the context of opportunities at the bank and the challenges of finding them— something that was not good for her or for the bank.

No matter which approach you take, raising the costs of the status quo and making your value visible must always be done carefully. And it is in these situations that allies can be so helpful.

ENLISTING ALLIES

Mika Brzezinski starts her book *Knowing Your Value* with a story about the role of allies. After working two years with Joe Scarborough on their MSNBC morning show, she sat with him at a café in Rocke-feller Center and told him of her plans to leave the show. Over the two years, she had tried without success to negotiate with the network to increase her salary and indirect compensation (defeats she describes colorfully in the book).[34] Scarborough, recognizing her critical role on the show, helped her directly from his own bonus and made her value known to the network so that she was emboldened the next time she tried to negotiate.

In some ways, this is a story of how Brzezinski raised the costs of the status quo with Scarborough by telling him that she would resign. However, it also shows the importance of the role of allies in making one's value visible. Allies can also help raise the costs of the status quo. Although we are not sure exactly how Scarborough handled the discussion with the network, he likely communicated Mika's threat to resign. In this section, we explore how allies help in making your value visible and in raising the costs of the status quo and why that is so critical, especially for women.

Allies Make Your Value Visible So You Don't Have To

Sally, a colleague of ours who is a dean at a major business school, described her surprise at the process some department chairs used when the time came for negotiations with faculty over salaries, course loads, research assistants, and other issues. Sally noticed that in certain departments, she would get a visit from that person's department chair prior to a review meeting with a faculty member. During this "premeeting," the chair would extol the accomplishments of the faculty member about to be reviewed. Sally was surprised at this process because she knew this had not happened on her behalf when she was a faculty member being reviewed by the dean. But she acknowledged the practice had a significant effect on the upcoming review meeting. The faculty member had already been positioned as an asset by a leader in his department. This meant that the faculty member did not have to promote his own accomplishments, which was quite helpful given it was an organizational culture that did not appreciate self-promotion. Although Sally was aware of what was going on, she still knew that her opinion and the decisions she might make were heavily influenced by the visit from the department chair. Sally also noted that these premeetings had so far only been arranged on behalf of men.

Sponsors: More Than Networks or Mentors

Much has been written about how critical networks are in navigating organizations.[35] Recent research suggests that women have good networks for advice and support—that is, mentors—but that they lack sponsors like Scarborough who have the position and authority that can ease negotiations.[36] As Pat Fili-Krushel, now the chair of NBC

News describes it, "Their authority allows them to speak to your strengths, make a case for your advancement, and be heard in your absence."[37] The faculty members in Sally's school played that role for the male faculty—but there didn't seem to be anyone doing it for female faculty members.

Sponsorship can be particularly valuable for women, in part because promoting one's own accomplishments has the potential to trigger a double bind. Those cultural assumptions that expect a woman to act "feminine"—to be nice, collaborative, and warm—can sometimes cause self-promoting moves to undermine the value she is trying to make visible. Allies help with this. They helped when Charlotte was able to have the new client attest to her role in selling the deal in chapter 2. They surely helped Isobel when the leaders in the operations group went to her boss to tell him that they needed Isobel on the government work. When she made her value visible, it was to point out the outcomes of her work. The leaders in the operations group made her value clear by discussing how they could not succeed without Isobel.

So many of the women I have spoken to cite the help of others in enhancing their role in negotiations. One of the leaders I most admire likes to say that she is never the first or obvious choice for stretch senior leadership roles, but she is the ultimate one—because she has a network of sponsors who sing her praises.

Allies Can Raise the Costs of the Status Quo

If self-promotion can potentially trigger a double bind, raising the costs of the status quo presents an even bigger challenge—because doing so suggests an implied threat. This is what makes allies so helpful in bringing reluctant negotiators to the table; they can say things that you might not be able to say yourself. In Alicia's case from the Introduction, her mentor might tell the chairman—with whom Alicia wants to negotiate—that the candidate he's considering might not be up to the job but Alicia would do it well. In Cheryl's case from chapter 3, leaders in the field operation might tell her boss how relations between corporate and the field might be compromised if a deal could not be worked out. Similarly, in Faith's situation, a trusted ally might tell her managing partner that Faith is likely to leave the firm if the new schedule is not finalized.

Setting the Table

James Sebenius and David Lax, well-known leaders in the negotiation field, talk about an overlooked dimension in negotiation that they call setting the table. They consider this an essential part of negotiating: the moves taken before the negotiation to ensure the most favorable conditions once negotiating has begun.[38] A big part of this during n-negotiations requires having allies who can help you get negotiations off the ground. Obviously not every member of a network is a potential ally; there seem to be two major attributes that are important. The first is the quality of the relationship you have with the potential ally. It should be someone with whom you have a good and trusting relationship—a mentor or a sponsor.

But a relationship can also be based on mutual need, as was the case with Isobel and the operations group. It was a combination of both for Joe Scarborough and Mika Brzezinski: they seemed to have a close relationship, and Scarborough also recognized how critical Brzezinski was to the show. In addition to the relationship, an ally must be credible to the person you are trying to get to the negotiating table. In other words, they must have that person's ear. When these two attributes are present, allies can play a helpful role in getting negotiations off the ground.

SECOND-GENERATION ISSUES AND SMALL WINS

The role of invisible work figures prominently in the experience of women leaders. Invisible work refers to the tasks that women often get asked to do or the ones they volunteer for. People typically attach invisible work to negative connotations: being asked to get the coffee or take the notes at a meeting. The advice given is to learn to say no more often. Yet the problem is not these kinds of situations in which it is logical to resent being asked to take up these traditional feminine roles.

We approach invisible work in a somewhat different way: it is work that is important to you and to your organization but not valued as such. Tasks might include mentoring other women, serving on diversity committees, helping others complete their work, and preventing crises. Joyce Fletcher writes about women engineers who do this work: though they anticipate and often prevent problems, this part of their work is "disappeared" in the sense that it is not credited as "real work"—but something women just "do."[39]

Isobel was in such a situation. She didn't want to stop helping, as she enjoyed it: "I loved the rush of jumping in during a crisis and loved that they specifically wanted me and that we made a real difference to the company." She said it was difficult not to continue doing the invisible work. Indeed, this kind of work is important. To tell people to stop because it is women's work fails to recognize the contributions that this type of work makes to an organization. It also fails to account for the projections that women may be experiencing as others continue to expect the same behavior from them even as they've moved into new roles.[40] In this chapter, we can see how one can claim value for that work by initiating a negotiation about it.

For this and other materials, visit www.deborahmkolb.com.

Putting *Negotiation-Launching Techniques* to Work

Make Your Value Visible
- Consider what is most valuable to your counterpart.
- Look for creative ways to highlight that value on an ongoing basis and in your negotiation.

Enlist Allies to Help Make Your Case
- Develop relationships with people—sponsors—who can promote your accomplishments.

(*Continued*)

Raise the Costs of the Status Quo (Iron Fist and Velvet Glove)
- Stop doing extra "invisible" work (a risky move, which must be done carefully).
- Allies can help deliver difficult messages about the cost of the status quo.

Use an Iron Fist to Bolster Your Power
- Prime yourself to feel powerful by reflecting on a situation in which you felt powerful.
- Use power poses to feel confident.
- Relax.

Wield Power Carefully with a Velvet Glove
- Smooth out your BATNA. Make it clear you know your options without making a threat.
- Use questions—for example, what are the consequences of no agreement?
- Connect your issue to the good of the organization.

PART TWO

PUTTING n-NEGOTIATIONS INTO PRACTICE

Building Rapport and Shifting Gears
The Power of a Good Opening

Openings matter. It's one thing to get the other party to the table where negotiation might be a possibility; it is another to actually get the process started. The way that negotiation gets started can have a significant impact on the agreement reached and the process by which it is reached. Research on traditional negotiation contexts—buyer-sellers, employers-applicants—demonstrates that what happens in the first few minutes of a negotiation not only predicts the process that will be followed but also foretells the outcome.[1]

Such research gives us insight into several dimensions of openings. They help us understand something of the strategy of opening offers: who should make them, what information one should have to make them, what constitutes a good opening offer, and the relative advantages of making them.[2] The research also helps us recognize certain scripts we're likely to follow: those that are more opening and trusting (often among acquaintances), problem solving or creative exploration of the issues, or haggling over price.[3]

OPENINGS WORK DIFFERENTLY IN
n-NEGOTIATIONS

When negotiations lack such clear structures, openings take on a different character. The context matters. In collective bargaining, opening moves are likely to be characterized by angry posturing as a way to show the various constituencies, especially on the labor side, that the bargainers are going to fight for their interests.[4] In hostage negotiations, opening moves are intended to contain the hostage taker's anxieties and calm the person down. So rather than opening offers, one might witness moves like mirroring, self-disclosure, and paraphrasing.[5]

In the same vein, openings in n-negotiations are also likely to be different.[6] They often entail shifting a request, assignment, or even dialogue from a routine meeting into something that resembles a negotiation. And these negotiations do not take place between strangers; the potential parties are likely known to each other.

In the first part of the chapter, we discuss some basic principles of opening as they've been described in the literature. These are the kinds of moves that build rapport and are crucial in n-negotiations. The second part of the chapter explains how you can shift gears by turning a meeting about one matter (say, a status update or a planning meeting) into a negotiation. In the third part of the chapter, we discuss the ways to put the preparation on mindfulness to work.[7] Finally, we deal with a special kind of situation where negotiation is unanticipated: you are asked to do something—sit on a diversity committee, take on a new project or role—and you are not happy about it. These are the situations when you are asked or assigned to do something and the expectation is not that negotiation will begin but rather that you will say yes. Based on our experiences, this kind of negotiation requires a different kind of opening.

BUILDING RAPPORT

People frequently emphasize the importance of rapport in the negotiation and dispute resolution fields. Building rapport is about creating a connection or getting in sync with your negotiating counterpart. People tell stories about the ways strangers build rapport—how they discover some connection between them, like a mutual friend, common interests, or similar backgrounds. In their book on the emotional dimensions of negotiation, Roger Fisher and Dan Shapiro suggest that these moves build structural connections between parties.[8] These connections contribute to creating a context where parties can work together despite their differences. These rapport-building moves seem especially important when you do not have a relationship with the other party—situations where you are if not strangers, at least not well known to each other. But what about n-negotiations, where you most likely not only know the person you will be negotiating with but already have a working relationship with her?

In these situations, rapport is still important.

The Costs of Lacking Rapport

Mika Brzezinski gives us a sad but humorous picture of the failure to build rapport when she tells of how she went into the office of MSNBC president Phil Griffen in the interest of securing a raise: "I sat down on his couch and proceeded to tell him in no uncertain terms that my salary was a joke and he'd better change it." She proceeded to raise her voice and even "tossed in a few F-bombs."[9] According to Brzezinski, the conversation unraveled to the point where she and Griffen stood six inches apart, jabbing each other in the shoulder. She described this incident as a failed attempt to emulate Joe Scarborough's masculine approach, which is surely true. But Scarborough's approach with Griffen was likely based on a bantering form of rapport that the two men had established. Brezinski, in contrast, had done nothing to establish a rapport of her own.

You probably have a relationship with the person you plan to negotiate with in n-negotiations—a boss, a peer, or a person who reports to you—so rapport exists at some level. However, the possibility of a negotiation, where interests are likely to diverge and where one person expects a negotiation while the other may not, calls for some care in setting the stage for a negotiation to begin. This stage setting is important; it creates a kind of holding environment for proposals to be heard.

Building Rapport: The Power of Schmoozing

The first step in building rapport, even with current coworkers, managers, and employees, is to set up some form of routine meeting to accomplish a number of things. First, as we suggest in chapter 4, these meetings provide an opportunity to update your boss about the status of ongoing projects, presumably in a way that emphasizes the value that you and your team consistently contribute. But second, they can create potential occasions for introducing a subject that might be ripe for negotiation. This can take the pressure off by eliminating the need to hold a special meeting, one that may raise the stakes.[10]

There are several ways to initiate a process of rapport building. People talk about the value of schmoozing—a word that comes from the Yiddish *schmeusen* or *shmoos*, which means to converse. Although people use the term to mean a host of networking activities, we refer to it to mean talk informally or to make small talk.[11] I'm always surprised that people know this word when I teach in other countries, since I tend to associate it with my background growing up in New York. Schmoozing, it turns out, makes a difference in negotiations. One study found that negotiators who engaged in small talk for just a few minutes before negotiating felt more cooperative and were more likely to come to an agreement than those who did not schmooze.[12]

Schmoozing is not an alien concept. Most of us start conversations by engaging in some kind of informal chitchat. We ask about each other's families, catch up on the local sports team, or in more benign fashion bemoan or applaud the weather. Schmoozing pretty much comes naturally in our normal day-to-day relationships. Yet we tend to be anxious to cut right to the chase when we're going into a negotiation—and so we forget to schmooze. In his book on improvisation in negotiation, Mike Wheeler describes a real estate negotiation role play: experienced real estate professionals were videotaped negotiating the terms between a developer and a major tenant. In one instance, the obviously anxious developer launches right into a discussion of the issues; in the second video, he spends time connecting with the tenant by talking about what they have in common. Wheeler suggests that the differences in how the tenant responds— the first in a rather hostile manner, the second more collaboratively— can be traced to these opening moves.[13]

Creating Rapport Routines

People establish rapport routines. The ones that get the most press are probably discussions of Monday-morning quarterbacking about local sports teams. People who use their weekends in other ways don't feel as comfortable participating in these discussions. But schmoozing can be about anything that connects you and the other person. If you don't know the person that well, you can talk about your business's recent performance. If you notice photographs on the wall or on a bookcase, you can ask about the family. In situations where you already know the other person well, maybe because it is a regularly scheduled meeting, schmoozing involves picking up on some of the standard topics of conversation you have usually engaged in.

Schmoozing isn't just for strangers. It is important even in well-established relationships because it allows us to get a read on where the other party is that day. One reason schmoozing is important is that it gives you a sense of what's happening with the person at the moment. You might, for example, want to know that your boss was involved in a car accident on the way into work before you broach the idea of a bonus. Let's say you do find out from schmoozing that this is not a good time—that something untoward has happened to the person with whom you've planned to negotiate and he or she is stressed or late or otherwise distracted. Under those circumstances, it might be a good idea to postpone the conversation. Schmoozing gives you some sense of how the other person is likely to perceive what you propose to negotiate.

Nonverbal cues. Though schmoozing is obviously about the words we use, it is also about the nonverbal cues we send. Researchers have found that when people are in each other's company for just a few minutes, their behaviors subtly start to converge.[14] So the other party is likely to mirror actions like leaning in and making eye contact. And when others respond in kind, we are more likely to trust them. As a result, we should be wary of basing trust only on people's responses; sometimes we need to use other means to assess how truthful a person is being with us.[15] This advice is critical when we are dealing with strangers or people we do not know very well. This may be less true with colleagues or bosses with whom we conduct n-negotiations. We have other criteria we can draw on to assess trust-worthiness in those situations, since we are likely to have some form of ongoing relationship with them, or at the very least we know them by reputation, giving us other means to judge trustworthiness. Our goal in the opening few minutes of the conversation is to establish a relatively comfortable connection before we start actually negotiating.

SHIFTING GEARS

You're able to shift gears when you have an idea about what you want to negotiate and recognize a potential occasion to do so. That potential occasion might have a different purpose—a status update, a planning meeting, or an off-site retreat. Shifting gears requires that you find a way to repurpose the meeting. In the general course of doing your work, you identify an issue about which you want to negotiate—perhaps your workload or the structure of your role. Maybe it is an idea you have to fix a persistent challenge: a morale problem in the unit, a well-resourced project that keeps underper-forming, or a new structure that does not seem to be working. Or maybe you want to advocate for more resources in your role. It might even be a promotion that you think is due. Shifting gears typically involves repurposing a meeting—such as a status update, standing one-to-one, or a planning meeting—and turning it into a negotiation.

Successful Gear-Shifting Moves

In our interviews and work with women leaders, we have seen a number of successful moves that shift gears from what might be a typical meeting into a negotiation. We've also seen a number of unsuccessful moves. Too often people jump right into their ask (even after some schmoozing) without thinking hard enough about how to shift gears. They may start out by asking very directly for what they need—more resources for their team, more compensation for themselves, a new opportunity—without creating a context that is more likely to move the other person into a negotiating frame of mind. We have observed several approaches that seem to work better in making this shift.

Picking the right time and place. We explored in chapter 4 one of the challenges in getting a negotiation off the ground: when the other person tells you that the time is right. You don't need to be rebuffed to plan ahead for what might be the right setting to start an n-negotiation, especially an unexpected one. Should you meet in an office, or would a less formal setting be more conducive?

That was the decision Meera, a partner in a pediatric practice composed of several physicians, had to make when she wanted to introduce a new compensation structure to her partners. The practice's income is basically fee-for-service, and the partners had a bonus formula to divide profit based on the number of patients each doctor treated. However, Meera believed that the compensation structure did not contribute to the practice's overall effectiveness: the doctors were not rewarded for things they did to help the practice outside of seeing patients. Partners who took on extra responsibilities (overseeing finances, working to help set insurance policies at the state level) ended up working just as much, if not more, yet they earned less compensation because they spent less time with patients.

Meera thought there might also be an opportunity to adjust their compensation plan because it failed to take into account revenue from their nurse practitioners. But she knew her proposal—that they instead base compensation on hours worked, not patient caseload—would be controversial because it would affect some of her partners' income. She also knew that if she proposed it during a regular staff meeting, her agenda could easily get hijacked by other pressing practice issues. So she decided that the annual off-site retreat where they meet at someone's house, rather than the office, would offer the most auspicious setting for her controversial proposal. The setting helped, the group was able to discuss her proposal on its merits, and ultimately they agreed that it would be more fair.

Connecting to what is happening in the organization. With this opening, the person starts the conversation by talking about something important in the organization. Tanya, a country leader in a financial services firm, wanted to renegotiate expanded areas of autonomy for her role. She began the negotiation by saying, "As you know, we are hearing from the CEO that budget is a big focus this year and we need to reduce expenses. We in Peru could manage to cut some substantial costs if we look at new ways to deal locally with our vendors." With this opening, she positions her ask in the broader context.

Connecting to the organization's overall activities is also a potential way to advocate for a promotion, even though that might seem self-serving.[16] Kristin, a director of human resources, believed she deserved a promotion but knew that there was only a small window to make that happen because her boss was leaving the company. She opened the meeting by saying, "You know, I don't often come with an ask, but I want to take our one-on-one agenda and put it aside." Kristin then went on to introduce the topic of her desire for a promotion to vice president by anchoring it in the context of two departures—that of her boss and of her counterpart in China—and the need to continue the work they had been doing by integrating different functions.

It can sometimes be difficult to advocate for a promotion for oneself; locating it in the context of what is occurring in an organization can make such an ask somewhat easier.[17] Still, it's never entirely easy.

Providing an update on a new role. The moment of taking on a new role is obviously a good time to negotiate. If you let that opportunity go by, will you be stuck with the role description you agreed to? Suggest that you want to take some time (maybe three months) to evaluate it, and then schedule time to negotiate what changes might make sense. That's what Amari did. She was three months into her role in a newly merged business development unit when she found that she was overwhelmed with day-to-day operational work and wanted more resources. She began the negotiation by stating, "I want to catch you up on how the new role is going. I really enjoy it and am so glad that you gave me the opportunity. But having spent a few months in this position, I think I see a way to deal with how stressed the group is." In this way, Amari paves the way to negotiate for hiring a new project manager so that she can spend less time on day-to-day operations and be more strategic in how she develops this new unit.

Enlarging the context for negotiating. Amari also enlarges the context for the negotiation. Yes, she wants more resources—but not just for herself. She argues that it will likely help the team, and her opening sets the stage for that.[18] Sheryl Sandberg provides a nice example of this in *Lean In*. She explains that in negotiating her role as chief operating officer for Facebook, she was prepared merely to take what the CEO, Mark Zuckerberg, offered. But her brother-in-law pointed out that a man would not consider taking the first offer. Equally interesting in this anecdote is how she opened the conversation: "Of course you realize that you're hiring me to run your deal teams, so you want me to be a good negotiator. This is the only time you and I will ever be on opposite sides of the table."[19] We know she did quite well in the negotiation, but how she opened was an interesting way to draw him in and connect their negotiation to the broader role.

DISCOVERING THE OTHER PERSON'S "GOOD REASONS"

In chapter 3, we discussed the importance of mindful preparation for a negotiation. We introduced the notion of considering your counterpart's perspective as well as any reasons she might have for taking these positions. Those reasons are the hidden agenda of any negotiation: the things that can potentially derail a negotiation if they are left unsaid. Because we are likely to be the initiator of a change in n-negotiations, the other party may become defensive. If you claim that a new structure is not working, for example, are you implicitly blaming your boss by bringing it up? If you have been overlooked for a development opportunity, are you implying that some type of bias was involved? Obviously you do not want the other party to feel blamed. But this person might—and could adopt a defensive posture, which makes it difficult for him to attend to the options you plan to propose. You find the party is defending more than listening.

Putting Good Reasons to Work

How can you mitigate this potential effect? One way is to mention one of your counterpart's good reasons early in the meeting so that you can discuss it.[20] Remember, we all have our own good reasons for taking the positions we do. When Cheryl wanted to negotiate about her schedule and locale in chapter 3, she knew her boss would likely have some significant reservations: among other things, it could mean that her job performance would suffer. She legitimates his concern by mentioning it early on in the conversation; then they can talk about it. When she introduces the option of a "tri-office," they can discuss how they will ensure that her performance does not suffer. Once Isobel (chapter 4) got her boss to the table to negotiate an expanded role for her, she expected that he would be concerned about the costs of the restructuring. When she brought it up, he confirmed her suspicions: he was concerned. From there, they can agree to discuss the financing of the new arrangement. The advantage to Isobel is that she has prevented the objections from coming up later in ways that might derail the negotiation. She's addressed the elephant in the room right off the bat.

In the workshops I teach, I always suggest that people consider mentioning a good reason early on in the negotiations. Although people appreciate the advice to *consider* the other party's good reasons for saying no, they often disagree with my advice to *mention* a good reason early in the negotiation. I've heard several objections:

- *First objection: Tipping your counterpart off.* The first concern (and the one that's the easiest to deal with) is whether you will mention a good reason that the other person hasn't even considered. That is always a possibility; however, when you know the person with whom you are negotiating and are familiar with the situation, you are unlikely to introduce an idea he has not thought about. This is not always a good strategy in N-negotiations, but in most n-negotiations, our familiarity with our counterpart and the situation make it unlikely we will raise a concern he hasn't already considered.

- *Second objection: There are likely to be many good reasons.* And what happens with the reasons you didn't mention? Will the other person raise them as objections later in the negotiations? This person well might, but by starting the conversation with a good reason, you signal that you have thought about her perspective and that you see her opinions and reactions as legitimate. That is more likely to prompt your counterpart to do the same and set a problem-solving tone for the negotiation.

- *Third objection: Ceding control.* A final objection that people have is that you've ceded control of the situation by starting with your counterpart's potential objections. Our executives tend to believe that it's preferable to control the agenda so you can best make your case. That is a legitimate point of view. However, mentioning a good reason and giving your counterpart space to air her potential objections actually does give you the best opportunity to take control. Recall our discussion of anchoring and that what happens early in the negotiation often anchors the conversation and determines both the scope of the negotiation and its outcome. Objections can work in this way as well. When you introduce one of your counterpart's good reasons, you're not just signaling that you are empathetic and problem solving; you also anchor the negotiation on whichever of their objections you wish to focus on. While others may come up, it's likely the focus will be on the issue you have raised.[21] Of course, this does mean you need to be strategic when you consider which "good reasons" you choose to introduce.

What Cheryl's Case Teaches Us

When Cheryl mentions that her boss will be concerned that any change in her locale will affect her performance, she makes it easier and more comfortable for them to discuss the issue. In doing so, she has created a space to introduce her proposal of the tri-office. And because her preparation helped her anticipate his reaction, her proposal includes ways to ensure that her performance doesn't suffer. Similarly, when Tanya opens with her wish to discuss how they handle local vendors, she mentions her boss's likely concern that this would change how the corporate office deals with country divisions. They can discuss this, and then when she introduces her proposal, they can discuss how they will sell this new idea to the corporate leadership.

Setting the context through opening moves is an important part of any negotiation. We have suggested that an opening has three parts: building rapport, shifting gears to set a context for negotiation, and mentioning a good reason to get potential defenses out in the open. Let's look at how one individual put all of these into practice.

I recently worked with a group of senior women using a short case involving a woman named Alexandra that exemplified the challenges of opening an n-negotiation in the context of an ask.

Alexandra's Case: Responding to an Ask

Alexandra is a director in her company, whose boss asks her to help out a vice president in another area who is having personal problems. In this case, the ask is ambiguous. Rather than be a director, Alexandra will have an interim title—director of special projects—and will also take over two major projects on an interim basis.[22] In addition, responsibility for an important initiative she is leading will pass to her subordinate.

This obviously creates a dilemma for Alexandra. On the plus side, her boss is expressing confidence in her leadership—she will be able to pull off this role and help out the division. It is a great opportunity for her, he says. She will get to work with a promising vice president in the division. Her boss clearly expects Alexandra to agree, and she is tempted to do so.

Of course, the women in the program were not pleased with the boss's ask. They reasoned that Alexandra was being asked to give up her initiative just when her hard work would pay off. Credit for the initiative's success would pass to her subordinate. And she was being asked to exchange that for an ambiguous role with no assurances about where it would lead. The women saw this as a request that was ripe for negotiation.[23] They developed creative options about the role, the title, the future, and the project she would be leaving.

We then set up a role play, and those playing Alexandra had a difficult time getting negotiations off the ground. The boss, wanting and anticipating a yes, did not expect to negotiate. Most of those playing Alexandra were frustrated that they could not open the negotiation. As the boss flattered her about how perfect she was for the role and how good she would be in it, Alexandra consistently tried to discuss other options. She wanted to actually get the title, or at least assurances about the role in the future, as well as some form of continued role in (and credit for) the initiative she had led. A skilled role player, the boss easily deflected these opening overtures, and the negotiations did not get off the ground.

What Alexandra's Case Teaches Us

While this case may not be specifically typical of n-negotiations, it does reflect a significant category of situations where people are asked to do something—take on a new role, a seat on a diversity task force, or a new subordinate—with an expectation that they will assent. We saw this situation in Marisa's case from chapter 1, when the managing partner was willing to engage with her and the advice to respond with "Yes, and…" seemed straightforward. But that is not always the case. Indeed, recent research suggests that women are more likely to be asked to do work that might not be beneficial to their careers.[24] Another example is when a company announces a reorganization and a subset of people are put into new roles. As part of that process, the expectation that accompanies these announcements is that there will be no negotiation. Indeed, in the case of reorganizations, we are sometimes grateful to still have a role at all. Launching these presumably nonnegotiable situations requires setting a context that will shift the conversation—one wherein it is a more difficult challenge to shift gears.

Similarities between Opening Moves and Responding to an Ask

As we have interviewed people about these situations and observed them role playing, we see these occasions as ones that make use of similar principles of opening moves yet deployed in slightly different ways.

Use gratitude carefully. Obviously schmoozing still applies because you want to connect with the asker. But a trap we have observed people fall into all too frequently is continuing in that vein by expressing gratitude for being asked. There is nothing wrong with expressing gratitude in general. But in this context, it can give the impression that you are prepared to say yes, whereas you want to either say no or more likely make it a "Yes, and…"

We have observed that people speak appreciatively too often when they are not really appreciative. Alexandra is not particularly happy about being offered an ambiguous role where the reward for doing so is not at all clear. If anything, rather than expressing gratitude for the opportunity, you can express gratitude in a way that legitimates your competence. "Thank you for recognizing I am qualified to take over the vice president's role" can be much more effective than "Thank you for this opportunity."

When you should question the other person. In contrast to the examples we already gave regarding shifting gears and connecting your ask to a broader organizational context, you want to do the questioning in this situation. You want the asker to answer your questions and connect the request to the organizational context. Alexandra needs answers to her opening questions so that she will feel that she can say yes. She wants to know several things: Why is she being asked to do this only temporarily? How long will this assignment last? Why is she being offered only an acting role? What happens after it ends?

In our experience with these types of conversations, it's common to get only vague answers to these sorts of questions. Remember, the other party is expecting her to say yes and would rather not get too specific. So, then, what should you do—and what can Alexandra do?

Shift the balance: When you should get the other person to question you. At this point, it's helpful to remind yourself that this person came to you, not someone else, for this assignment. Presumably he or she thinks you're the right person for this role. You might not be able to say no outright, but you do have some power here. Your boss's BATNA might not be so good in this situation; remember, there's a vice president who has to take a leave of absence and a scramble to pick up the pieces.

When you're not getting answers to your questions, it helps to shift the balance and the direction of the questions. Ultimately, you want your counterpart to start asking you questions about what you want. Once you can get that to happen, a negotiation can begin.

We have observed some useful opening moves to create this shift in the balance and prompt the asker (boss) to start doing the asking. Alexandra might respond:

- "Thank you for this offer, but I don't think I can say yes under the terms you are suggesting." The boss responds with, "What terms would make it possible for you to say yes?"
- "I don't think I can take this role in the way you have described it." The boss responds, "What would make you change your mind?"
- "I have some concerns about the role as you have defined it." The boss responds, "What are your concerns?"

With each of these openings, Alexandra shifts the conversation so that the boss has to question her. This shifting of gears gives her an opening to put her options on the table. Obviously the degree of directness with which you make these kinds of openings depends on the situation and the relationship you have with your negotiating counterpart. In situations like Alexandra's, where you are offered an opportunity proposed uniquely to you, you have more leeway in how you open as a way to get the other party to ask you questions. You can be more direct. However, there are other situations where the first opening might prompt the other party to say, "Fine," and move onto the next person. In situations where you realistically see that your bargaining room is limited, the third and more oblique opening is likely to work best. Whichever opening you use to switch gears from an ask to a negotiation, you need to be clear that just because a person expects you to say yes directly does not mean you have to do so.

SECOND-GENERATION ISSUES AND SMALL WINS

Openings in n-negotiations are important and tricky because they involve a situation where the other person is not expecting a negotiation. It may be a routine meeting or simply that the other person expects acquiescence. The issue of asks is particularly important. We know from the research that women get asked to do many things because of their position in an organization. If they are one of few women, they may be asked to sit on various committees to bolster diversity—especially true for women of color. It may also be that women get asked more because people expect them to say yes—not just because there is a general expectation that women will say yes, but also because people get reputations for doing so. Indeed, Isobel (chapter 4) told us that she had to ask a friend to make sure that she did not say yes the next time the operations group asked her to do something.

Negotiation over asks is important so that you, like Isobel, can keep focused on the work that matters to you and is recognized. And if you do respond affirmatively, you need to think of it as a "Yes, and..." in order to ensure that you are not overloading yourself. It's critical to figure out what the "and" is. For Isobel to continue to do the extra work would not be good for her or the organization. That's part of how you prepare yourself to come up with creative options and anticipate the reactions to your ask. But equally important is to have a way to open these kinds of negotiations so that the other person is ready to discuss the options you have prepared. Once Alexandra responds to her boss with what it will take for her to agree to the temporary role, they can negotiate a good agreement for her, for her boss, and for the organization. These examples are small wins for the women who negotiated them. They put a value on the work they are being asked to do and so are more likely to get credit for work that might have been invisible.

For this and other materials, visit www.deborahmkolb.com.

Putting *Openings* to Work

Rapport Is Important: Take Time to Build Relationships
- Schedule regular check-ins with your manager, subordinates, and peers.
- Don't underestimate the value of schmoozing during both everyday interactions and within the negotiation itself.

Be Prepared to Shift Gears
- Plan for the right time and place.
- Look for ways to repurpose an existing meeting.
- Make connections to what is happening in the organization or in your work.
- Enlarge the context of your discussion. How does what you want help you do a better job? How does it help your team?

(*Continued*)

Put Your Counterpart's "Good Reasons" to Work for You
- Introduce one of her "good reasons" for saying no to you.
- Show that you understand and can address these concerns.
- By legitimating her perspective, you encourage her to do the same for you.
- Focus on the "good reasons" you want to discuss.

You Don't Have to Be Grateful for Bad Opportunities
- When your boss expects a "yes," you can still negotiate the "and."
- Determine the conditions you'd need for success: duration, title, buy-in, clear metrics of success, promotion time line, increased resources, and so on.
- Manage the conversation such that your boss is the one asking questions.
- Your goal is for her to ask you, "What would it take for you to say yes?"
- Remember the value of "Yes, and...," as in, "*Yes*, I'll take the role, *and* in order to be successful, I'll need X, Y, and Z."

Power at Play in Negotiations
Moves and Turns

Menacingly, [the Chinese negotiator] leaned forward across the table toward Barshefsky and said flatly, "It's take it or leave it." Barshefsky, taken aback by the harsh tone, surprised her counterpart by sitting quietly. She waited thirty to forty seconds—an eternity given the intensity of the negotiation—and came back with a measured reply: "If the choice is take or leave it, of course I'll leave it. But I can't imagine that's what you meant. I think what you mean is that you'd like me to think over your last offer and that we can continue tomorrow."

—From a 2001 Harvard Business School case by James Sebenius and Rebecca Hulse[1]

US trade representative Charlene Barshefsky faced a threat in trade negotiations with China over intellectual property. She didn't respond to the scenario described above by issuing a counterthreat; rather, she waited and then reframed the threat (a move) into an action (a turn) that would drive the negotiations forward. These kinds of moves and turns are the subject of this chapter.

In the normal byplay of negotiations, parties say things that can throw you off balance. We call these "strategic moves."[2] Jim Sebenius has a related concept, which he calls the "hardest question."[3] Coming in several varieties, these are the questions you don't want to have to answer. They might be innocent questions, or they could be strategic questions designed to throw you off guard: "How can we be sure your family responsibilities won't get in the way of you doing your job?" Or "Aren't you too inexperienced for us to risk giving you this contract?" They're questions that call for a response; some might even ask you to provide what you consider confidential information: "What is the minimum salary you would take?" or, "What other offers do you have?"

This chapter focuses particularly on the types of questions and statements that, usually by design, could cause you to become defensive—strategic moves. Because these moves can make you feel defensive and questioning of yourself, they can make it challenging to pursue the options you've proposed. If the negotiation is to continue, such moves need to be turned, as Barshefsky did with her silence.

SPOTLIGHT ON STRATEGIC MOVES—AND HOW TO TURN THEM

Strategic moves happen in all negotiations. In the first section of this chapter, we discuss how n-negotiations raise the kinds of issues that often lead to resistance. Resistance is frequently expressed in strategic moves that can have an impact on negotiators directly, as well as the options they propose. In the next section, we identify the several types of moves that can come up in n-negotiations. These moves are part of the normal interactive byplay of negotiation; they come up naturally as parties deal with the issues that are raised. We're mostly interested in the moves that potentially challenge a negotiator's own presentation of self and make it more likely that he will be put on the defensive, which will make it more difficult to advocate credibly for the options proposed or to be open to other possibilities. There are things a negotiator can do to prepare for these moves, and we discuss these in the third part of the chapter.

Our tendency in these situations is often to become defensive and simply push back, using what we call *countermoves*. Yet this can keep the focus of the negotiation within the frame of the moves. A different approach is to "turn" the moves, which can refocus the negotiation. In the fourth section of the chapter, we describe a variety of turns and show how to phrase different turns to shift the conversation, so that you can credibly stay in the conversation and move the discussion forward. That was the challenge Rosalie faced during her annual performance review.

Rosalie's Case

Rosalie has a PhD in economics and is a senior research fellow at a global nonprofit, where she's worked for five years. She has two young children and works at home one day a week. Research staff members in her group are evaluated on their scientific contributions to their field, which are gauged by several criteria: the ability to generate funding for significant research projects, implementing complex multiparty research projects that produce significant findings that also have policy implications, publishing the results in prestigious journals in the field, and then publicizing the results in policymaking forums.

By most of these criteria, Rosalie had a very good year. Her major grant was renewed based on its impressive findings across several research sites. A multiauthored article that had been submitted a year ago had been accepted in a good journal with only minor revisions. This was a relief to Rosalie, because it was a challenge to translate the seventy-five-page research report into a journal article. Despite her accomplishments, however, she had not received opportunities to present her work publicly, either to policymakers or to colleagues in her field. This is important for her career in her organization, but also more generally because people in her field move back and forth from nonprofit development work into academia. Visibility and connections are critical, and gaining them has been a perennial problem for junior researchers in her organization. The same small group of people always take over the presentations; that

(*Continued*)

> is, other people would present Rosalie's work to donors and at large international conferences. Rosalie wants to take the occasion of her upcoming review with the associate director of her center; she wants to shift gears and negotiate to present her work at two international conferences with support and funding from the organization.

Resistance and Strategic Moves

A gamut of topics fall in the category of n-negotiations. Typically compensation is the most prominent topic we associate with employment relationships. However, studies of negotiation at work show that both women and men also negotiate to achieve change for themselves, their groups, their functions, or their divisions. They may seek a new role or leadership opportunity. They may want to experiment with new working arrangements or extend their authority beyond their current areas of responsibility. They might have an idea or plan for which they want support or resources,[4] or, like Rosalie, they want a specific opportunity.

In the previous chapters, we've laid out strategies to prepare for negotiations—to position yourself and develop creative options and approaches to get negotiations off the ground by getting the other party to the table and opening the conversation in ways that start to build collaboration and commitment. But no matter how well you've followed the steps of preparation and tried to get negotiations off on the right foot, issues will inevitably bubble up.[5] After all, most of these potentially negotiable issues challenge—or at least question—the status quo. That's what Rosalie's request for conference support does: challenges the current situation in which only leaders get to present.

Of course, we can expect at least some resistance to new ideas under such conditions.

Sources of Resistance

People resist change for a host of reasons. They may feel they will lose control over areas important to them, or that this kind of change will make them appear incompetent or bring more work for them. They may have technical reasons to resist: they don't think what you propose will work, or they worry that it will create too much uncertainty or that the costs will outweigh the benefits. Maybe they fear a change might marginalize them, or maybe they are just surprised about what you propose. Or maybe what you propose is beyond the scope of their authority to change.[6] These sources of resistance can hold true for any kind of change. But the n-negotiations that concern us here add other complications to our thinking about resistance.

The forms that resistance takes in n-negotiations can be a bit more complicated. If we are overlooked for an opportunity, raising that issue can make the other person feel defensive. Women are often discounted when overseas assignments are being made because the assumption is that they won't want to or simply cannot relocate their families. Like Alexandra in chapter 5, we may be asked to take an ambiguous or lesser role we don't especially want but are expected to say yes to. Like Isobel in chapter 4, we are doing more work and not getting recognized for it. Or, like the associate director in Rosalie's case, our boss is happy with the current arrangements and will be surprised that employees see it as discriminatory for younger researchers.

When we negotiate about these kinds of issues, we recognize a problem that the other party likely does not. Second-generation gender issues are by definition unconscious because they are built into the organization. And when organizational processes are gendered, people in power don't recognize that there's a problem.[7] By negotiating around these types of issues, we're likely to get resistance as a result. When people resist in these situations, they push back on us and our ideas. And when this happens, we can become defensive.

We've described this process as one of moves and turns. We use strategic moves to position ourselves to advantage. We described some of these moves in chapters 4 and 5—how to get people to the table and open the negotiations in ways that work to our advantage. The other party is similarly using strategic moves to position herself advantageously. One type of strategic move discussed widely in the literature is so-called dirty tricks where negotiators employ some familiar tactics, such as good cop/bad cop, in order to throw the other negotiator off.[8] We've described other moves that are so demeaning to a person—calling somebody a "bitch"—that they verge on harassment.[9] While these kinds of moves can occur, they are rarer; therefore, we concentrate on the routine moves that occur typically as the other party positions herself to her advantage and reacts to the options you propose in ways that can put you on the defensive.

Strategic Moves

The concept of strategic moves and turns is central to understanding the shifting power dynamics in a negotiation. At the same time as we are explicitly negotiating over the issues—presenting proposals, making the case for them, and having the other party respond—a parallel process is occurring: we're engaged in what we've called a shadow negotiation about the relative positioning of the parties. In the shadow negotiation, our identities as negotiators, the legitimacy that gets attached to our positions, the power and authority we claim, and the import of gender and race are always part of what is being negotiated alongside the substantive issues. To look at negotiations from the perspective of the shadow negotiation is to attend to how parties manage impressions of themselves, how they claim and maintain legitimacy and credibility, how they assert what power and influence they have, and how they shape perceptions of what is possible.[10] In the previous chapters, we've focused on some of the ways that you can manage these impressions through the strategic moves you use to get people to the table and to open the negotiation.

Of course, at the same time that you're using strategic moves to position yourself, so too is the other party—and his actions can make you feel defensive. These are critical moments when your legitimacy and the legitimacy of your positions are challenged.[11]

From research and our experiences, we have identified a number of common moves:

- *Challenging your competence or expertise.* This occurs when the other party makes a comment that explicitly or indirectly questions your competence or expertise. For instance, Rosalie seeks to make her value visible by describing her publication successes, while the associate director comments that this seems like an average year. He then says that the journals she's published in are not that prestigious. When Charlotte (chapter 2) asks to be appointed to the vice president role she's already been doing, the CEO tells her she's not ready. While you base your proposals on your value, these moves undermine your value, causing you to back off. After all, the other person is challenging your competence to do what you are asking.

- *Demeaning your ideas.* This is when the other person attacks the ideas or options you propose in ways that give you little room to respond. In making this move, the other person can express disbelief or even outrage at what you have proposed. Saying something like, "You can't be serious about this proposal," makes you and your idea sound ridiculous. When Amari (chapter 5) wanted to negotiate for more resources after she'd been in a new role for several months, her boss said, "I'm surprised. You spent so much time researching this idea and estimated what it would cost. You can't be serious about asking for more now." The party may demean your ideas by pointing out all the flaws in your proposal, suggesting that you have not adequately thought it through. When Cheryl (chapter 3) proposes her alternative working arrangement of the tri-office, her boss raises objections to the plan: it will cost too much; it won't work; she'll be unable to do her job. Obviously these moves make it difficult to argue for what might otherwise be a reasonable idea.

- *Criticizing style.* When other parties use phrases such as, "Don't get so upset," they're casting you—who you are and how you act—as the subject of the move. Such a move casts a negotiator as overreacting or inconsiderate and positions that person as irrational—someone who cannot be reasoned with or who is selfish or not nice. Mika Brzezinski recounts her experiences with a female manager who told her that if she persisted in her request for a higher salary, she would offend people and get "a bad reputation."[12] While Brzezinski later regretted how naive she'd been, this manager's appeal effectively shut down Brzezinski's negotiation attempts because Brzezinski didn't want to become unpopular. This move can call forth such unfortunate stereotypes as the hysterical female.[13] When Rosalie was understandably offended that the associate director had derogated her accomplishments, he told her not to overreact and that she took things too personally. These moves can be profoundly unsettling. Who among us thinks of ourselves as unreasonable or difficult?

- *Threatening moves.* Threats can take many forms, ranging from explicit moves to end or cut off negotiations to suggesting the possibility of unpleasant consequences if the person doesn't back down. Threats are intended to force a choice on a negotiator: "Cut your rates, or there's no deal." The global leader told Claudia from chapter 1 that they were interviewing other promising candidates and needed an immediate decision, pressuring her to make a decision before she even knew what the client list would be. That threatening move undermined Claudia; she felt disempowered and backed into a corner, which made it difficult for her to think about proposing other options.

- *Appealing for sympathy or flattery.* The moves described thus far have been critical of the person or her ideas. But appeals for sympathy and flattery also can be quite powerful in n-negotiations. When the other party flatters you by describing you in a positive light, she is counting on you to acquiesce or back down. If Alexandra's boss is counting on her to say yes, then instead of threatening her, she tells her that she's so good at what she does, she's such a quick study, and she'll be able to help her colleague and bring her second-in-command up to speed so that he can take over her project. When Isobel approached her boss about restructuring her role in chapter 4, he used flattery to deflect her request: "You are so good at what you do, and everybody appreciates the work you are doing for the government group. You are so organized and work so hard that I know you can continue to do both roles." Appeals for sympathy can be even more powerful than criticism. With these moves, the other party is asking you to take her situation more fully into account and back down to save her face. When the associate director says to Rosalie, "I really need your support," he's asking her not to raise the issue of presenting at conferences. When Alexandra's boss says to her, "I know you won't let me down" or "I really need your help on this," she's counting on the move to silence Alexandra, making it difficult for her to advocate and press for a different outcome.

Strategic moves like these five and the many variants on them can be seen as situated exercises of power meant to "put a person in her place." In the interactive byplay, these moves are intended to position the negotiator in a one-down, defensive position. When the other party presses for advantage by questioning one's competence, motives, ideas, legitimacy, and style, the move not only challenges the potential argument or claim a negotiator wants to make; it can also undermine her sense of competence and confidence. It also makes it difficult for her, in a one-down position, to stay in the negotiation in a productive way. When they're taken unaware by these moves, negotiators tend to react, almost without thinking, by making a countermove.

The Trap of Countermoves

When taken by surprise by a move, we often respond automatically by defending ourselves with a countermove, which are comebacks in kind. The associate director told Rosalie not to get so upset, and she responded emphatically, "I am not upset." The CEO told Charlotte that she was not ready for the VP role, and she said, "Yes, I am." Although such a defensive countermove is quite common, it clearly reinforces the previous move; that is, the recipient of the move stays in the original, defensive position. Defensive countermoves are so common in part because negotiators do not recognize that a move is being used as a tactic; hence, they respond emotionally and defensively.

Another problem with countermoves is that they prompt you to act in accordance with the other party's definition of the situation; in other words, you're responding on his turf. Worst of all, countermoves can invite a tit-for-tat process that spirals the conversation downward. Rather than discussing the issues you set out to discuss, you find yourself in a heated debate, going back and forth about something that's not productive.

It is also possible to misinterpret a move. Sometimes a question to uncover your interests or pursue the problem can be genuine, but something you perceive as a move. For example, when Mia, a project manager in a financial services firm, brought up the need for more resources, she got push-back. She opened the negotiation by noting the growing backlog in the audits they were doing: "I'm worried that we're exposing the company to additional risks by not getting through the audits. I want to talk about getting an additional resource to help with that problem." Her boss responded, "This keeps coming up, and we keep adding resources. What's the problem?" Her boss may have just been inquiring, but Mia could read this response as a challenge to her competency. If she hears it that way, she could respond with a countermove: "There is no problem." Her boss might take this as an implied criticism and might escalate his response. Since my moves are dependent on my interpretations of your moves, we could go down a very slippery slope.

Of course, you can also ignore these strategic moves. When Amari's boss (chapter 5) challenged her ideas after they'd agreed not to pursue them, she could just ignore the comment and push on. Still, the move has been made, and it sits there. It's not clear whether Amari agrees. When seriously demeaning moves are made about sex or race, to ignore them is potentially to collude in that positioning.[14]

Preparing for Strategic Moves

Strategic moves can catch us unaware, but we can prepare for their possibility even if we cannot be sure they will happen. Jim Sebenius suggests that as part of your preparation, you take time to identify the kinds of questions that might be the most difficult for you to answer.[15] As part of the preparation we outlined in chapters 1, 2, 3 and 4, you will have a good idea of what forms strategic moves might take.

Know your challenges. Part of your preparation is to take stock of your strengths and figure out ways to make them visible. But just as critical is focusing on areas of vulnerability, since these are likely to come up as moves. For example, when Charlotte (chapter 2) puts herself forward for the vice president role, she can be pretty sure that the CEO will raise her inexperience as an issue. It may come out as a move: "You don't have the experience to do this job." Or he may ask why he should put her in the role when he can hire somebody more experienced from the outside. Since Charlotte can be sure these questions and challenges will come up, she needs to be prepared to deal with them.

Know what you know about the person you are dealing with. As we know, one of the characteristics that distinguish n-negotiations from N-negotiations is that you're likely to have some relationship with the other person in the former. You know this person's style and how she responds to different kinds of requests. You know what might make her defensive and push her to employ a strategic move that might put you on the defensive. It's something of a problem that despite Charlotte's doing the VP job in addition to her own, the CEO does not like criticism. To surface the suggestion that he's been overlooking her—indeed, is taking advantage of her—might be met with push-back.

Rosalie knows the associate director and how he deals with her in performance reviews. She wants the session to focus on what she's accomplished and not on her problems—which has been her experience in the past. She also knows that she can expect him to downplay her accomplishments in getting the grant and in the acceptance of her paper. She has a pretty good idea about the kinds of strategic moves he'll make, so she can come prepared to deal with them.

Know the other person's "good reasons" for saying no. As part of the preparation to be mindful of the other person that we discussed in chapter 3, we cited how important it is to discern their good reasons for saying no to you. If you understand these reasons, you can expect them to come up as strategic moves in the negotiation. Cheryl was pretty clear about the reasons the CFO could use to say no to her. He would be afraid the proposal would not work and would likely demean her idea. Because he is relatively new to his position, he might appeal for sympathy and ask her to postpone her plan. He might worry that she lacked the expertise to pull off the role in such a complicated manner. Since Cheryl had prepared for these reasons, she was ready with ideas to meet them. By going through the process of delineating them, she was also preparing herself for his push-back. Likewise, Rosalie has a good sense of why the associate director would say no. Simply raising the issue that the entire junior research staff were not being sponsored to attend important conferences is an effort on her part to change the status quo, so she can expect such a move to meet resistance. And given her experience with the associate director, she should be pretty sure about the forms the resistance might take.

Preparing for the possibility of the difficult question or strategic moves is important for building your confidence going into the negotiation. Having a map of what to expect takes some of the uncertainty out of a negotiation that means a lot to you. Even if the moves never happen, at least in preparing for them, you're likely to provide a reservoir of strength going into the negotiation—which gives you a way to plan for your responses with what we call *turns*.[16]

CULTIVATE YOUR REPERTOIRE OF TURNS

You can think about turns as akin to turns in a road: they indicate a shift in direction. And that's precisely what turns can do in a negotiation. They are responses to strategic moves that reframe the move. They are moments of potential resistance. Rather than staying in a defensive position and responding with a countermove, a turn changes the conversation's direction.

Turns also have the potential to change a meaning and so reposition the other party. Where the meanings and intentions behind statements can be unclear—since two or more interpretations of them may exist at any given moment—these indirect methods or turns can reframe how parties are viewed. A repertoire of turns is a set of tools a negotiator can use to resist being put in a defensive position, as well as a means to shift the conversation into a more productive space.

Six Major Turns

When you turn a move, you're shifting the negotiation in a number of possible ways. For one thing, you go from being on the defensive to being on a more equal footing, which gives you more agency. And we know that the possibility for achieving good agreements for both parties is more likely to come when there is some parity between the parties.[17] Turns help you achieve that parity. Second, turns can create an important break or transition in the negotiation that can shift what might be opening posturing and debate into a more collaborative mode of problem solving. From our work, we have identified six major turns: interruption, naming, questioning, correcting, diverting, and focusing on the future.

Interruption. When you interrupt a move, the mere fact of doing so breaks the action of a move. People often misunderstand this definition and assume it means to cut off somebody who is talking. Instead, this kind of interruption means creating a break in the action, which does three things. First, it introduces a pause, which gives you a chance to collect your thoughts so that you don't make an unproductive countermove without thinking. Second, even the shortest break can reset the conversation; you never return to exactly the same place afterward. Third, research suggests that many negotiations actually benefit from some form of interruption. When negotiators who were concerned for both themselves and the other took a break, even as short as three minutes, they engaged in more cooperative negotiations—and also reached more agreements—afterward.[18]

Interruptions can take many forms. They can be a pause. You can sit silent for a minute or less. You can stand up, get a cup of coffee, or take a restroom break. A break of any length changes the dynamic. When Cheryl introduced her plan to negotiate a different work schedule, she knew the chief financial officer (CFO) would reject the idea out of hand. So she let him vent, then sat silent. Research has shown that most people are uncomfortable with silence and often feel the need to cover up awkward silences.[19] This was true for Cheryl's CFO, who felt the need to fill in the empty space. Realizing that his strategic move did not have its intended effect (she had predicted and planned for it), he asked her how she planned to handle the complications a different office arrangement would entail. She was prepared for that.

Interruptions can also last longer. Taken by surprise at the reaction to an idea or even shocked by a threat or insult, rescheduling a meeting might be the best course. Charlene Barshefsky, from the chapter's opening, used an interruption beautifully—pausing thirty to forty seconds to defuse the take-it-or-leave-it threat. Then she indicated that she was going to take a break to think through the offer. You cannot always be totally prepared for a strategic move that undercuts your plan and potentially puts you on the defensive. In those circumstances, interruption is an important move on your part. When you are in a defensive mode, you defend. Interruption makes that much less likely.

Naming. To name a move makes it clear that you recognize the purpose behind what's being said. Naming can take many forms, but its major purpose is to show clearly that you recognize the tactic. You can name by using humor or irony. Our favorite example comes from professor and editor Silvia Gherardi. After returning from a conference, one of her senior male colleagues went to open the door for her, then paused. "Do you want me to open the door for you," he asked, "or will you react as if I'd grabbed your arse?" Gherardi observes that she was put in a position of being perceived as either a hysterical feminist or a sweet and docile lady who knew her place in academia, as well as society. "I decided on sarcasm and told him emphatically that I formally authorized him to open that door and all the other doors and obstacles that might stand in my way."[20]

You can name a move by revealing its ineffectiveness or showing that it has unintended consequences. When you name in this kind of way, you need to be careful that you do not blame the other person. Indeed, you try to supply a reasonable motive to his move. When the associate director tells Rosalie that she is not ready to attend the international conferences, she could say, "The way I see people getting ready is by actually preparing and going to the conferences." By naming the move in that way, she tries to open up the possibility that he will rethink and give her the opportunity. Charlene Barshefsky named the move by insinuating that the Chinese negotiator could not have been serious about the threat because the outcome was not what he would want. In naming it, she provided a good intention for him.

Another way to name a turn is to highlight a move's inappropriateness in a way that reinterprets the intention behind the move in a positive way. The Introduction told the story of Alicia, who wants to negotiate with the vice chairman of her company for a position as regional vice president of sales. During the negotiation, the vice chairman is likely to question her ability to do the job because of her family responsibilities. As Jim Sebenius suggests in his discussion of difficult questions, you can respond to what is an inappropriate question—or, in our context, a strategic move—by addressing the concern without explicitly mentioning its inappropriateness.[21] Alicia might say, "Although how I handle my family is a private matter, I think your comment implies that you are concerned about my ability to devote the time to the new role. I can assure you that I have always managed the commitments in my jobs and would continue to do so in this one." Statements like, "As you and I both know...," or "If this were true, I would be uncomfortable," allow you to name the move and set it up for a turn.

Questioning. When you question a move, you are in essence throwing it back to the mover. As with naming, you recognize the move as a possible tactic. But in questioning the move, you take a more inquiring stance. The most benign reason for questioning a move is simply to gather more information. When the CFO raises multiple objections to Cheryl's plan as something that will not work (in chapter 3), indicating that she has not thought through what she's proposing, Cheryl can use inquiry to solicit more information about his objections. She can ask, "What really concerns you? Which of the issues is most critical?" Her questions allow her to discover that he was really concerned that she would tire of an arrangement. By questioning the strategic move, she learns more about what is critically important to him.

You can use a questioning turn as a means to pressure the other person to justify a demeaning assertion he may have made. Rosalie opens the negotiation by asking the associate director whether he's read the summary she prepared about what she has accomplished this year. In a move that challenges her accomplishments, he says that he only got a chance to skim it, but it looks like an average year. Of course, Rosalie is set back on her heels because this opening was her attempt to make her value visible. In a questioning turn, she could ask him to justify his assertion: "How would you define an excellent year?" What she might learn from that question was that he hadn't thought about his response to such a question and had only a vague answer—which would make Rosalie feel that she was back in the negotiation.

Questioning turns can help other parties see beyond their own perspectives and actions. This turn, which basically asks the other party what she would do in your situation, is often a subtle way to call a bluff. For example, in Charlotte's situation (chapter 2), the CEO tries to diminish her accomplishments—in bringing in a new client, he said, she just closed a deal already in the pipeline—as a way to get her to back off her proposal to be appointed to the vice president's role. When she asks him what he would do if he were in her situation, she effectively silences him because he knows he would do precisely what Charlotte is doing. Similarly, when Rosalie gets rattled as the associate director diminishes her accomplishments, he tells her not to overreact. She too asks him how he would respond if the tables were turned. These kinds of turns can give the other person pause and change the direction of the conversation.

Correcting. A correcting turn substitutes a different version or motivation to the one the move has implied. These turns suggest different ways of seeing things. Moves often imply criticism or some ways you or your ideas are lacking, and dispute the merits of your positions or options. They make you wonder whether the way the other party sees the situation is actually reasonable. Maybe your proposal is not so good after all. With the budget so tight, maybe you are being greedy. Correcting turns bring these distorted impressions back into focus. You can correct an impression by providing a positive version of the situation. When the CEO tells Charlotte that she only closed a deal that was already in the pipeline, she can correct that move: "Let me tell you what I did to get the client and how I was able to close the deal, which was not at all a sure thing." When the associate director suggests that the success Rosalie has had in getting her work published is not a major accomplishment, she could correct the move by providing data on acceptance rates for the journal.

You can correct a move by providing a different, more legitimate motive to your actions than has been implied by the strategic move. When Marisa entered into negotiations with the regional managing partner in chapter 1, she had a long list of both financial and organizational issues to be resolved. After all, taking the position in the Southeast was going to be a major disruption for her. Even though Alice, the regional managing partner, very much wanted her to take the role, she was not happy with some of the demands Marisa was making. "You are focused only on yourself, not accounting for the firm's situation. If I give you what you're asking, it will create a real problem for me going forward." Alice's move was intended in part to lower Marisa's aspirations. Marisa provided context for her ask: her concerns about leaving her community of support, the compensation she would need to move to a high-priced area, the resources she would need to build up the declining business. By elaborating on her motivation through her correcting turn, she provided more information to the partner.

Finally, you can use correcting turns to counter stereotype moves. We often make assumptions based on people's gender, race, background, or function. When these assumptions enter the negotiation as a strategic move, they can put the person in a very difficult situation—because to correct it can make salient a certain bias behind the move. In *Tempered Radicals*, Debra Meyerson uses the example of a female executive responding to her colleagues' plan for an evening meeting.[22] In making a correcting turn, the executive would point out that she has other responsibilities that cannot easily change without notice. By doing this, she subtly questions her colleagues' assumption that people should be available for work 24/7.

Correcting turns can be tricky to implement because they can often come across as a defensive countermove. Meyerson suggests that people may perceive correcting turns as confrontational when they're used to counter stereotypes, as in the example. When we discuss moves and turns, people often mention correcting turns. It is almost the most accessible comeback to a move. When someone says, "Don't get upset," our immediate comeback is to reply we are not upset. While that is a correcting turn in some ways—because it corrects a perception—it does not function as a turn because it doesn't change or reframe the dynamic.

Diverting. A diverting turn shifts the focus to the problem itself; therefore, it is a way to depersonalize a move. In that regard, it echoes a well-known dictum from *Getting to Yes*: focus on the problem, not the people.[23] One diverting turn is simply to substitute a better idea. If you've prepared by thinking through multiple options, you can divert a turn by introducing one that has not yet been discussed. When Alexandra (chapter 5) prepared for her meeting with her boss to discuss the ask that she take on a temporary role and give up the leadership role in her current project, she both flattered her—"You are so good at picking up new roles and doing them"—and appealed for sympathy. She diverted the move by proposing some other workable solutions.

Focusing on the future. Another way to turn a move is to shift the focus to the future. You may acknowledge the past and admit a mistake or a problem, but then move past it to the current problem. Recall that Mia, earlier in this chapter, got a push-back when she requested more resources to deal with the backlog of audits. Her boss challenged her as to why she kept coming back for more resources. To use a diverting turn, Mia could acknowledge that she had failed to forecast the need for auditors accurately or that business grew more rapidly than expected. By owning the problem, she can then divert the move to talk about the current problem. "I underestimated our needs, and I apologize for that. But in the current environment, we run risks if we don't devote more resources to building up our auditing capacity." She can then put forth her proposals for how to deploy the needed resource.

Finally, you can divert a move that is personal and shift it to the problem by reminding a person of your contributions. When the CFO challenged whether Cheryl would be able to keep up the pace of multiple offices (a veiled allusion to her age), she suggested that they focus on ways they could ensure that the new plan would work. In Rosalie's review with the associate director, things got quite personal. He denigrated her contributions, suggested that she took things too personally, and said she was not at all ready to present her work to international audiences. When he said she wasn't ready, she could have diverted the move by saying, "I'd like to get better. How can you help me?" In shifting to the problem, Rosalie is trying to ally herself with him and encourage him to help her develop so that he will support her desire to attend the conferences.

Many Ways to Turn a Move

There are many ways to turn a move. Let's look at how these various turns could work in response to the same move. Many of the executives we interview recount the experience of being told, "Don't get so upset." Sometimes they are trying to reorganize their teams, or they might have been asking for a new opportunity. One attorney was trying to rectify the fact that her direct report, who was hired at the same time, was making a higher salary than she was. In each of these cases, their counterpart shut them down with this remark.

Here are some ways they have used these turns to counter the "Don't get so upset" move:

- *Interrupt:* Sit silently. Allow the void to get uncomfortable, and wait until the other person fills in the gap. It's possible he will do so with an apology. Either way, you've interrupted the move.
- *Name it:* "I'm surprised you said that." In this way, you're signaling that you recognize a tactic is being used.
- *Questioning stance:* "Upset? I'm not clear what you mean. Can you explain?" Questioning prompts the other person to consider your perspective and think beyond her own point of view.
- *Correct it:* "I always get excited when issues matter to me." This allows you to substitute a different version of reality from what they've suggested. Of course you're excited; you see an opportunity to improve the business. Why wouldn't you be?
- *Divert it:* "Let's not get stuck on me. We have a problem to deal with." Now you've shifted the focus away from whether you're upset and back to the issue you're discussing.
- *Focus on the future:* "Let's not focus on my emotional state. Instead, let's figure out what we need to do about this." It really is about the problem and what to do about it. Challenging your emotional state is just a diversion.

Reflections on Turns

Recognize turning possibilities.   You will have noticed that protagonists appear several times in our discussion. They could name a move, question it, correct it, or turn it. The reason we show possibilities for the same situation is that there are always turning possibilities. When somebody mentions a move in a case discussion in our seminars on moves and turns—perhaps, "You are not ready for this position"—we always ask for three different turns to reinforce the message that there are many ways to turn a move.

Incorporate your own style. This second observation has to do with style and comfort with different types of turns. We may have individual style differences that may make us more comfortable using some turns over others. In addition, hierarchy may matter: those lower on the totem pole may be more comfortable using questions and corrections and eschew naming, which may seem too bold a turn.

It's important to keep cultural norms in mind as well. We have sometimes observed that women in Asian countries were uncomfortable with naming and correcting moves, preferring to divert instead. Women who attend our trainings in Africa have said that they would not name a move and would not feel comfortable using a perspective-changing question such as, "What would you do if you were in my situation?" Their feelings might be cultural in part, but it's also possible that the leaders with whom they work could be insulted with that type of question. As white European men working with black African women, these leaders might not be able to even conceive of the women's experiences. Therefore, asking them what they would do in that situation would just cause a disconnect for them.

The reason we emphasize choice is to encourage people to understand the dynamic of moves and turns, but not rigidly focus on any one choice. Find a turn that you are comfortable using and that fits the situation.

Hear how you say what you say. As with all other strategies in negotiation, how you say something is as important as what you say. Moves and turns can function as breaks in the action and serve as an important transition in the process. So you always want to turn a move in a way that can bring the negotiation forward and not mire it in a back and forth of moves and countermoves. Some have suggested that a naming turn is high risk because of this.[24] Again, naming does not have to be an attack accusing the other of bad tactics. It can be done humorously, collaboratively (in the sense of "We both understand"), and in the service of learning (in the sense that somebody sees something they had not seen before).

Prepare for surprises. Finally, people inevitably mention that they always think about these turns right after they leave the room. Of course, no one can ever fully anticipate what moves or difficult questions might be asked; however, we've suggested many ways to prepare. That preparation will always account for what you know about the other person, your situation, and the context within which you operate. Because Rosalie was fully aware of what the associate director might say to her, she was prepared; yet she was still surprised. She expected, given what she knew about him, that he was unlikely to have read her research summary or the actual papers. But what she was not fully prepared for was his denigration of the work. When you are blindsided, you can always interrupt by introducing a pause or a longer break. But do not let a move keep you in a defensive position. That is when you will defend, and moves and countermoves will not get you very far.

SECOND-GENERATION ISSUES AND SMALL WINS

Moves and turns present interesting opportunities for small wins. When other parties make a move—whether it challenges competence, ideas, style, or appeals for sympathy—you have a clear window into how the other party sees you and the situation. Those moves are often rooted in their good reasons for saying no to you. You may have introduced one or more of these in your opening (chapter 5), but certainly not all of the good reasons. These good reasons for saying no take form in the moves that are made. And so they give you an opportunity to react to them in a way that can both change the direction of the conversation and lead to moments of learning.

Consider a few examples. When Charlotte responds to the CEO by asking him what he would do in her situation, he can see several things. First, he would be very unlikely to keep doing two jobs without title and bonus. Second, he can see that despite her performance, he does not consider a woman who has come up through the ranks as vice president material. That was an eye-opener for him. Similarly, the associate director in Rosalie's situation might come to see the ways that junior staff are being held back in their careers by a practice that prevents them from attending and presenting at conferences. Not only is that a problem for Rosalie and her fellow junior staffers; it can also reflect badly on the center as a whole and might interfere with their recruiting, among other issues. Indeed, Rosalie could have used a diverting turn to make this very case. So moves and turns are moments in the negotiation when potential learning can occur, which opens up the possibilities for change.

For this and other materials, visit www.deborahmkolb.com.

 Putting *Turns* to Work

Cultivate Your Repertoire of Turns
- Interrupt by using silence.
- Name the other person's tactic.
- Question the assertion of her move.
- Correct what she has said by giving a different version of the story.
- Divert the conversation back to the issue at hand.
- Focus on the future by moving past prior mistakes or assumptions.

Prepare for Moves and Turns
- Consider where you are vulnerable so that you have turns in mind.
- Practice turns in advance to determine what you're most comfortable with.

(Continued)

- Know what you know about the person and how he has dealt with you in the past.
- Consider your counterpart's "good reasons" to anticipate how moves might come up.
- When caught by surprise, you can always interrupt.
- Remember that context is important. Some turns, like naming, can be risky in hierarchical situations and in some cultures.

Managing the Negotiation Process
Fostering Problem Solving

Several years ago, I ran a negotiation program for labor judges in Denmark. Already extremely accomplished negotiators, the judges wanted to learn more about negotiating within their highly bureaucratic organizations. One of the mainstays of the negotiation programs I run is an activity in which people role-play a negotiation about a likely situation at work. They usually perform these role plays in small groups: one pair negotiates, while the other pair observes. Because I don't speak Danish, I had some of the group act as observers. Afterward, we discovered one overall observation: the parties talked to and at each other—but they never asked any questions! Each person was involved in what we call "telling and selling," something that's often confused with negotiating but is not that. Indeed in a study that compared expert negotiators to novices, asking questions was a major dimension on which the negotiators differed.[1]

Framing for Problem Solving in n-Negotiations

The way we use questions, and indeed the way we create an environment for problem solving, depends on how we frame the n-negotiating process.[2] In chapter 3, we described two forms of preparation following the work of Mary Parker Follett. The first, what Follett describes as integration, requires identifying the interests of both parties and coming up with possible trade-offs that meet those interests. In the example Follett uses about the library, one reader wants more air circulation in the room, while the other wants to make sure that her papers do not blow around. The integrative solution Follett proposes is to open a window in the adjoining room: it gives one reader air and the other protection from blowing pages.

Preparing to propose these kinds of trade-offs or packages is one thing; actually managing this dimension of problem solving is another. But there's more to problem solving than proposing good trades in n-negotiations because of the contexts in which they occur.

Integration in n-negotiations is different. Remember that in n-negotiations, one person is often raising an issue that the other party does not necessarily see as a problem. In other words, one party is set to negotiate and the other may not be. Charlotte (chapter 2) wants the official role she has been doing informally. Cheryl (chapter 3) wants a different work arrangement, but her boss doesn't want to rock the boat. Isobel (chapter 4) wants the informal work she's doing folded into her formal responsibilities. Alexandra (chapter 5) wants to convert an ask into a negotiation about a formal role. Rosalie (chapter 6) wants to engage the associate director of her organization in a negotiation about her external role.

Anticipating the resistance. The other person is not expecting to negotiate in each of these situations. While we have discussed helping our counterpart make this shift into a negotiation, openings only set the stage for the way the rest of the process unfolds. When we introduce these topics—asking for opportunities after being overlooked, seeking an alternative work structure, claiming value for invisible work, asking for resources or buy-in for projects—we are asking the other party to change something about established practices, whether formal or not, in our organizations.

Under these circumstances, we can expect to encounter some kind of resistance, either overtly through outright objections or even covertly by ignoring the overtures. Dealing with these forms of resistance demands that we go beyond merely proposing possible trades. It requires a different mind-set, which can lead to different ways to connect with the other party.

SHAPING YOUR STANCE TO THE CIRCUMSTANCE

This chapter covers the various ways to create a problem-solving process that incorporates best practices for mutual-gains negotiations and for the kinds of n-negotiations where we can meet resistance. It begins with our stance coming into the negotiation. How should we be thinking about the task and what we know or don't know is coming? The attitude we take influences the types of questions we ask. Are we seeking information or trying to use questions to foster a different kind of working relationship that might come out of the negotiation? And, finally, we consider what happens if or when negotiations get stuck. How can we put them back on track?

We begin by introducing Margaret and the challenge she has in negotiating with a colleague.[3]

Margaret's Mandate

Margaret Margolis is vice president of global joint ventures for ABCO, a large biotech company where she's responsible for monitoring and managing the firm's portfolio of joint-venture projects. In her previous positions with the firm, Margaret had always been a vocal supporter of ABCO's emerging global markets strategy and so was excited when CEO Jim Drake asked her to lead the newly created division. Jim gave her a mandate in her first year to use the financial modeling strategies she had developed to examine the performance of existing joint ventures worldwide: to invest in the profitable ones but also "clean house" by disbanding the unprofitable ones.

Her latest challenge is determining how to deal with a struggling marketing initiative in Argentina that ABCO had jointly undertaken with one of its South American partners, Sorso Inc. Although other joint-venture initiatives with Sorso continued

(Continued)

---

to be reasonably successful in South America, this particular project had had problems since it was created three years ago. With losses on the books, Sorso was requesting a further infusion of capital. Although Margaret had faith in the abilities of Ricardo Cortez, the head of operations in South America, who reported to Margaret's peer, Alex Bass, vice president of the international division, she was concerned that he was not on top of this problem. Her analysis showed that additional funding was not warranted until the political and economic climate in the region improved. She began to push Ricardo hard on cutting back, but he resisted. The currency crunch, he argued, was a temporary setback; the venture would ultimately succeed. Although he agreed that revenues were slow to materialize, he pointed out that they had invested significant sums in order to build distribution channels in the region, which would be put at risk were they to scale back. Margaret thought that Ricardo was too heavily involved with Sorso in this and other ventures to be able to see the benefits of shutting down this one losing proposition.

Impatient with Ricardo's foot dragging, Jim told Margaret to "take care of it." Although she knew that Ricardo thought that he should control what happened in his area, Margaret decided that it was her job to intervene directly in the negotiations with Sorso to disband this project in Argentina. She felt she had no choice; she was under pressure from Jim on the numbers and needed to move quickly. She planned to ask Ricardo to set up a meeting with Sorso's senior management to discuss closing down the venture. But she was worried. Before ABCO could negotiate with Sorso, she would have to negotiate with Ricardo to get his buy-in. She hoped that by continuing the other South American joint ventures with Sorso, Ricardo would see this not as a harbinger of things to come but rather as phasing out one leg of a larger operation. She wasn't convinced he'd see it that way.

Your Stance Going into the Negotiation

So much of this book, and indeed many of the others written about negotiation, encourages you to prepare, prepare, prepare. And preparation is important. But I've often observed that as we prepare, we can tend to get locked into our own way of thinking about the issues. Although we've spent time thinking about the other person's interests, context, and good reasons for saying no, we may still not be ready to truly hear and connect with the other party, for several reasons.

Heroes of our own stories. One of these is that we tend to be the heroes of our own stories. We often think of our take on a situation as the right one and the other party's as somehow out of sync. As I explained in chapter 3, I often use a pictorial example to make this point when I teach. On the left side of the picture, I list words we use to describe ourselves: we take the long-term perspective; we see the big picture; we are flexible and collaborative. On the right side of the picture, I list the words we use to describe the other parties. They are short-term thinkers with narrow vision; they are rigid and out for themselves.

People chuckle with recognition when I put the slide up. We all see ourselves in that positive light—never as narrow, rigid, or myopic. But the other person? She's difficult, hard to reason with, stuck in the old ways. Once we see things this way, we realize how easy it is to perceive the other person as the problem.

One story, different versions. When Cheryl from chapter 3 began telling me about her boss, she described him as very smart, frugal, and results driven—but also as a risk-averse person who has difficult peer relationships, lacks self-perception, is not approachable, and can be a bully, prone to emotional outbursts. As Doug Stone and his coauthors of *Difficult Conversations* point out, when we tell stories in which the other person is a problem, he is likely telling a different version of the same story—one where he sees us as the problem as well.[4]

Margaret clearly sees Ricardo in this way. From her perspective, he is protecting his turf—an empire builder who is thinking only in the short term and not for the good of ABCO. Margaret perceives herself as looking out for the company's best interests and as having truth on her side. She has her financial and market analyses to support this version.

And although we don't have Ricardo's full side of the story, our guess is that he sees Margaret as interfering (without sufficient knowledge) about the operations in Argentina. When we discussed mindfulness in chapter 3, we discussed considering our counterpart's "five good reasons" to mitigate our tendency to see the other party in a negative light. But there are a few other steps we can take to see the other party in a more appreciative light.

Having that stance makes it more likely that we can create a negotiating environment that fosters problem solving.

Stances That Help in n-Negotiations

Preparing well for a negotiation can give us a sense of confidence that we know what to expect. To adopt a stance of curiosity is to focus on what you don't know or aren't sure about. But it is also about the stance we take toward the relationship.

A stance of curiosity. *Curiosity* comes from the Latin, *cura*, which means "handle with care." This puts the relationship front and center. In the negotiation field, this perspective is captured by the concept of empathy. Robert Mnookin and his colleagues define empathy as having two components: the ability to take the other party's perspective and the ability to be nonjudgmental in considering these perspectives.[5]

While empathy is important, taking a stance of curiosity means more than just knowledge about the other parties and their interests. It means being able to consider how open we are to change and learning. Sara Cobb, a communications scholar, describes it as being able to live in the position that we, as negotiators, construct for the other party. It requires our being reflective about the stories we tell about ourselves—where we are the heroines and heroes—as well as those we tell about the other party.[6] From this perspective, Margaret not only needs to delineate the "good reasons" Ricardo might have to reject her plans; she also needs to reflect on why she is so convinced of the rightness of her situation. If she can do that, she has a much greater chance of entering the negotiation in a position where she can really listen to what Ricardo is saying without focusing on their areas of disagreement. Only from that position will she be able to learn, and likely so will he.

Role reversal. It isn't easy to develop a stance of curiosity when we focus only on ourselves. It helps if we can take the other party's position and really engage in her processes of thinking and feeling. As part of the programs we run, we ask people to role-play a consequential negotiation that is likely to occur in the near future. The first part of the exercise has them first role-play the person they'll be negotiating with; they actually take on the role of their real-life negotiating counterpart. We call it the phase of enrolling[7] and describe it in the following way: "Let's say I'm going to negotiate with my boss, Natalia, to get more resources for a project. My role-play partner will need to know enough about Natalia and the situation to play my boss. Therefore, I play my boss in the first phase of the exercise. My role-play partner interviews me, as Natalia, while I play Natalia's role in the first person like this: 'I'm worried Deborah has too much on her plate.'"

What enrollment brings. There are a number of reasons that this enrollment through role reversal helps foster a stance of curiosity. First, it helps me both understand and feel how the other person sees me and what I want to negotiate about. By really trying to get inside my boss's head, I become more empathetic toward her and more mindful of her perspective.[8] The act of role-playing serves the function of a mirror in which I can more fully appreciate how my boss sees me. And when I look at the issues from her perspective, I can begin to understand how what I'm asking for might create problems for her and her bosses, create equity issues for my peers, or create time binds for those who report to me. Because I'm now mindful of my boss's point of view, I can better anticipate what she might bring up, which might prevent me from becoming defensive. Also, because I'm now more empathetic, I can remain open to new information. The role reversal changes my perspective on the situation. Finally, as a practical matter, by taking the part of my boss, I can provide enough information and insight from that perspective so that my role-play partner can convincingly play that role. People who participate in this activity find it incredibly useful because they come to see their counterpart in a very different way.[9]

Enrolling: Margaret and Ricardo. Let's use Margaret as an example of how this works. When Margaret enrolls as Ricardo, it is likely a revelation to her. First, she recognizes that he sees her involvement as encroaching on his territory in an officious, noncollaborative way. Second, she comes to see his motivation quite differently: he thinks that he's doing what's best for the company, that there are good reasons for thinking the situation in Argentina will turn around soon. In fact, Ricardo believes Margaret doesn't understand the situation very well at all. Based on her enrolling experience, Margaret can come to see her understanding of the situation quite differently. She will then be more open to thinking with Ricardo about how to handle the situation.

A stance of appreciation. The final element of the stance we take toward the negotiation is about relationships. In 2002, the Program on Negotiation at Harvard Law School honored Lakhdar Brahimi, the United Nations special envoy to Afghanistan, with the Great Negotiator Award. In his acceptance speech, Brahimi challenged some of the conventional ideas about negotiation as a rational search for mutual gains or the notion that we separate people from the problem. For Brahimi, a precondition for negotiating is to know the parties deeply. In his work, he deals with parties in armed struggle with each other. But he recognizes (and wants the parties to recognize) that each wants peace in its own way.[10] In chapter 5, we discussed building rapport as part of opening moves. But a stance of appreciation takes us a step further. As Brahimi explains, those involved in n-negotiations need to appreciate from the start that both sides want what is best for the company—even though they disagree in the short term on what that might be.

Thinking like this is a big leap for Margaret. She assumes that Ricardo is taking a short-term view, missing the big picture, and therefore not working for the good of the company. Adopting a stance of appreciation prompts Margaret to shift her perspective, attribute good and legitimate motives to Ricardo, and assume that his intent is positive. She has altered her thinking to acknowledge that she and he are working toward the same end, albeit by potentially different paths. For Margaret to acknowledge Ricardo differently would mean that her goal to close down the operation in Argentina would have to shift. Together they would have to define the problem differently: specifically, how to handle the problem of an operation that is losing money. That would be the stance Margaret would have to take going into the negotiation with Ricardo, which would prepare her to learn more during the negotiation.

USING QUESTIONS TO PROMOTE PROBLEM SOLVING

Nobody doubts the importance of questions in problem-solving negotiations, and there is a great deal of advice out there on using questions and how to listen. We are advised against asking closed-ended questions—those with just yes or no as possible answers—because they cut off rather than open up communication. We are told it pays to lean in and nod appreciatively as we listen. (While this can be useful advice, it's important not to go overboard and become a parody.) Active listening has three main components: paraphrasing your counterpart's main ideas, using open-ended questions and prompts, and acknowledging feelings that your counterpart surfaces.[11]

Open-Ended Questions Are Best

What Edward Miles calls the WH questions—who, whose, what, when, why, which and how—are the most effective in negotiations.[12] How we question is typically tied to the type of negotiation we are conducting. If it is a distributive negotiation—that is, one where the size of the pie is fixed and a gain for one party is by definition a loss for the other—then revealing information about true preferences can give the other person a strategic advantage. In these situations, our questioning is more likely to support our position than to seek out more clues about theirs. In integrative or mutual-gains bargaining, our intent is to seek information about the other's interests. The more we know about the other's concerns, the more likely it is that we can propose ideas that meet our mutual needs.

Questions promoting mutual-gains problem solving. The goal in a mutual-gains approach to problem solving is to identify possible trade-offs that will satisfy both parties' interests and create value for them. We learn about possible trade-offs by asking open-ended questions. People are often tempted to start by asking "why" questions. However, we've found that others tend to misinterpret those types of questions. We might intend to show appreciation and concern, but the other person might hear it instead as a challenge or an attempt to lower his aspirations.[13] His response—why do you want to know?—doesn't get us very far.

Contextual questions. More contextual questions can capture some of the conditions that underlie a person's position. A variety of questions will help Margaret understand Ricardo's concerns. She would want to start with more benign questions first, such as those about time: For how long do you foresee the economic problems in Argentina continuing? The answers she receives might help her frame a proposal that is based on time. She might ask "what" questions: What will happen if the problem continues for longer than expected? Answers to this could help her propose an agreement with a deadline attached. She might ask him about the other Sorso ventures: How might they be able to use more funds? From that answer, she might be able to propose a trade: cutting back on Argentinian operations in return for greater contributions in other regions. She might ask: What makes you confident that the situation will turn around? This may lead to a potential contingent agreement: they continue operations, but if the situation doesn't turn around in a specific period of time, they agree to close it down. This trade would be based on their differential assessments of the likelihood of success.

Hypothetical testing questions. "What if we...?" These questions are actually proposed options in the guise of a question. They invite the other person to think with you about making an idea you have work. It isn't a guarantee, but it is a way to jointly design an agreeable outcome.

Cheryl (chapter 3) used hypothetical testing questions to good advantage. Recall that she had formulated options she wanted to propose to her boss to create a more workable work arrangement for herself. Rather than ask a set of open-ended questions, Cheryl centered questions on the option she had in mind: the idea of the tri-office. Her question to José Garcia was, "What if we created a tri-office, where I split my time between the home office, the field, and my home in Pennsylvania?" Through her hypothetical testing questions, Cheryl learned about his concerns regarding cost, his connection to the field, and her performance. His responses to her hypothetical question enabled them to develop the full plan that took account of both of their concerns.

Margaret could also use a hypothetical testing question, but in her situation, she would have to be careful that it could be one that Ricardo could build on and not reject out of hand. Hypothetical testing questions—what if we did it this way?—are a way to link the other person's ideas to yours. But it's important to remember that this is still an open-ended question to which the other person is intended to contribute. It can be a risk to use this approach unless you have enough information about the other person's interests and concerns such that the question focuses and extends the discussion but does not derail it.

Hypothetical questions can be expanded to include multiple equivalent offers. Research has shown that instead of posing one idea and testing for the reaction, you increase the odds of coming to agreement if you can propose multiple equivalent offers simultaneously.[14] There might be several ways to meet your interests, and you want to see which makes the most sense to the other party. Giving the other party a choice of offers shifts his thinking. Rather than having the other person focus on whether to say yes to something or reject it, you are asking him to make a choice. Research shows that using hypothetical multiple equivalent offers improves outcomes and increases parties' satisfaction.[15]

Reciprocity questions. The norm of reciprocity is one of the most prevalent ways we exert influence. People feel indebted to somebody who has done something for them; therefore, they feel some pressure to reciprocate.[16] While this can play an interesting role in negotiation, we use the concept here in a slightly different way.[17] We think of reciprocity questions as "if-then" questions that serve several functions in a mutual-gains negotiation. First, they make unilateral concessions—those in which you give in without getting something in return—less likely. Second, they build into the conversation the notion that we are discussing trades and frame the conversation in this way. Marisa from chapter 1 uses a set of if-then questions to build the agreement over her taking the new role. If she agrees to take a marketplace role, what will Alice be prepared to do to support her efforts in the marketplace? If Marisa agrees to relocate, what kind of family support will Alice provide?

Reciprocity questions might be critical for Margaret because Ricardo appears to reject negotiation as a possibility. By asking if-then questions, Margaret can attempt to establish a norm of reciprocity with Ricardo. She shows herself willing to make concessions. Will he reciprocate? Of course, we can never be sure. But if she agrees to concede something of what he wants—more time to see if the situation turns around—then what will he agree to in return? He might still say no, but it's more difficult to do that when somebody has invoked a norm of reciprocity.

Different forecasts need not prevent an agreement. Questions in mutual-gains negotiation are intended to build toward agreement based on the parties' distinct interests. It is quite likely that Margaret and Ricardo could come to some agreement. Since they have different forecasts about what will happen with the economic situation in Argentina, these might be the ingredients for contingent agreement. Perhaps they agree to keep the Sorso investment going for a period of time with no further investment, but then they agree to close it down if there is no change after that time. Or they could make an agreement to close down the Argentinian operation in return for greater investment in Sorso operations in other countries.

Still, while these agreements are feasible, Margaret and Richard might not realize the problem-solving potential in this situation. A different form of inquiry is needed in order for that to occur.

Questions That Promote Collaborative Problem Solving

Mutual-gains agreements are often very good: they can resolve the issues at hand for both parties. While Margaret and Ricardo can reach an agreement, it fails to fully resolve both of their concerns. Margaret, who is under a directive from the CEO to close down the Argentinian initiative, will have to account for either a delay or a larger infusion of capital elsewhere in South America. Ricardo runs a risk if the economy takes longer to turn around or of cutting off the Argentinian relationship altogether.

In part, because these negotiations occur in the same organization, it might be possible to develop a more systemic agreement that is not based on trades but rather emerges from a different form of questioning. This manner of asking questions creates both a deeper understanding of the situation and a greater sense of interdependence between the parties. It offers the potential for an outcome that goes beyond a mutual-gains agreement to also solve both of their problems.

Circular questions. Circular questioning is intended to expand the problem and make connections between it and the larger system surrounding the particular issues being negotiated.[18] We call these questions circular not only because they accomplish a broader and deeper understanding of the issues but because in so doing, they also create a different form of connection and collaboration between the parties. Circular questions can start with understanding the history of the situation.

Margaret would want to ask Ricardo questions about the evolution of the Sorso initiative and his role in it. How does it differ in the various countries in South America? Why has the Argentinian initiative been the most affected? Is it likely that others will be as well? Ricardo will want to ask Margaret about her financial models. How does she use them? Has she used them in other situations?

Circular questions can create a deeper connection between the parties. Connections can deepen as each party inquires about the impact her stance has on the other beyond the immediate outcome of the negotiation. We often posture as we advocate for what we want. A shift to circular questions moves us to a more connected frame. We know that Margaret and Ricardo seem to have a great deal riding on the outcome of this decision. What does Ricardo mean precisely when he says it would jeopardize relationships with other Sorso initiatives in South America? Would it compromise his professional connections with the leaders in the other countries? Would they worry that they couldn't count on him?

Margaret, for her part, is in a new role. Is this situation in South America a test for her? If she doesn't succeed, how will that affect the CEO's confidence in her? Is the pressure so real for her that she thinks she must close the operation down?

If Margaret and Ricardo were able to ask these questions, the answers could shift their thinking about the negotiation. Rather than look for trades that might or might not work, they are more likely to become invested in looking for a more systemic solution to the situation at hand. They would be both reframing the negotiation and revaluing each other. Indeed, they are telling a new story about their disagreement. They are beginning to own it together.

Root-cause questions. Root-cause questions shift the discussion from the domain of concrete proposals—what we discussed in hypothesis-testing questions—to a more abstract level of consideration. They seek to understand more about the underlying bases of a conflict. We move from a question like, "What if we did this? Would it work for you?" to one that says, "What are the possibilities that we can think of if we consider this as an organizational issue?" or "How do we deal with problems in our relationships with subsidiaries?"

Root-cause questions shift the discussion from the specifics of a possible trade to the broader principle. For Margaret and Ricardo, it could mean simultaneously holding her need to deal with a money-losing subsidiary alongside Ricardo's interest in preserving his relationship with all the Sorso subsidiaries. Agreement on this principle, which shifts the discussion to a more abstract level, might help Margaret and Ricardo back away from focusing exclusively on their own interests and consider ways that they could integrate both of their needs.[19]

Indeed, that's what they did: considered the root cause of their disagreement. When they did that, they recognized that they could trace a great deal of the problem to the CEO, whose anxiety and ambivalence about subsidiary relations tended to promote a short-term view of underperforming units. Because of this, he pressured people like Margaret to overreact. Once Ricardo and Margaret understood the problem together, they considered how they could handle this short-term problem in a way that wouldn't undermine either Margaret's position in a new role—how to get a losing proposition off her books—or Ricardo's relationship with Sorso. This is a good example of the principle that principles unite and specifics divide.

Too often in negotiations, we find ourselves disagreeing about the specifics of a deal. Margaret and Ricardo's specific disagreement was over how long they would keep the status quo with Sorso. Ricardo wanted more time and Margaret less time. Once they agreed on the principle—the root cause that the CEO took a short-term view— they could collaborate to find a unified solution.

The results are in. Margaret and Ricardo reached a good agreement: Sorso South America agreed to take over the problem venture and carry losses on its books in the short term while they outsourced other pieces of the business. Margaret didn't have to explain carrying a losing affiliate in her portfolio, and Ricardo was able to use his good relationship with the South American partner to solve the problem and set the stage for growth in the future.

In fact, their agreement went further in dealing with the root cause of the problem. They decided that they needed to begin to address the systemic problem—pressure from the CEO that prompted short-term reactive responses. They began a process, starting with Ricardo's boss, the vice president of the international division, to develop criteria for assessing performance in joint ventures.

In thinking about these issues, we are reminded of Virginia Woolf's impeccable hostess. "Dinner parties," Mrs. Dalloway says, "are a time to risk one's own little point of view for that immeasurable delight in coming together, a time to create, rather than manipulate, to combine instead of separating."[20]

That's what we think *collaborative* problem solving can accomplish in negotiation.

NAVIGATING PAST BUMPS IN THE ROAD

So many stories in this book imply that following our suggestions will lead to smooth sailing. Obviously we know that this isn't always the case. We all encounter bumps in the road.[21] No matter how well you've prepared, how much you've tried to anticipate problems, how creative your options, or how well you've considered where the other party is coming from, you may still face obstacles you hadn't considered. One trait of n-negotiations is that they potentially open up areas that people might not have negotiated about before: flexible work arrangements, credit for taking on extra work, changes in policy, clarifying criteria for promotion. And resistance to such changes can take many forms.

We've already discussed several approaches to dealing with resistance. We mentioned in chapter 5 how naming a "good reason" can be helpful. Chapter 6 discussed some turns you can use when the other party's resistance takes the form of moves that put you on the defensive. In this chapter, we've covered strategies that demonstrate you understand and are curious to learn more about the sources of resistance. But it's still possible that whatever you propose will still result in the other party saying no. And so you find yourself stuck.

Tips for When You're Stuck

There are a number of steps you can take to get unstuck in a negotiation.

Take a break. The first prescription is to step back and see if you can understand what is happening. William Ury describes this in *Getting Past No* as "going to the balcony."[22] In chapter 6, we suggested the idea of an interruption: when you seem to be at an impasse, take a break and see if you can understand better what's going on. In doing so, you're forced to consider what you may have done to precipitate an impasse. If Margaret and Ricardo get stuck, it would be helpful for them to take a break and consider the ways in which her directive to close down the Argentinian operation might have made Ricardo dig in his heels. A time-out can keep frustrations from getting the best of you and the other person.

Name what's happening. This means taking some of the responsibility for why the other person is saying no. You're puzzled at the stalemate because it isn't what you intended; in this case, you want to reframe what's happening. You can shift the conversation from the attributions—that is, the tendency to say who is at fault—to the impact it is having on the two of you. You might want to review how it is that the negotiations came to an impasse, which can shift the discussion from blame to the contribution that each party may have made.[23] If Margaret and Ricardo were to do that, they'd recognize the ways that each had contributed. Naming might give them a pause and a way to restart their negotiation.

Ask for advice. Sometimes asking for and getting advice can help make it a shared problem. Seeking guidance can actually help you prompt your counterpart to engage in perspective taking—meaning she might be better able to understand your interests and help find a creative solution. Asking for advice can also help your advisor feel a greater sense of commitment, which increases the odds that she will follow through on your agreement.[24]

A well-known radio journalist told us about a negotiation she had with her boss about a charity event she wanted to host. Although other decision makers at the station had signed off on it, her boss repeatedly said no. According to the journalist, her boss had no good reason for the refusal: the two were just at an impasse. Her boss simply didn't want her to do it, and the journalist threatened to do so anyway. Things got heated, and her boss offered some advice: "Threats are not a great way to get me to change my mind."

That forced the journalist to step back and realize their dispute had become a standoff. It was no longer about the issue at hand; it was simply that neither wanted to back down. The journalist acknowledged her role in the situation—one she hadn't intended—and they were able to get the discussion back on track.

Explore assumptions more deeply. As part of our preparation, best practice has us look at our own assumptions—the story we tell ourselves—as well as those of the other party. We can identify her "good reasons" for saying no and try to keep ourselves open by coming in with a stance of curiosity. But these are assumptions we are exploring ourselves.

When you're stuck, one way out is to explicitly share the assumptions you're making about the other. This compels you to ask: What don't we know that we need to consider? Cheryl from chapter 3 had prepared well when she negotiated with her boss, but it is easy to see how they might have gotten stuck. For example, her boss was worried that she might tire of the travel in making a dual office work. Although she didn't think this would be the case, it is an assumption that was worth exploring because it might have been a deal breaker.

Consider small steps you can take. It is not always possible to come to full agreement in an n-negotiation at the time you undertake it. A full agreement might be a step too far for the other party to take, for many reasons. Maybe it would violate an important precedent, as was the situation with Charlotte (chapter 2). As a director, asking for a bonus for bringing in a new client would violate the policy that bonuses are only for vice presidents. It is understandable that the CEO would resist giving in to her request because it would mean that others would want the same treatment. Focusing on officially getting the job she was doing allows her to achieve a significant part of her goal in the negotiation.

When you are asking somebody to take a big step in agreeing to your proposal, you can position your proposal as a trial. That is what Cheryl did: she proposed the tri-office solution as an experiment for three months and came up with metrics to judge its efficacy. That her boss knew it was a trial made it easier for him to agree. Alicia, whom we met in the Introduction, might similarly propose that she take the regional vice president role in an acting capacity, which might make it easier for the chairman to accept.

Proposing your suggestions as a pilot or experiment in n-negotiations—where one is introducing often complex and precedent-breaking proposals—makes it much easier for the other party to say yes. Indeed, granting early small wins like these contributes to building trust.[25]

Another reason to take small steps is that the time might not be right for fully achieving what you want. We often end presentations by saying that "no may be just the beginning." What you learn, and maybe some of the small wins you do achieve, can position you for revisiting the issues in the future. Even with a no, you've learned a great deal that you can use another day.

Explore consequences of no agreement. Throughout the book, we have noted the role that BATNA plays in your preparation and how smoothing out its presentation can help get a negotiation under way. But the way you use BATNA when negotiations get stuck is somewhat different. Asking the question, "What happens if we can't reach agreement?" requires both parties to be more realistic. People are often quite unrealistic about these consequences and don't ask, "Compared to what?"[26]

What will happen to us, to our clients, to the company if we can't reach agreement? Margaret could propose this question to Ricardo: "If we can't find a solution, what are we going to be forced to do?" Margaret would likely have to appeal to Ricardo's boss or even the CEO to pressure Ricardo to close down the Argentinian operation, something that neither she nor Ricardo wants. She might have to go to his boss to ask for help. This option forces both Margaret and Ricardo to admit that they are not capable of dealing with this issue—not a good alternative for either of them.

Bring in others who can help. It may be that the n-negotiation has implications for individuals besides you and the person you're negotiating with. We discussed the role that allies can play in helping you make your value visible and get the other person to negotiate with you (chapter 4). But you also want to consider the ways that allies might have an interest in an agreement and so might be helpful.[27] They might have working relationships with you and your counterpart, which may make them willing to find other options that you hadn't thought about. They might be in a position to supply added resources that might expand the pie and so make it easier to come to agreement. It may also be that the person you are negotiating with lacks the authority to make a decision—something that might be the case when significantly more resources for a project are the subject of the negotiation. Finding ways to bring in a more senior leader might help.

In the ABCO case, Margaret and Ricardo might enlist another senior leader who has good relationships with the CEO; perhaps she could help convince the CEO to take a longer-term perspective in judging the capacity of international affiliates. Stretching out the time line would make it easier for Margaret and Ricardo to come to agreement.

Finding yourself stuck in a negotiation can be discouraging. Despite all your preparation and efforts to collaborate and take the other person's interests into account, you can still get a no. But from what we know about negotiations that get stuck—the research is primarily in the international sphere—these can be times when things can start to turn around.[28] They are critical moments that can shift the negotiation to a more productive place. The reason is that the moves to get negotiations unstuck focus on the process itself, not the issues in dispute. When we work together to analyze why we're stuck, we set the stage potentially for a shift in how we are working together. And in attempting to break a stalemate, we open the possibility for more collaboration. Parties that use stalemates as moments to build toward more cooperation can improve their outcomes.

SECOND-GENERATION ISSUES AND SMALL WINS

Leading change is always a challenge for leaders. And it can be especially challenging when you're in a newly created role that carries limited authority. Margaret's position is an interesting one. In a staff role, she has to influence leaders on the ground who do not report to her. Many, like Ricardo, generally have little faith in her understanding of the true situation. This is complicated by a number of factors. First, this is a new role; in filling it, Margaret is inherently encroaching on the turf of others who previously had discretion over these decisions. By definition, she'll be challenged in exercising her authority in this role. Second, as a woman in this role, she'll be judged according to the culture where she's trying to intervene. In this case, that is South America—a place where Ricardo may understand in a way that she does not that she might not have the standing as a woman leader to negotiate with Sorso. He may think he's helping her by discouraging her from proceeding. Finally, the situation with Ricardo is one that will likely be replicated in the many regions where a global company like ABCO has operations. What Margaret learns from this will be important to her and to ABCO as a whole.

The agreement that Margaret reached with Ricardo, and especially their agreement to try to change the time horizon used to judge affiliates in unstable economic environments, will give her more leeway in the other negotiations she'll inevitably have down the road. And if their agreement creates clear criteria by which to judge performance, it will limit the difficult negotiations that Margaret will have to do. Under both scenarios, Margaret will be more likely to succeed in this role.

We know from research that women are more likely to be asked to lead in situations of crisis or where there are performance issues—the glass cliff—and that those roles are very risky.[29] And because they are risky, it is likely that women in these roles will try to exercise tight control to ensure that their agenda is successful. We can see this tendency in Margaret. But what we also see are the ways that she can negotiate to build collaboration and get others, like Ricardo, to join her in dealing with the significant problem they face.

For this and other materials, visit www.deborahmkolb.com.

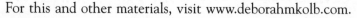

Putting *Problem-Solving Techniques* to Work

Prepare for Problem-Solving Negotiations
- Take a stance of curiosity.
- Practice role reversal for important negotiations by putting yourself in the other party's position and mind-set.

Use Questions to Promote Mutual-Gains Problem Solving
- Ask open-ended questions.
- Ask contextual questions to learn more about interests.
- Use hypothetical testing questions to link your ideas to theirs.
- Use reciprocity questions to establish a trading process.

Use Questions to Promote Collaborative Problem Solving
- Use circular questioning to establish joint ownership of the problem.
- Use root-cause questions to understand the conflict more deeply.

Tips for When Negotiations Are Stuck
- Take a break.
- Name what is happening.
- Look for small steps—"small wins"—you can take.
- Explore assumptions more deeply.
- Explore consequences of no agreement.
- Bring in others who can help.

NOTES ON CHANGE

From Small Wins to Bigger Gains

Throughout *Negotiating at Work*, we've introduced a way of thinking about negotiations as they play out in organizations. As distinct from many N-negotiations, which are identified as distinct events—a buyer-seller transaction, a labor-management contract, a peace agreement between nations—n-negotiations take place in the context of negotiated orders that are themselves the product of previous negotiations.[1] As we discussed in the Introduction, second-generation gender bias, which shows up in a variety of forms, can shape the negotiated order within which an individual negotiator negotiates. In many instances, these negotiated orders reflect and legitimize existing arrangements that benefit those who have traditionally dominated in these organizations. These are evident in the policies, practices, and belief systems that justify the very arrangements that may not create level playing fields or promote organizational effectiveness more generally.[2]

Those who have benefited from these arrangements often struggle to envision alternatives. This is where n-negotiations, as well as the subtitle of the book—*Turn Small Wins into Big Gains*—come in. While the interactions we've described in the book reveal some of these negative patterns, they also create potential opportunity. A negotiation presents the chance to challenge assumptions, norms, and practices that have been previously taken for granted.[3] These can take the form of small wins, which we've described at the end of each chapter.

SMALL WINS: CATEGORIES AND MECHANISMS

In these notes—and we use word *notes* deliberately—we want to extend our consideration of small wins and connect them to larger efforts that can potentially alter the negotiated orders within which future negotiations play out.[4] First, we cluster the small wins we've discussed into categories:

- Making processes and practices more transparent so that critical information is more widely available
- Demonstrating the ways these negotiations highlight practices that fit certain parts of an organization's population but may create challenges for other groups
- Suggesting a stance that leaders might take to actually promote negotiation as a part of decision making

These categories suggest some of the ways that the negotiation stories engage existing practices and arrangements and point us toward places where changes might have more impact.

In the second part of the chapter, we consider some of the mechanisms by which small wins might spread and so have potentially broader impact. In raising the issues in the context of a given negotiation, there are potential moments of learning as those who have benefited from existing arrangements may come to appreciate a situation from a broader perspective. But these lessons can spread as well when those directly involved tell new stories—success stories, we hope—that continue to publicly question aspects of a negotiated order. Some may pick up these examples and use them explicitly as pilots to more directly work toward change, allowing us to come full circle: what starts as an individual negotiating in the context of an existing negotiated order might yield to more systemic changes, which may create an entirely different playing field for those negotiators who follow.

SMALL WINS: THREE CATEGORIES

We've seen several types of small wins in our interviews with professionals and executives, all of which begin as an individual negotiation but have the potential to accumulate to greater change. These cluster into the three broad categories we mentioned above, which we now look at in detail: increasing transparency, questioning assumptions, and opening dialogue.

Increasing Transparency

In chapter 1 we explored one of the long-standing axioms of negotiation theory: information is power. Having information allows us to make good offers, form creative solutions, anticipate our counterparts' concerns, and negotiate more confidently. We've also seen how a lack of information can lead to a weaker negotiating position. This is perhaps easiest to recognize when it comes to compensation: without good information, it's difficult to credibly advocate for a competitive salary.[5] But there are a host of other critical pieces of information, often tacit, that people need in order to do their jobs well and advance in their careers.[6] And just as individuals can be disadvantaged without this type of information, so too can the lack of information contribute indirectly to inequality at a more systemic level.

We've discussed several ways our protagonists had to negotiate without good information in the previous seven chapters. The type of information covers a gamut of subjects—criteria used for making promotion decisions and the kinds of roles or activities that are most likely to pay off in your career. By negotiating around these issues, every one of us has an opportunity to question the negotiated order and increase transparency around criteria, opportunities, communication channels, and rewards. Going forward, this act of questioning makes it easier for others to negotiate. This is how negotiated orders are built.

Clear criteria. One of the challenges of negotiating for criteria is that they often don't exist before you do so, at least not in a formalized way. By negotiating for criteria, whether it is for performance or advancement, we make it more likely that organizations consider objective criteria going forward. This was the case for Alicia, whom we met in the Introduction. Alicia wanted to negotiate for a promotion for which she knew she wasn't on the radar—largely because the decision maker, Bob, planned to tap someone without stepping back to consider what the criteria for the position should be. By putting herself forward for the job, Alicia may influence Bob to consider the criteria for the position itself, making it more likely he will realize that she is a viable candidate.[7] Charlotte was in a similar situation in chapter 2—negotiating for an official move to vice president after serving in an acting role. By doing so, she forced the CEO to clarify the requirements for promotion to the vice president level, which may help others who are planning their career paths as well.

Having clear criteria for promotion is essential for mapping out career progression and development plans, particularly for women.[8] Yet it's also important to have clear expectations for the position you're already in. This was the case for Isobel, in chapter 4, who wanted to expand her role to include the crisis work she was already doing. Isobel made the case that since her internal clients valued her aid, that work should be included in her job description and performance reviews. Elena, in chapter 3, faced a similar challenge when she was asked to lead the women's initiative in her firm. She knew that saying yes could slow her career progression and compensation, since the internal role was not valued as much as rainmaking and client work. Elena negotiated with a "Yes, and ..." strategy to rectify this; she suggested that her performance metrics be adjusted to recognize the value of her work in reducing women's attrition, thereby reducing costs for the firm. Both Isobel and Elena made what we call invisible work visible, thereby paving the way for others to do the same.[9]

Alexandra, in chapter 5, needed to accomplish a similar goal when her boss asked—almost demanded—that she fill in for a vice president who had to take a leave of absence. Often when we're asked to take on a new role, it's not clear what that role will look like, when it will be over, or how our success in it will be measured. This lack of clarity can contribute to what has been called the "glass cliff"—women being placed in high-risk assignments with low odds of success and a high amount of visibility.[10] When Alexandra was negotiating with her boss, she had to define the criteria for success in this interim role. Having clear criteria, particularly for an interim or temporary assignment, will help her avoid being pushed off the cliff—and will also set a precedent for others in interim assignments in the future.

Clear opportunities. In many organizations, large and small, opportunities for professional development, relocation, and flexibility are not obvious. This was the case for Rosalie in chapter 6, who wanted to present her work at international conferences. She knew this would help her organization and her own career, but she didn't know the process for junior researchers to get approval for these opportunities. By negotiating for that opportunity for herself, she also became an example for other junior researchers. They could see that there was the prospect of presenting at conferences and understand the process for doing so because Rosalie had changed the negotiated order to include asking for these types of opportunities. Marisa, in chapter 1, also changed the negotiated order when she negotiated conditions for her next move that took account of her family situation.

A lack of information about opportunities for relocation made it difficult for Claudia, in chapter 1, to negotiate for an assignment in the London office. When she started to explore her options for relocation, she didn't even know where to start. She'd heard rumors about an ex-pat package, but it wasn't clear what that was and how to find out about it. Once she did gather some details about this option and negotiate her transfer, she was able to let others who wanted to pursue international assignments know that resources were available.

Clear communication channels. Claudia's negotiation for a relocation package was made even more difficult by the lack of clarity around how to get information. While she knew her local human resources lead would have that information, she did not want to tip him off that she was thinking of leaving the Chicago office before she had an agreement with London. Claudia needed to find someone to talk to outside her HR department; luckily, she had a human resources contact in London.

One of the complexities about negotiating at work is that it is not always clear whom to approach for information—or even whom to negotiate with. If you lack connections, you may not even know what you do not know.[11] In addition, your immediate boss or human-resources officer could have mixed motives because she doesn't want to lose you; so having access to networks and sponsors who can help you navigate is quite helpful. In some organizations, an ombudsman can help provide information about whom to talk to, as can leaders in diversity efforts.[12] In universities, there might be what Columbia Law School Professor Susan Sturm calls an "organizational catalyst," whose function makes critical pieces of information available in institutional contexts.[13]

Negotiations can help increase transparency about whom to go to for consultation or information. In one organization we worked with, a very senior woman recognized a dearth of women in the pipeline. She negotiated to form a women's network as a forum for female colleagues to share their experiences and support one another. One of the benefits of the network was that it allowed women to share information about opportunities across the organization and clarify organizational knowledge around good partners with whom to negotiate and connect.[14]

Clear rewards. It almost goes without saying that if we had clear information about salary and compensation, negotiating about those issues would be much more straightforward. If I know the range of salary paid to other people in my position, I'm much more likely to stay in the negotiation to get a good deal. While there are now several online sources of information to help benchmark rewards such as compensation and benefits, nothing beats having inside information that you know you can really count on. However, sharing information about rewards can be tricky in many organizations. One survey found that roughly half of all US workers were employed by organizations that discourage and even punish employees from discussing wage and salary information.[15] In an attempt to increase transparency around these issues in the United States, in 2014 President Obama went so far as to sign an executive order that prohibits federal contractors from retaliating against employees who choose to discuss their compensation.[16] Transparency about wage and salary information not only helps us negotiate better as individuals; it also helps to ensure that individuals are compensated fairly at an organizational level.

When women negotiate about rewards, they have the opportunity to change the negotiated order simply by noting that they've done so and setting an example for others. Just hearing that your colleague negotiated when she was offered a promotion can help you feel empowered to do the same. And we take this a step further when we share information about what we actually negotiated for. When Cheryl negotiated for a tri-office arrangement in chapter 3, she signaled to others in the company that they could negotiate around issues of flexibility. Even when we're uncomfortable sharing exact salary information, there are often other aspects of your compensation package that are easier to share in order to help others in their own negotiations. By increasing transparency around the types of issues we negotiate for—vacation, tuition reimbursement, bonus, support staff, professional affiliations, development opportunities, flexibility, profit sharing—we pave the way for others to consider those issues when they negotiate their own packages.

Questioning Assumptions about Existing Practice

Increasing transparency is not the only way negotiations can lead to small wins; negotiating at work also helps to question assumptions about how certain facets of work are done. Think of policies or practices in your organization that seem misguided or out of date: the report that needs to be filed on multiple forms, a policy about booking travel that makes no sense and wastes a lot of your time. Like people, organizations can get set in their ways and don't always review whether policies are still relevant.

Challenging outdated policies. Cheryl's request for a tri-office is a good example of how we can use negotiation to challenge potentially outdated organization-wide assumptions. Senior leaders at Cheryl's manufacturing company were required to work out of the headquarters with the implicit assumption that they could work more effectively by being colocated. Yet Cheryl recognized that it was her relationships with people in the field, not other executives, that were most instrumental for her to be effective. When Cheryl argued that she could be just as effective working from a tri-office, she was not only reframing her own position; she was challenging the company's assumption that leaders should work from the same office. Given the global nature of her company, that assumption was no longer true: senior leaders did not need to be based in the same place. Cheryl's challenge to this notion likely helped other senior leaders become more effective as well by setting the precedent that one's home office should be based on the nature of one's work. It also legitimated the notion that family concerns mattered for executives.

Showcasing an organization's deep bench. Rosalie's negotiation to present at international conferences had a similar component. In the past, junior researchers had not been encouraged to present; senior researchers made the presentations, even when the more junior members of the organization had completed the actual research. This may have been based on an assumption that senior researchers would better represent the organization. Yet by broaching this topic in her negotiation, Rosalie helped the company reassess whether this was the right practice. For instance, perhaps donors would give more generously if they saw how knowledgeable the junior researchers were, thereby indicating a promising future for the organization. Perhaps junior researchers would be more likely to stay at the organization longer if they had a chance to present their own work. In this way, Rosalie's negotiation was not just about her own career needs; it was also about changing the company's policies and practices to be more effective in meeting their mission.

Honing an organization's messages. Cheryl and Rosalie's cases illustrate how negotiations that highlight assumptions can be particularly useful in creating small wins for the organization. Another favorite example of this came from Spencer, an executive at a global media company who had been challenged to recruit more women. Yet he quickly became frustrated: every time his colleague posted a job opening, they received far more applications from men than women. Spencer's theory was that men were more likely than women to exaggerate their qualifications to fit the job requirements. He argued that rather than writing a description of an ideal candidate, they needed to write a realistic description based on their actual needs. He met resistance: his company's human resources practices were ingrained, and his colleague was averse to change. But in the end he prevailed and succeeded in making the adjustment. And once he did, Spencer received far more applications from women, and they were able to meet their target of increasing women staff.[17]

Unexamined practices can have dramatic effects, even to the extent of blocking people's careers. There are often specific experiences that a senior leader is expected to have in order to progress to the top. One such experience that has become increasingly important is to have had international assignments. Often there is an assumption, spoken or otherwise, that women with families will not be able or willing to relocate for these experiences. And because that is the assumption, women are not offered these assignments. We heard a variant of this story from Miriam, one of the international scientists we met in Addis Ababa (chapter 1). Miriam realized that people assumed she would not move to Nairobi from rural Kenya because that would disrupt her family. As a result, she had to negotiate for the opportunity to relocate to Nairobi; afterward, she let others in the organization know of her experience.

Another side of this expectation for international experience is that women may take themselves out of contention for such opportunities. But by recognizing that being offered an opportunity is a chance to negotiate, one can often find creative ways to manage a family and a global assignment. Rhonda, a procurement executive in an energy company, did just that. Whereas her predecessors had moved to Dubai to do their work, she negotiated to find another option. Rhonda managed to find a way to accommodate her work and her family by spending one week a month in Dubai and managing the rest long distance. Marisa (chapter 1), unsuccessful at the time, tried to do the same thing. Changes like these can accumulate to make people rethink outdated practices and change expectations.

Opening Dialogue

As much as leaders might want to encourage open dialogue and input, it's easy to skip that step in the reality of day-to-day work. This is what happened with Alexandra's boss in chapter 5 when she asked Alexandra to fill in for a vice president without considering what Alexandra would need to be successful. Alexandra's boss had a problem, she thought of Alexandra as a solution, and she approached her as if it were a done deal. Yet as with many other decisions, this was an issue that would benefit from a dialogue around options in order to form a plan that would best support the vice president, Alexandra, and the work itself. By initiating a negotiation, Alexandra helped her boss become more mindful around Alexandra's concerns and turn to a perspective-taking stance. This allowed them to come to an agreement that Alexandra could confidently accept—which was particularly helpful since she couldn't really say no. Even in cases when you can't say no, negotiating around alternatives that will benefit both parties more than the original ask is always an option.

As we've noted throughout, the more we build trust and rapport, the more we are able to have productive negotiations that uncover creative options and actually create value. Establishing a stance of open dialogue with our peers, bosses, subordinates, and teams helps build trust such that negotiating—creative problem solving— becomes integrated in how we do our work. Alexandra's boss likely felt good about their negotiated outcome; she realized that by structuring Alexandra's temporary role with more authority (or clear promotion path), it would not only be better for Alexandra's career—it would also serve the company better because Alexandra could be more effective.

MECHANISMS TO DISSEMINATE SMALL WINS

Creating Moments of Learning

In most of the negotiations we describe in this book, the potential exists to create a moment of learning or a teachable moment. These are times when someone says something or an event occurs that presents an opportunity for somebody to open up the dialogue. In her book *Tempered Radicals*, Debra Meyerson provides many examples of people creating moments of learning. The "tempered radicals" she refers to in the title are leaders who want to create change from within their organizations without jeopardizing their positions there. As she describes them, "They want to rock the boat, and they want to stay in it."[18] This means they're often confronted with a dilemma: when someone says or does something that might be contrary to their values, do they address it or let it slide?

We heard about this sort of dilemma from Indra, who told us about a talent review she'd attended. Indra noticed that the words *nice* or *likable* came up for each of the women but never for the men during these discussions. She started keeping track in her notes of how much this happened and decided to speak up. After an hour, she told her colleagues she'd noticed that they'd used these words for six of the women being reviewed and none of the men and asked them what they thought of that. The group then had a conversation about what that meant. They didn't rush out and immediately change the review process, but it did help people become more attentive to whether there might be some unconscious bias in the reviews.[19]

In their study of workplace interventions, Rhona Rapoport and her colleagues describe a teachable moment in the context of an engineering group.[20] As one of their sunset meetings was about to occur, the engineering manager told one of the female engineers that it was fine if she went home to be with her family. A witness to the encounter asked the manager if he realized that he had just told her that her input did not matter. That moment of learning resulted in changing the schedule for those meetings to take place during the workday.

In each of these examples, somebody external to the situation took advantage of a potential teachable moment. Yet it could also be the negotiator who recognizes a teachable moment. After Charlotte (chapter 2) negotiated to be permanently appointed to the job she was already doing, she could ask her boss to reflect about how he judges who is ready to be a vice president.[21] Rosalie (chapter 6) could also talk to her boss about the criteria the nonprofit uses to award travel grants for professionals to present their work at international meetings.

Spreading Wins with Stories

Storytelling has a rich tradition in the domain of organization change.[22] Narrative has been an important component of creating change in the small-wins projects with which we have been involved.[23] Narratives are the stories that organizations tell themselves that make sense of how things work. Many of these stories concern the kinds of second-generation bias that we have discussed throughout the book. An example is that people like Marisa (chapter 1) should be willing to relocate without reference to her family or community or that leadership roles go to those like Alicia (Introduction) who promote themselves. Many companies also operate with a narrative that time is a free resource—and people like Isobel in chapter 4 should be willing to expend it without consideration of other work, or that people like Alexandra in chapter 5 should say yes when asked and blindly trust that her boss has her best interests at heart. These are the types of stories that become so accepted throughout organizations that they go unquestioned and become an invisible part of the culture.

Just as narratives can describe, so can they be revised. We use narrative in our work as a way to show how these accepted stories can have differential impacts on men and women and different groups of men and women.[24] In our study of an international non-governmental organization (NGO), for example, we found that people worked very long hours because time was seen as an unlimited resource. It was expected as part of how professionals showed their commitment, and no one questioned it.[25]

We were able to show the ways that the dominant narrative that time was an unlimited resource had negative consequences for different groups of professionals—particularly dual-career families who were constrained in the hours they could commit.[26] It also had harmful and unintended consequences for the NGO, diminishing its ability to create cross-institutional collaborations. Change was not immediate. However, over time, as people told and retold stories about time and the problems it was creating for individuals and the organization, small wins spread. Individual professionals felt emboldened to push back on unrealistic requests by using a "Yes, and…" approach. If a leader wanted them to take on more work, they needed to identify the trade-offs. A major systemic change also followed. In the past, as professionals created their work plans, all expected them to be "unrealistic"—it was part of the culture of unlimited time. Going forward, it became the policy to approve only "realistic" work plans and to make sure that budgets could actually support the promised work.

A story is a simple way to build on small wins. Narratives have the potential to build on small wins even without external analysts. Each of our protagonists has the capacity to tell her story in ways that challenge and potentially revise the status quo. Let's consider an example from one of our women's leadership development programs.

Lucy's case: Small wins built on story. Lucy is an operations leader in a western mineral and gas company. Like a number of her (relatively few!) female colleagues, she noted a tendency to promote women with children into staff roles, especially in human resources. And that is what happened to her several years ago in her own career.

Using the strategies she honed in the leadership development program, Lucy negotiated for a new, more senior role in operations. Then, spurred by her own experience, she researched the question of how common that story of women with children being moved into staff roles was within the organization. It turned out to be quite routine. She discovered that women were often counseled to move into staff roles after they had children. Lucy worked with leaders in other facilities to look at these patterns in her new role. Although she found that women represented about a quarter of the workforce in the facilities, very few were in any supervisory roles; two had even left the company recently. The pipeline for these leadership roles was no better because of the belief that women with children should be in less-taxing roles. Lucy worked with these leaders to review the job criteria, such as a requirement of being constantly on call. Was this accepted assumption truly critical for supervisory roles? From this review, Lucy and the leaders identified nine women who had the potential to move into operational roles and developed action plans for them to do so.

Changing your organization with stories drawn from your own experience. The protagonists in this book could, like Lucy, use their experience to tell stories that expand their individual small wins, which they can achieve one-on-one by mentoring other women. But an even greater opportunity can take place in the context of what we and our colleagues have called "safe-identity workspaces."[27] Indeed, Lucy's experience with other colleagues from her company helped her recognize the existing narrative that mothers needed lesser roles. She recognized it because it had happened to each of them. Claudia (chapter 1) has since shared her experiences with the women's leadership group in her bank so that they can create informational networks that allow others to be better prepared than she was. Isobel from chapter 4 has played a leadership role in her company to bring female leaders—who have participated in various women's leadership development programs—together to tell their stories and determine how they can use them to help others (and critically stem the departure of senior women). Rosalie (chapter 6) used her experiences to join the more junior members of the research staff to start a working group so that they would be better prepared to present at international conferences. Cheryl (chapter 3) worked with a cohort from a leadership program she attended to create a repository of small wins that women in the company had achieved. Lisa (chapter 4) shared her story of negotiating with the CEO at a leadership program for women in her company to demonstrate not only how she negotiated, but also what types of issues could be negotiated in that firm. These kinds of women's leadership development programs often build into them a collaborative endeavor to create and spread small wins.[28]

THE IMPLICATIONS OF BUILDING SMALL WINS

This book has laid out a set of strategies to help people, both women and men, negotiate about issues that are not the standard fare of bargaining. These negotiations present challenges in part because the people raising the issues are actually challenging established practices that others might not see as problems. To the degree that these negotiations raise awareness and result in small wins, there is the potential that smaller wins can become bigger gains. We mentioned the issue of workplace flexibility in the Introduction. If you are the first person to request a tri-office, as Cheryl was, then it is up to you to make your case. But if there is a policy in place that makes it legitimate for a person to request such an option, you'd be doing it against that background. It could still be a challenge; your boss might be reluctant and even resistant. But suppose that beyond a policy, there was actually a change in practices that involved more than you and your boss. Then negotiating small wins becomes something else indeed.

One such example comes from the Boston Consulting Group (BCG), a global management consulting firm.[29] In the consulting industry, people are generally expected to work long hours and be accessible to their clients and project teams 24/7. Even when there are policies supporting flexible work options, people are often reluctant to take advantage of them for fear of signaling that they are less committed to their work. It's therefore understandably difficult to negotiate for more time with your family in a setting like that.

To try to address this problem, which was contributing to attrition among high-potential workers, BCG began experimenting with ways to improve work-life balance at the firm.[30] One experiment required all five members of a project team to take one night (or equivalent unit of time) off work each week. That meant also disconnecting from their cell phones and e-mails. They were expected to collaborate with each other to make the time off work and to share their experiences of being "off" at weekly team meetings. Doing so meant team members were able to bring their full selves to work and to talk about their lives outside work in a way they had not been comfortable doing before the experiment.

The story does not end with a small win, though. After this project, the team's story was told throughout their office, and other teams joined the "experiment." What started as a small win for five people evolved into a global initiative and series of policy changes, a big gain for the firm and its employees.

The power of small wins to accumulate to big gains. When the first experiment started at BCG, negotiating for personal time was not a part of the negotiated order of the firm. In fact, many felt it was hard to negotiate even around issues of project scope and priorities at that time. With each negotiation for flexible time or a new priority, the negotiated order expanded, and the definition of what was acceptable to talk about began to include personal lives and questions about the work. As the negotiated order expanded, policies and practices in the firm changed to support this new order. Where people had previously been hesitant to negotiate for personal time, they now felt it was safe to do so because the negotiated order had changed. The firm's policies and practices changed too, to support the new negotiated order and reward people who protected personal time for themselves and their colleagues.

It's clear that you can make a difference for your own career by recognizing opportunities for n-negotiations at work. You can negotiate for credit, opportunities, buy-in, and the other things that you need to be successful and ultimately to progress in your field or your organization. You can also use n-negotiations to address problems—to make your value visible or rectify an oversight. What's important to keep in mind is that each negotiation gives you the chance to change the negotiated order. And when you do, your small wins become a precedent for those who negotiate after you. This opens up the opportunity for small wins to become bigger gains, for individuals and the organizations in which we work.

NOTES

Introduction

1. *Merriam Webster Online*, s.v. "negotiation." Accessed February 11, 2014, http://www .merriam-webster.com/dictionary/negotiation.
2. See Fisher, Ury, and Patton, *Getting to Yes*. Written by the founders of the Harvard Negotiation Project, this is probably the best-known book on negotiation. The authors lay out strategies for "principled negotiation" in which the negotiators focus on the merits of the issues and look for mutual gains: outcomes that are advantageous for both parties or for multiple parties. These strategies—such as using objective criteria and focusing on interests, not positions—have become widely used best practices. William Ury's follow-up book, *Getting Past No*, offers advice for breaking through resistance in negotiations. Even in negotiations that do not start cooperatively, Ury shows how we can help others overcome their resistance by managing our own reactions, diffusing their reactions, reframing issues, and engaging them in problem solving. Also see Malhotra and Bazerman, *Negotiation Genius*, which offers strategies to create value, not just claim it; it includes the idea of "investigative negotiation." The authors note on page 102 that negotiation is an "information game." By approaching the task of gathering information almost as a journalist would, they assert, we can obtain knowledge to help structure attractive deals.
3. See Raiffa, *The Art and Science*; Mnookin, "Why Negotiations Fail"; and Bazerman and Neale, *Negotiating Rationally*. Also see Susskind, *Good for You*.
4. See Lax and Sebenius, *3D Negotiation*. The authors draw on their own research to identify three dimensions of negotiation: tactics, deal design, and setup. While the concepts of tactics and deal design are well known, their focus on actions and interactions away from the table provides a helpful framing for thinking about preparation as well as methods to reset negotiations once they've begun.
5. Strauss, *Negotiations*, 7.
6. This is a dimension of negotiation that laboratory studies have a hard time capturing. In most controlled studies, situations are predefined, and subjects have specific power ascribed to their role. In organizations, though, the status and power of the negotiators affect the definition of the situation, determine what's negotiable, and establish appropriate negotiation behavior.
7. See Felstiner, Abel, and Sarat, "The Emergence and Transformation of Disputes." In order for an issue to be raised for negotiation, someone must first recognize that there is an issue. The processes by which people in organizations come to recognize an issue that is worthy of negotiation (or of making a claim or grievance) parallel what the authors describe as "naming, blaming, and claiming."

8. See Bowles, Thomason, and Bear, "Women's Career Negotiations." The authors surveyed 264 professional women about their actual negotiation experiences and coded them based on whether those experiences were opportunities or problems in the negotiations. They found that women had negotiated for solutions to such problems as not being given recognition for an accomplishment, being blocked from advancing, and being undervalued, as well as what we would call style issues—not fitting in and facing negative stereotypes. On the opportunities side, women were prompted to negotiate to seek new positions, change their work to advance their careers, ask for broader authority, and seek special assignments or new opportunities.

9. Kanter, Men and Women of the Corporation.

10. Sandberg, Lean In. Sheryl Sandberg's book hit a nerve and spent thirty-one weeks in the top ten on the New York Times nonfiction best-seller list, with twenty-two of those weeks in the top five. Sandberg, the chief operating officer of Facebook, reflects on ways women unintentionally hold themselves back in their careers. She offers lessons including, "Don't leave before you leave," noting that many women take their feet off the accelerator simply in anticipation of family needs such as maternity leave, rather than continue full stride until there is actually a reason to step out temporarily. Sandberg also offers advice on the importance of picking a supportive partner or spouse, communicating authentically, capturing the attention of potential mentors, and negotiating effectively.

11. Catalyst Knowledge Center, "US Women in Business," accessed March 3, 2014, http://www.catalyst.org/knowledge/us-women-business.

12. See DeGroot, Mohapatra, and Lippman, "Examining the Cracks in the Ceiling," 3.

13. Based on data from the United Nations, accessed May 12, 2014, http://www.unwomen.org/en/what-we-do/leadership-and-political-participation/facts-and-figures.

14. See Equality and Human Rights Commission (UK), "Sex and Power 2011," 3. This 2011 report by a UK commission estimated that at the current rate of change, it would take seventy years to achieve gender balance on boards of directors in the country and up to seventy years to achieve gender balance among members of Parliament. Also see Catalyst, "Historical List of Women CEOs." In the United States, the proportion of Fortune 500 board seats held by women increased by less than 2 percent between 2010 and 2013, from 15.7 percent to 16.9 percent. From 2010 to 2013, the percentage of Fortune 500 companies helmed by a woman CEO increased just 1 percent, from 3 percent to 4 percent.

15. Sandberg, Lean In, 8–9.

16. Before we go further, we should define the word gender. First, it's important to distinguish gender from sex. Sex refers to biological differences and traits that are male or female, whereas gender is widely understood to describe the social construction of what is considered masculine or feminine, definitions of which can vary among cultures. In the popular view, gender is an individual characteristic that is reflected in who people are, how they behave, and how they see themselves. See Wharton, The Sociology of Gender, 9. Here Amy Wharton identifies three important features of gender, all of which are relevant to our understanding of gender in organizations. First, she notes, gender is "as much a process as it is a fixed state." Gender is not simply a static characteristic that is expressed; it is constantly being reproduced. Second, she notes that gender is located not only in individual characteristics; it is also a system of practices and assumptions that can become embedded in organizations. Third, gender is one of the dimensions used to distribute social resources and organize inequality. While the distinction is often made that sex is a biological category and gender a social one, based on socialization and occupancy of different social roles in the negotiating field, these terms tend to be used interchangeably. Also see Kolb and Coolidge, Her Place at the Table. For a still more thorough understanding of gender, we recommend Jean Baker Miller's Toward a New Psychology of Women; Eagly, Sex Difference

and Social Behavior; and Ely and Padavic, "A Feminist Analysis of Organizational Research on Sex Differences."

17. See Babcock and Laschever, *Women Don't Ask*, xii. While from 1980 to 1990 the wage gap between men and women had narrowed by over 10 percent, in the next decade the gap decreased by less than 2 percent. The authors' research found that while 57 percent of male students leaving Carnegie Mellon with a master's degree attempted to negotiate their compensation packages, only 7 percent of their female counterparts had done the same. Those who negotiated had increased their salary by 7.4 percent on average, which translated to a difference of $4,053 in real dollars and seemed to account for the gender gap among graduates' starting pay. However, research on graduating MBAs suggests that when information about compensation is widely available, gender differences in negotiating disappear. Also see Bowles, Babcock, and McGinn, "Constraints and Triggers."

18. There has been a great deal of attention paid to the wage gap in the United States in the past several years. In 2014 President Obama issued two executive orders that protect individuals who share information about their wages and direct federal contractors who provide compensation data broken down by race and gender. Analysis of the wage gap suggests a number of contributing factors, including the number of hours women work relative to men, the professions that women are more likely to work in, and the financial impact of career interruptions. See Bertrand, Goldin, and Katz, "Dynamics of the Gender Gap." The authors did a particularly interesting study of MBA graduates from the University of Chicago Booth School of Business, finding that differences in pre-MBA experience, increased career interruptions, and working fewer hours could lead to dramatically lower annual pay for women compared to men ten to sixteen years after graduation.

19. See American Association of University Women, "The Simple Truth." The wage gap is even more pronounced for women of color, who on average earn less than non-Hispanic white women and Asian American women. In 2013, non-Hispanic white women with advanced degrees (beyond a bachelor's degree) had median weekly earnings of $1,193, compared to $1,116 for African American women and $1,045 for Hispanic women. While the gap between men and women of the same race/ethnicity is often not as extreme, compared to non-Hispanic white men the gap can be quite large. Asian American women have the lowest gap when compared to white men, 87 percent, which is a smaller gap than that of white men and white women, 78 percent. On the other end of the spectrum, African American women earn just 64 percent of white men's earnings, and Hispanic or Latina women earn only 53 percent of that of white men.

20. See Blau and Kahn, *The Gender Pay Gap*. Economists Francine Blau and Lawrence Kahn performed an in-depth examination of the causes of the gender pay gap, noting that even when comparing male and female full-time workers, there was an earnings differential of 20 percent. This gap is despite women having a higher level of education than men, without which the gap would be even wider. Blau and Kahn find that a substantial portion of the gap is due to occupation, industry, and union participation, which combined make up 53 percent of the gap. They suggest that if women had the same education, experience, occupation, and industry distribution, they would still make 91 percent of what men with the same characteristics do. While career interruptions might explain a portion of the remaining gap, Blau and Kahn note that the effect is reduced for mothers who have maternity leave coverage. They posit that some portion of the residual gap can be explained by subtle forms of discrimination that create barriers for women at some levels and in some industries or firms.

21. See Babcock and Laschever, *Women Don't Ask*, 2. Note 17 describes differences in salary negotiating patterns between male and female students on completion of their master's

degrees. The authors found similar patterns in other studies. In one laboratory study, researchers found men were almost nine times as likely as women to directly ask for more money.

22. See Babcock and Laschever, *Women Don't Ask*. One survey of 227 people found men had initiated negotiations two to four times more recently than women. Other studies found women much more likely to be intimidated by negotiating than men were, though this difference went down significantly if the task was framed as "asking" rather than negotiating. Another laboratory study by the same researchers found that while women were less likely than men to initiate a negotiation for higher payment, the results varied depending on cues and framing. One group was a control that received no cue, one group of subjects was given a cue that participants could "negotiate" for higher payment, and the third group was given a cue that participants could "ask" for higher payment. Men who were cued to negotiate were the most likely to initiate requests for more payment and were 25 percent more likely to do so than their female counterparts given the same cue. Yet when the cue was to "ask," women not only closed the gap, they actually requested higher payment slightly more often than men in the same group. See Small et al., "Who Goes to the Bargaining Table."

23. See Kray and Thompson, "Gender Stereotypes."

24. See Watson, "Gender versus Power"; Kay and Shipman, *The Confidence Code*.

25. See Stevens, Bavetta, and Gist, "Gender Differences in the Acquisition of Salary Negotiation Skills." After noting that men achieved higher outcomes than women in simulated salary negotiations among MBA students, Cynthia Stevens, Anna Bavetta, and Marilyn Gist conducted research to explore whether these differences could be mitigated by negotiation training. They gave participants a four-hour primer on negotiation strategies, after which men were more likely to set higher goals and negotiate better salaries than women. Even after attending an additional two-hour training about setting aggressive goals, women's goals were consistently lower than those of men in the study. Although women's goals were higher after the goal-setting workshop, the goals of men after that training were also higher, so the gender gap prevailed.

26. See Martin, "Gender Differences in Salary Expectations." This study presented undergraduate business students who were about to graduate with detailed data about starting salaries in several business fields: accounting, business administration, finance, marketing, and personnel. The students were then asked what they expected their starting salary to be. In four of the five fields (all but business administration), women expected their starting salaries to be significantly lower than men did, despite having identical information on salaries in each field. Also see Major and Konar, "An Investigation of Sex Differences in Pay Expectations." These authors surveyed students in management programs and found women expected to earn about 13 percent less than men in their first year working full-time and 32 percent less at their career peaks. Also see Jackson, Gardner, and Sullivan, "Explaining Gender Differences in Self-Pay Expectations." This study asked college seniors to estimate "fair pay" and found that women's estimates were 4 percent lower than men's for their first jobs and 23 percent lower than men's estimates of fair pay at the peaks of their careers.

27. See Kamen and Härtel, "Gender Differences in Anticipated Pay." In this study of business students, Vicki Kamen and Charlene Härtel found that men expected higher salaries for a specific management trainee position than their female counterparts expected. Also see Jost, "An Experimental Replication of the Depressed-Entitlement Effect among Women." John Jost found similar trends and theorized that disadvantaged groups can internalize the justifications for their disadvantage. Thus, women might internalize that their work is less valuable than a man's, so they are not entitled to the same compensation. Also see Barron,

"Ask and You Shall Receive?" Lisa Barron conducted an interesting study of second-year MBA students to better understand beliefs around salary expectations. She interviewed the students after a simulated salary negotiation and found a significant difference in their beliefs about entitlement. Seventy percent of men made comments suggesting they were entitled to more compensation than others, whereas 71 percent of women made statements that they were entitled to the same as others. Those who were oriented toward the same compensation as others tended to make lower salary requests than those who felt entitled to more compensation than others.

28. See Eckert, "Cooperative Competition," 34. Penelope Eckert suggests the historical emphasis of women's worth as being based on "her ability to maintain order in, and control over, her domestic realm," in contrast to men's worth, which has historically been based on his "accumulation of goods, status, and power in the marketplace." As a result, women are more likely to assess their worth based on their character and behavior and to place less value on pay than other aspects of their jobs. Also see Desmaris and Curtis, "Gender and Perceived Pay Entitlement."

29. See Stevens, Bavetta, and Gist, "Gender Differences in Acquisition of Salary Negotiation Skills."

30. See Watson and Hoffman, "Managers as Negotiators." In a simulated negotiation between practicing managers, Carol Watson and Richard Hoffman found that women managers expressed less confidence and were less satisfied with their negotiation performances than the male managers, despite having used the same behaviors as the men and achieving the same outcomes.

31. See Stevens, Bavetta, and Gist, "Gender Differences."

32. See Stuhlmacher and Walters, "Gender Differences in Negotiation Outcome."

33. See Ely and Padavic, "A Feminist Analysis of Organizational Research on Sex Differences." Embedded in much of this research is the notion that one's gender is an essential and stable attribute of individuals. Although the claim is typically made that the focus is on gender—hence, a social, nonessential category—the effect is the same. Differences are attributed not to biology but to socialization, role theory, or entitlements that are never explicitly tested nor connected to the findings. In response to these shortcomings, scholars have moved away from explicitly examining differences between men and women as negotiators to focus more on the social and institutional processes that might activate gendered behavior.

34. See Bowles, Babcock, and McGinn, "Constraints and Triggers." The type of negotiation seems to matter a great deal. When negotiations are distributive, that is, the parties are negotiating over a single issue—typically something of economic value like price or salary—research indicates significant gender differences. This is the type of negotiation that dominates much of the research. Also see Kray and Thompson, "Gender Stereotypes and Negotiation Performance." In this review of the gender and negotiation literature, over two-thirds of the studies involved distributive negotiations over pay. Also see Walters, Stuhlmacher, and Meyer, "Gender and Negotiator Competitiveness." This meta-analysis of negotiation research found that gender differences were greater in experiments based on explicit bargaining with face-to face communication and less pronounced in matrix games that forced less direct communication among subjects. Distributive bargaining has been seen to value a more masculine style (assertive, competitive, analytical) over approaches that are more associated with the feminine (compassionate, intuitive, collaborative). Also see Solnick, "Gender Differences in the Ultimatum Game," and Stuhlmacher and Walters, "Gender Differences in Negotiation Outcome." Because gender issues are more likely to be studied in distributive contexts, it is not surprising that women have not fared as well as men.

35. See Deaux and Major, "A Social-Psychological Model of Gender," and Ely and Padavic, "A Feminist Analysis of Organizational Research on Sex Differences." Rather than being an essential property of the self, the degree to which a negotiator takes up a gendered role and how that role is expressed is likely to be fluid and fragmented. See Holvino, "Intersections." As negotiators, we have multiple social identities. Which aspects of identity are salient in a particular negotiation depends on a number of factors: the interplay of identities of each party, power differentials, and the topic being negotiated, among others. This more complex notion about the simultaneity of identities means that in understanding what happens between, say, a white European male boss and an African woman scientist in his employ, we must think beyond simple gender distinctions. In response to this understanding of intersecting identities, researchers have moved away from examining individual men and women to focus more on social and institutional processes that might support gendered behavior. Also see Buzanell and Liu, "Struggling with Maternity Leave," and Greenberg, Ladge, and Clair, "Negotiating Pregnancy at Work." There are other dimensions of identity that intersect with gender and have an impact on who comes to the table and what happens there. One obvious category is motherhood. When women negotiate for maternity leave and other aspects of work related to pregnancy and birth, they find themselves negotiating about roles, responsibilities, and more generally about perceptions of themselves in the workplace. Also see Correll, Benard, and Paik, "Getting a Job," and Roth, "Selling Women Short." When women do negotiate around aspects of work related to maternity or family leave, it can be from a position of disadvantage. Mothers are routinely offered less-desirable assignments and lower compensation than women without children. Negotiating about work and personal life is a topic that we address throughout this book.

36. See Amanatullah, "Negotiating Gender Role Stereotypes." Emily Amanatullah found that women who negotiated aggressively on behalf of themselves were perceived more negatively than men who did the same. She studied MBA students who were coached to aggressively claim value in their negotiations. While there was no significant difference in the negotiated outcomes—women and men achieved similar results—women provoked more negative reactions from their counterparts than men did. This difference in impression applied only to women who were negotiating for themselves; when women were negotiating as agents, they were not perceived more negatively than men. Amanatullah suggests that when women negotiate on behalf of others, they are perceived as helping and communal and less likely to trigger a backlash for violating gender stereotypes.

37. See Bowles, Babcock, and Lai, "Social Incentives for Gender Differences." This fascinating study reinforces that a one-size-fits-all approach—one that simply encourages women to negotiate as much as men—is ineffective. The authors conducted a series of experiments in which participants evaluated written accounts and videotaped negotiations of men and women either accepting or negotiating compensation packages. Not only did participants consider women who initiated negotiations to be demanding and less "nice," they were less likely to want to work with women who initiated negotiations than with men who'd done the same. The authors call this the "social cost of asking."

38. See Kulik and Olekalns, "Negotiating the Gender Divide."

39. See Heilman and Okimoto, "Why Are Women Penalized for Success at Male Tasks?" Madeline Heilman and Tyler Okimoto found that women who were described as successful in masculine-typed jobs were disliked and viewed as undesirable bosses, but when they were described with communal qualities—understanding, supportive, caring—evaluators' negative feelings were suspended. In another experiment, the authors found that successful female managers were viewed more negatively than comparable male managers, yet when female managers were identified as mothers, they were perceived much more

positively. By being identified as mothers, the women managers were associated with communality and considered to be more desirable as bosses. It's not clear whether this holds true for all women, though. Also see Holvino, "Complicating Gender." Evangelina Holvino notes that most research on gender in organizations has privileged gender as the relevant aspect of identity and failed to examine the intersection of gender with race, class, and ethnicity. While women are generally associated with communal traits—helping, caretaking, nurturing—the similarities and differences between how white women and women of color are held responsible for this behavior are worthy of further study.

40. See Amanatullah and Tinsley, "Punishing Female Negotiators." Emily Amanatullah and Catherine Tinsley examined the backlash women can receive from negotiating aggressively for themselves. As in other studies, they found that women who negotiated aggressively on their own behalf were judged more harshly than men who did the same. Ironically, when women did not negotiate aggressively on behalf of others, they were also judged harshly.

41. Kolb and McGinn, "Beyond Gender and Negotiation"; Ely, Ibarra, and Kolb, "Taking Gender into Account."

42. US House of Representatives, History, Art & Archives, "The Lindy Claiborne Boggs Room," accessed April 23, 2014, http://history.house.gov/Exhibitions-and-Publications/Statuary-Hall/Lindy-Boggs/Lindy-Claiborne-Boggs-Room/.

43. See Anthony and Dufresne, "Potty Parity in Perspective."

44. See McKeon, "Women in the House Get a Restroom."

45. See Heil, "Senate Women's Restroom Expanding."

46. See Banaji and Greenwald, *Blindspot*, 115. Researchers at Project Implicit, a network of scientists who study implicit associations, have designed implicit association tests (IATs) to help people understand their unconscious biases around race, gender, weight, religion, and a number of other issues. In their book *Blindspot*, Mahzarin Banagi and Anthony Greenwald are careful to stress that having an unconscious association is different from being prejudiced. They note it is not just men who hold unconscious biases about gender roles. Of those taking the gender-career IAT, 75 percent of men and 80 percent of women make some implicit connection between men and careers, and women and families. Taking the IAT can be a useful way to understand stereotypes in general, as well as to become aware of our own unconscious associations. A full selection of IAT tests can be explored at Harvard's Project Implicit website (https://implicit.harvard.edu/implicit/).

47. See Klos, "The Status of Women in the US Media." As an example, in coverage of the 2012 US presidential election, male bylines outnumbered female bylines three to one.

48. Ibid.

49. Ibid. The number of actual protagonists is even lower—only 11 percent of movies in 2011 had a female protagonist.

50. Hewlett and Luce, "Extreme Jobs."

51. See O'Donnell, *Mogul, Mom, and Maid*, xii. Liz O'Donnell notes that although men have doubled their contribution to housework and tripled their percentage of child care, women still do 30 percent more housework and child care on average than their male spouses. Also see Groysberg and Abrahams, "Manage Your Work." It's worth noting that male leaders are far more likely than women to have a stay-at-home spouse. A survey of executives in a Harvard Business School executive program revealed that 60 percent of the male executives had spouses who didn't work full-time (outside the home), whereas only 10 percent of female executives had spouses who worked less than full time. Women executives were also less likely than the men to be married and had fewer children, suggesting women were forced to make trade-offs between family and career that male executives

were not faced with. It's also worth noting that research in this area seems either to focus on heterosexual couples or to ignore whether couples are same sex or opposite sex; there is not a good understanding of how same-sex couples manage work and caregiving.

52. See Bohnet and Grieg, "Gender Matters."

53. See Correll, with Benard and Paik, "Getting a Job." The authors note that the concept of the ideal worker, one who will drop anything for work and put in long hours on evenings and weekends, creates tension with our ideas of motherhood, in which "good" mothers are devoted to their children and invest in them without limit. Those cultural assumptions can create penalties for individual women, who are assumed to be less committed to work and even less competent simply because they are also mothers. The authors designed an experiment in which participants read applications for a marketing position, with the applications being similar except for parental status. Mothers were consistently rated as less committed and less competent, offered less salary, and deemed less worthy of promotion than women who were not identified as mothers. Only 47 percent of mothers were recommended for the position, compared to 84 percent of female nonmothers, who were otherwise identical candidates. In an interesting twist, men were rewarded for being fathers; men with children were considered more committed than men who were not fathers and offered higher salaries. Also see Miller, "Motherhood Penalty," in which the author posits a "fatherhood bonus."

54. See Fletcher, "Relational Practice." Joyce Fletcher studied female software engineers, logging every activity they enacted throughout the day. She categorized a number of activities as being "relational work"—tasks that did not fit the standard definition of work yet were integral in getting the job done. Examples of relational work include preserving the well-being of a project, even if that meant helping with lower-level work, or taking time to teach others and help them develop. While relational practice helps with professional development and efficacy, it's not always recognized as work. Also see Fletcher, *Disappearing Acts.*

55. See Mizruchi and Stearns, "Getting Deals Done."

56. See Fernandez and Weinberg, "Sifting and Sorting."

57. See Seidel, Polzer, and Stewart, "Friends in High Places." The authors examined data from over three thousand actual salary negotiations at a US high-tech company. They found that members of racial minority groups negotiated lower salaries than their white counterparts, but that these differences were reduced when the minorities had social ties in the organization. This study suggests how critical networks are to successful salary negotiations.

58. See McGuire, "Gender, Race, and the Shadow Structure."

59. See Ridgeway, "Gender, Status and Leadership."

60. See Joy et al., "The Bottom Line." A Catalyst study found that companies with the most women board directors outperformed those with the fewest women board directors on return on sales and return on invested capital by 16 percent and 26 percent, respectively. Their findings show a clear correlation between gender diversity at the highest ranks and financial performance. While it is a stretch to suggest a causal relationship, it does seem reasonable to assert that companies that create conditions for women (and others) to thrive and ascend outperform their rivals.

Chapter 1

1. Babcock and Laschever, *Ask for It*, 20.

2. Bear in mind that the attributes cited here are based on the executives' own self-reporting. In the moments when I ask these questions in seminars, I have no way of assessing whether

the attributes they cite have a real bearing on their actual negotiations. Still, the executives' answers reveal how they perceive themselves in negotiations.

3. See Mnookin, Peppet, and Tulumello, *Beyond Winning*, 30. The authors identify many of these same differences between agents and principals. Principals are often invested in matters like saving face, improving their reputations, and preserving relationships they'll need going forward. Agents tend to have a different set of incentives and different set of relationships in which they're invested, as well as different access to information.

4. See Mitchell and Hesli, "Women Don't Ask?" Analysis of almost fourteen hundred responses to an American Political Science Association survey found that women were more likely than men to be asked to take on additional responsibilities in service to their universities. In addition, the types of responsibilities women were asked to take on were different from those for men. Women were more likely to take on more token forms of service to their institutions, whereas men were asked to serve in roles that help further their careers, such as department head or committee chair.

5. See Vesterlund, Babcock, and Weingart, "Breaking the Glass Ceiling with 'No'," and Braiker, *The Disease to Please*. Linda Vesterlund and her colleagues found that women and men tended to differ in their emotional response when being asked for favors. Men were more likely to experience calmness and happiness when considering favor requests, whereas women were more likely to experience anger, fatigue, and guilt and to worry that they would be seen as not helpful if they were to say no.

6. See Andreoni and Vesterlund, "Which Is the Fair Gender?" Using an economics exercise called the dictator game, James Andreoni and Lise Vesterlund found that while men were likely to be altruistic when the cost to do so was low, women were more likely to be generous when the cost of doing so was high.

7. See Bergeron, "The Potential Paradox of Organizational Citizenship Behavior." While women are more likely to acquiesce to these types of requests, doing so does not necessarily help their careers. In fact, these types of tasks tend to be unrecognized in performance reviews and to detract from time spent on tasks that are recognized and measured. Bergeron's paradox is that by helping others in the organization with these types of tasks, women can in fact hurt their own career trajectories.

8. See Salmon et al., "Negotiating to No." Elizabeth Salmon and her colleagues found that women were less likely to resist requests from female supervisors for fear of a backlash. They then researched how supervisors reacted to subordinates who resist requests and found that while both male and female supervisors penalized women for using direct tactics in refusing requests, female supervisors penalized them more harshly.

9. See Weirup, "Favors Feel Different for Females."

10. See Ridgeway, "Gender, Status and Leadership." Gender-status beliefs that presume men are more deserving of rewards can make it more challenging for a woman to raise issues of fair treatment or question whether she has been overlooked for an opportunity. Status beliefs are widely held cultural beliefs that "imply both difference and inequality." Higher-status groups (men, whites, professionals) are linked with greater competence and more valued skills than lower-status groups (women, people of color, manual laborers). Higher-status groups, however, do not generally recognize their privilege. In the workplace, members of lower-status groups are held to higher standards than members of higher-status groups, who are automatically considered competent and skilled. As lower-status people move up in an organization, they not only face higher performance expectations, but their legitimacy is also likely to be questioned when they exercise authority over others. Thus, while women are more likely than men to be overlooked for opportunities or promotions, should they speak up about this, they are susceptible to a backlash for acting assertively without the (perceived) legitimacy to do so.

11. See Introduction, notes 35 and 54, especially Correll, Benard, and Paik, "Getting a Job."

12. See Introduction, note 22; and Babcock and Laschever, *Women Don't Ask*. In that note we cited survey research indicating that men had initiated negotiations more recently than women. But other research has observed different patterns. Also see Bowles, Bear, and Thomason, "Claiming Authority." The authors found conflicting data in an interview with executives in the US government, with no difference between women and men in their recent negotiating experience. However, this may be because the interview defined *negotiation* more broadly: "By negotiation, we mean requests that involve some problem solving, creative tradeoffs, or compromise to be resolved. So, we are not interested in requests that are simply accepted or rejected."

13. See Small et al., "Who Goes to the Bargaining Table?" Recall the study that found women were less likely to initiate negotiations than men, though being cued to either negotiate or ask for more money did in fact prompt more women to do so. The prompt had the same effect on men, increasing their likelihood to initiate negotiations as well. That women responded to cues suggests they don't always perceive opportunities to negotiate. It's likely that men, through their networks and general exposure, are more likely to understand which circumstances are negotiable.

14. See Calhoun and Smith, "Integrative Bargaining." Patrick Calhoun and William Smith found that although women entered negotiations with strong opening offers, they were more likely than men to yield in the negotiation. An exception was when women had been primed to be concerned for their profit, in which case they were less likely to yield and experience aspirational collapse.

15. See Bowles, Babcock, and McGinn, "Constraints and Triggers." The authors explored the question of how information affects women, with the finding that women were outperformed by men in negotiations with high ambiguity. Yet when women had information relevant to the negotiation, there were no differences between men and women in their target prices, opening offers, or final agreement.

16. See Galinsky, Mussweiler, and Husted Medvec, "Disconnecting Outcomes and Evaluations." Researchers have found that staying focused on your aspiration produces higher negotiated outcomes. Also see Schneider, "Aspirations in Negotiation." Andrea Schneider notes that negotiators will rarely do better than their aspiration; setting high aspirations helps ensure we make more aggressive demands. She suggests that having high aspirations also increases our willingness to work hard in the negotiation and makes us more likely to stay in the negotiation longer.

17. See Bowles, Babcock, and McGinn, "Constraints and Triggers."

18. In addition to doing general research on the company, industry, and comparable positions, a number of websites are devoted to providing salary and compensation information for just this purpose. Glassdoor.com and Salary.com provide salary information as well as employee reviews of different companies. Recruiting services such as Monster.com and Careerbuilder.com also offer salary information for different professions and companies.

19. See Schneider, "Aspirations in Negotiation." Having good information allows us to set what Schneider calls "justifiable" aspirations, which help us to remain in the negotiation longer.

20. See Vesterlund, Babcock, and Weingart, "Breaking the Glass Ceiling with 'No'." In a study at a major university, the researchers examined faculty members' responses to a request that they volunteer for a university-wide committee. They found women were 2.7 times as likely as men to volunteer in response to the request. In a related study, the same researchers surveyed people about their experiences with work-related requests that they would have preferred to decline but instead actually agreed to. Women were more likely to feel pressured to say yes and more worried about the negative consequences of saying

no. Yet the researchers note there can be negative consequences of saying yes to undesirable tasks, which tend to be nonpromotable and might even lower one's job satisfaction and commitment.

21. See Kolb, Williams, and Frohlinger, *Her Place at the Table*. Chapter 2 has recommendations for garnering resources.

22. Schneider, "Aspirations in Negotiation."

23. Bazerman and Neale, *Negotiating Rationally*. Also see Kray and Gelfand, "Relief versus Regret."

24. See Seidel, Polzer, and Stewart, "Friends in High Places"; Mizruchi and Stearns, "Getting Deals Done"; and Fernandez and Weinberg, "Sifting and Sorting."

25. See Belliveau, "Blind Ambition." It is not just the access to networks that can influence this; negotiation outcomes are also susceptible to assumptions about network access. Belliveau found that female graduates of same-sex institutions received lower salary offers than female graduates of coeducational institutions. She suggests that employers assumed graduates of women's colleges would have less access to competitive salary information and be more likely to accept lower offers.

26. See Reskin and McBrier, "Why Not Ascription?" Networks are influential in hiring as well. A study of 461 organization practices found that over half of the organizations frequently recruited new employees through referrals and invitations rather than open recruitment. Companies that engaged in this network-based hiring were more likely to hire men than women. Also see Ibarra, "Personal Networks"; Higgins and Kram, "Reconceptualizing Mentoring at Work"; Podolny and Baron, "Resources and Relationships"; and McGuire, "Gender, Race, and the Shadow Structure."

27. See Groysberg, "How Star Women Build Portable Skills."

28. See Weick, "Small Wins." Karl Weick introduced the groundbreaking idea of small wins thirty years ago: "When the magnitude of problems is scaled upward in the interest of mobilizing action, the quality of thought and action declines, because processes such as frustration, arousal, and helplessness are activated. Ironically people cannot solve problems unless they think they aren't problems." Weick suggested that people can become paralyzed in the face of big problems but that by focusing on incremental change, the cumulative effect of small wins could be transformative. Also see Meyerson, *Tempered Radicals*.

Chapter 2

1. See Ury, Brett, and Goldberg, *Getting Disputes Resolved*. The authors suggest that three factors come into play in resolving disputes: interests, rights, and power. While some negotiations do center primarily on rights or power, most of the negotiations in organizations are interest based and can be framed as mutual problem solving. If instead we become grounded in focusing on which party is "right" or more powerful, it's more likely that one party ends up feeling like a loser. In my colleague's case, her focus on rights was a missed opportunity to explore mutual interests, which can strengthen relationships. When we focus on rights or power, relationships are often strained, as my colleague learned the hard way.

2. Babcock and Laschever, *Women Don't Ask*.

3. Ibid.

4. See Small et al., "Who Goes to the Bargaining Table?" Researchers found that women were much less likely to be intimidated at the prospect of "asking" than they were at the prospect of "negotiating." Men did not distinguish between asking and negotiating. The researchers suggest cuing women to ask might be more effective than cuing them to negotiate. Also see Bowles, Bear, and Thomason, "Claiming Authority" (see chap. 1, n. 12).

This study cited there were no reported differences between recent negotiating experiences of men and women when negotiation was framed more broadly as problem solving or trade-offs.

5. See Ibarra, "Homophily and Differential Returns," and Ibarra and Hunter, "How Leaders Create and Use Networks."

6. See Miles, "Gender Differences." Edward Miles examined four steps in a negotiation to determine which steps might reveal differences for men and women. He looked at aspiration (goal), intended opening offer, actual opening offer, and the actual counteroffer and found that while men and women set similar goals and intentions for opening offers, women's opening offers and first counteroffers were more likely to vary and be lower than those of the men. Even when women do aspire high, they can experience a gap between their intentions and the offers they actually make. Also see Calhoun and Smith, "Integrative Bargaining."

7. See Lax and Sebenius, *The Manager as Negotiator*. Henry Kissinger, who served as US national security advisor and US secretary of state in the 1970s, said, "If agreement is usually found between two starting points, there is no point in making moderate offers. Good bargaining technique would suggest a point of departure far more extreme than what one is willing to accept. The more outrageous the initial proposition, the better is the prospect that what one 'really' wants will be considered a compromise." Lax and Sebenius caution that setting outrageous opening offers can result in equally extreme counteroffers. Still, holding Kissinger's main point is important: it's rare to find agreement at a higher place than your opening offer.

8. Williams and Dempsey, *What Works for Women at Work*, 154.

9. Kolb, "Are We Becoming Part of the Problem?"

10. See Fletcher, "Leadership as Relational Practice." Joyce Fletcher explains that just as some leaders can enact dysfunctional nonrelational practice, such as being so focused on oneself and the task as to ignore others' opinions and needs, leaders can also practice relational malpractice and become so focused on others and on process as to become ineffective and sacrifice their own interests. Fletcher describes a (functional) relational leader as someone who focuses on learning, effectiveness, and reciprocal relationships. These are salient traits in negotiation; by focusing on mutuality and learning, we are more likely to come to creative, value-enhancing agreements.

11. For a full discussion on the differences between N-negotiations and n-negotiations, see chapter 1.

12. See Lax and Sebenius, *3-D Negotiation*. There are some analogies to international conflict where structure is not a forgone conclusion; for example, you need to get the right parties to the table.

13. See Malholtra and Bazerman, *Negotiation Genius*, and Thompson, *The Mind and Heart of the Negotiator*.

14. See Davies and Harré, "Positioning."

15. See Gerson and Peiss, "Boundaries, Negotiation, Consciousness," and Gherardi, *Gender, Symbolism, and Organizational Culture*.

16. See Rubin, "Negotiation."

17. See Fisher, Ury, and Patton, *Getting to Yes*; also see n. 16 in the Introduction to this book. The concept of BATNA was developed at the Harvard Program on Negotiation by Roger Fisher, Bill Ury, and Bruce Patton and has become a fundamental concept in negotiation. Understanding your alternatives gives you a standard that you can use to measure the worth of possible agreements. For instance, if you know you can buy a new car online for twenty-five thousand dollars, you can measure your negotiations with a dealer by that number to know whether to accept the deal or walk away.

18. Williams and Dempsey, *What Works for Women at Work.* This can be particularly important for women, who are more likely to be judged for their achievements than men, who are often judged on potential. In a similar manner, men's successes are more likely to be remembered than women's, which are more likely to be overlooked. This is because when a person's behavior conforms to our expectations, it reinforces our sense of his or her skill, and when a person's behavior violates our expectations, we attribute it to an external factor such as luck. So when it comes to identifying and documenting one's value, this is even more important for women who are less likely to have been credited for their achievements.

19. Sandberg, *Lean In*, 51.

20. Auletta, "A Woman's Place."

21. Ibid. Williams and Dempsey, *What Works for Women at Work*, recommend a number of ways to document your accomplishments to have them easily accessible should you need to make them visible. When people e-mail you their thanks, you can e-mail a response and save the e-mail chain. If you receive verbal praise, they recommend e-mailing a thank-you that repeats part of the compliment and, again, keeping your e-mail as a record.

22. Bowles, Babcock, and Lai, "Social Incentives."

23. See Adler, "Expecting International Success." In the leadership development programs we teach, we've heard over and over that women are less likely to be offered overseas roles, a phenomenon that has been documented in the research. Also see Lyness and Thompson, "Climbing the Corporate Ladder." Others have found that women's careers are often hindered as a result of having less overseas experience. When it comes to accepting over-seas assignments, women may often face additional obstacles to saying yes than those faced by men. For one thing, women are more likely to have spouses who work full-time and are more entrenched in their careers than are their male counterparts. Thus, women can be vulnerable in facing others' perceptions of their availability and interest in taking global assignments. In our conversations with executives, it seems that a willingness to take on global assignments is becoming part of what it means to be an "ideal worker."

24. Williams and Cuddy, "Will Working Mothers."

25. See Fletcher, *Leadership as Relational Practice.*

26. See Groysberg, McLean, and Nohria, "Are Leaders Portable?" The concept of firm-specific human capital was developed by economist Gary Becker, who distinguished between general knowledge that is useful in multiple companies or even industries and firm-specific knowledge, which is useful in only one company. Firm-specific knowledge includes formal policies and decision-making practices, knowing which relationships are critical, under-standing informal norms, as well as knowledge of the strategy and history of the organiza-tion. In economics, firm-specific human capital explains why companies value seniority to the extent that a senior employee would be paid more than she could receive (in the same position) at a competing firm; her seniority and company knowledge make her more valu-able to the organization than someone with an otherwise identical skill set. Groysberg et al. note that each of us has a portfolio of skills, and while industry or general management skills are portable, company-specific skills are not. Your company-specific skills are valuable to your organization, though, and can give you a source of leverage when it comes to your counterpart's BATNA.

27. See Fisher, Ury, and Patton, *Getting to Yes*; Malhotra and Bazerman, *Negotiation Genius*; and White and Neale, "Reservation Prices, Resistance Points, and BATNAs."

28. See White and Neale, "Reservation Prices, Resistance Points, and BATNAs."

29. See Neale and Bazerman, "The Effects of Framing and Negotiator Overconfidence." Researchers have found that people are likely to be overconfident and to underestimate

the strength of their counterpart's alternatives. This overconfidence can lead to being less concessionary in the negotiation itself, with less successful outcomes as a result. This is why it is so important to gather information and consider your counterpart's alternatives. We discuss this more in chapter 4.

30. See Emerson, "Power-Dependence Relations." Emerson suggested that power is a product of the social relations between two actors. It is not that actor A or B has an objective amount of power, or lack thereof. Rather, each actor's power is determined by his or her level of dependence on the other. Parties that are interdependent will have less of a power imbalance than those who are either independent or for whom one is dependent while the other is independent. Also see Bacharach and Lawler, *Bargaining: Power, Tactics, and Outcomes.*

31. See Diamond and Quinby, *Feminism and Foucault.* Power is exerted in more nuanced ways in social interactions. Following the work of Michel Foucault, scholars observe how knowledge and accepted truths, which appear natural and neutral, serve to discipline action. Certain discourses become dominant and hold sway in ways actors do not necessarily recognize as exercises of power. In negotiations in the workplace, accepted beliefs in a gendered negotiated order can discipline the negotiations. For example, the belief that an ideal worker is one who is available 24/7 can mean that negotiating for a less-demanding schedule is going against powerful beliefs.

Chapter 3

1. See Fisher, Ury, and Patton, *Getting to Yes;* Lax and Sebenius, *3-D Negotiation;* and Walton and McKersie, *A Behavioral Theory.*

2. A helpful way to understand mutual-gains negotiation is with the concept of enlarging the pie. In distributive negotiations, there is a fixed pie. Each party will get some portion of that pie, and what one party loses the other party will gain. Yet in most negotiations, it's possible to expand the pie by bringing in more and different options. For instance, in a real estate negotiation, a landlord and tenant could negotiate over rent with a fixed pie—the landlord wants X and the tenant wants to pay Y, and they need to come to agreement. But they could expand the pie if they consider other options. Perhaps the landlord lives far away and needs help maintaining the property. The tenant might take on property maintenance in exchange for a lower rent, which would still cost the landlord less than if she had to hire someone to do maintenance. By being creative, both parties walk away with more of what is valuable to them than if they had just negotiated over the monthly rental charge.

3. See chapter 1 for a full definition of N-negotiations and n-negotiations.

4. Fisher, Ury, and Patton, *Getting to Yes.* For a more detailed discussion of that book, see the Introduction, n. 2.

5. Follett, "Constructive Conflict," 68. Also see Kolb, Jensen, and Shannon, "She Said It All Before."

6. Follett, *Creative Experience,* 42.

7. Ibid., 75.

8. See Hammond, Keeney, and Raiffa, "The Hidden Traps." The authors introduce a useful illustration of how this works. They pose two questions: "Is the population of Turkey greater than 35 million?" and "What is your best estimate of the population of Turkey?" The authors note that the first question anchors people to the notion that the population is around 35 million. When they ask this question in groups, people's estimates are within the 35 million range. When they substitute 100 million in the first question, they find population estimates increase by many millions.

9. See Chertkoff and Conley, "Opening Offer"; Liebert et al., "The Effects of Information"; and Benton, Kelley, and Liebling, "Effects of Extremity." Countless experiments have shown that opening offers can anchor negotiations and influence the final deal.

10. Pruitt, *Negotiation Behavior*.

11. See Lax and Sebenius, *3-D Negotiation*, and Bazerman and Gillespie, "Betting on the Future."

12. See Ramarajan, McGinn, and Kolb, "An Outside-Inside Evolution."

13. Langer, *Mindfulness*, 22.

14. Follett, *Creative Conflict*.

15. See Maholtra and Bazerman, *Negotiation Genius*, especially chapter 2, "Creating Value in Negotiation."

16. See Bazerman and Neale, *Negotiating Rationally*. Max Bazerman and Margaret Neale explain that it's easy to get committed to one's original course of action, even when pursuing that course becomes irrational. When we are fixed in our expectations of the other party's concerns, we are likely to confirm those expectations in our negotiations because we do not explore other options. Our expectations can then become self-fulfilling prophecies.

17. Langer, *Mindfulness*.

18. See Kawakami, White and Langer, "Mindful and Masculine." The authors found that women can escape the double bind by being mindful. They note the double bind presents women leaders with a paradox: act "feminine" (warm, nurturing) and be liked but not respected; act "masculine" (assertive) and she may be respected but certainly not liked. Kawakami and her colleagues found that women who acted assertively *and* mindfully—that is, they focused on purpose rather than being concerned about their image—were able to escape this paradox of the double bind. This learning is particularly salient with regard to negotiation, in which women who negotiate hard on their own behalf can be prone to backlash for violating feminine gender stereotypes.

19. Goffman, *Interaction Ritual*, 7. Erving Goffman wrote extensively of *face*, bringing broader attention to a concept whose origin is Chinese. Goffman explained the tension that maintaining, or saving, face can present in situations such as negotiation: "Thus while the concern for face focuses the attention of the person on the current activity, he must, to maintain face in this activity, take into consideration his place in the social world beyond it."

20. Langer, *Mindfulness*.

21. Kolb and Williams, *Everyday Negotiation*, 176–193.

Chapter 4

1. See chapter 1 for a full discussion of n-negotiations and N-negotiations.

2. An exception is Lax and Sebenius, *3-D Negotiation*, which includes a section on setting up the negotiation "away from the table," though even this treatment is more about the structure of the negotiation itself than starting a negotiation with someone who is not primed to negotiate. (We discuss Lax and Sebenius's approach to "setting the table" later in this chapter.) The other main exception is within the subject of international relations–negotiations. See Stein, *Getting to the Table*. In both of these cases, the focus is on preparation for N-negotiations.

3. Zartman, "Prenegotiation: Phases and Functions." William Zartman describes prenegotiation as an important process but one that academics often overlook. Researchers who do explore the concept tend to do so within the domain of international relations and other N-negotiations. Yet the process of prenegotiation is relevant for n-negotiations as well:

prenegotiation begins when one party recognizes a problem that cannot be resolved uni-laterally. In n-negotiations, the task then becomes convincing other parties that there is a problem to be solved and that it can be solved cooperatively.

4. See Donohue and Roberto, "Relational Development as Negotiated Order." In a study of ten FBI transcripts from actual hostage negotiations, William Donohue and Anthony Roberto found that relational patterns between hostage takers and crisis negotiators were established early, most often by the negotiator. The most effective negotiators are able to quickly build a relationship in which the hostage taker likes and trusts the negotiator. Police trained as hostage negotiators must learn to build a relational context with hostage takers despite their institutional dislike for lawbreakers.

5. See Stevens, *Strategy and Collective Bargaining*.

6. See *Negotiation Newsletter*, "To Capture the Force."

7. See *Negotiation Newsletter*, "Lessons."

8. See Fast et al., "Illusory Control." Power has been linked to a sense of control, self-esteem, and an action orientation. On the flip side, those in lower-power groups are likely to feel less control and to have less of an action orientation. A study examining the relationship between power and control found that 78 percent of those with high power (manipulated for the experiment) took an action orientation compared to only 56 percent of those in the baseline group.

9. See Ridgeway, "Gender, Status, and Leadership."

10. See Bear, "Passing the Buck." Julia Bear's work shows that the type of issue being negotiated makes a difference in how men and women avoid or initiate negotiations. In a simulated workplace negotiation, she found women were more likely than men to avoid negotiating around compensation, whereas men were more likely than women to avoid compensating around lactation rooms. She suggests that we are more likely to negotiate around issues that are congruent with our own gender roles. This can add to the asymmetrical incentives to negotiate in n-negotiations, since many of the issues women negotiate for in organizations (compensation, promotions, status, credit, resources, new opportunities) are associated more with men.

   Also see Bear and Babcock, "Negotiation Topic." In another study, Julia Bear and Linda Babcock explored how the issues being negotiated relate to gender differences in outcomes. They took a commonly used negotiation exercise that asks participants to agree to a price for halogen lamps and created an otherwise identical exercise that substituted glass jewelry beads as the product being priced. When mixed-gender pairs negotiated using each of the two exercises, men outperformed women when they were pricing the more "masculine" product of halogen lamps, yet there were no gender differences in negotiating for the price of glass beads. Bear and Babcock suggest this is a particularly interesting finding in the context of negotiation training. They had students in a negotiation class rate the masculinity and femininity of a number of widely used negotiation exercises from Harvard Business School, the Harvard Law School Program on Negotiation, and the Center for Dispute Resolution Research at Northwestern University: 78 percent of the cases were rated as significantly more masculine. Bear and Babcock note that given their findings that women are likely to be outperformed by men in masculine cases, women and men in negotiation trainings may be getting skewed feedback about their performance.

11. See Amanatullah and Morris, "Negotiating Gender Roles." Emily Amanatullah and Michael Morris found that women who negotiated on their own behalf opened with significantly lower counterproposals than men negotiating for themselves. Yet when nego-tiating on behalf of a friend, men and women behaved similarly. Amanatullah and Morris attribute women's reluctance to negotiate as forcefully for themselves as they would for

others to a fear of backlash for violating gender expectations. They note negotiating on behalf of someone else is actually consistent with the stereotype of women as caregivers—wives and mothers who focus on others' needs over their own.

12. See Bowles, Bear, and Thomason, "Claiming Authority." In their fieldwork, Hannah Bowles, Julia Bear, and Bobbi Thomason found that women were just as likely to initiate negotiation as men when they perceived injustice or that they were not being treated fairly.

13. See Galinsky et al., "Power and Perspectives Not Taken." Adam Galinsky and his colleagues found that people with power were less likely to practice perspective taking—"stepping outside of one's own experience and imagining the emotions, perceptions, and motivations of another individual." Through a number of experiments, they found high-power individuals had a lower tendency to understand not only others' perspectives but also their feelings. This power-induced lack of empathy and perspective can make it particularly difficult to initiate negotiations with those in power; they are less likely to be able to see the issue from our perspective and likely to see the issue as a problem and to misread verbal and emotional cues during the negotiation itself.

14. See Kolb and Williams, Everyday Negotiation, chap. 2.

15. Frankel, Nice Girls, 130–131.

16. Brzezinski, Knowing Your Value, 116. For more suggestions on making your value visible, see the section "Taking Stock of Your Value" in chapter 2.

17. See Kolb and Williams, Everyday Negotiation.

18. See Coughlin, "The Time Is Now." Research has shown that even where there are formal promotion processes, men tend to be considered for promotion more often than their female counterparts. There are a number of factors for this; for example, men tend to have stronger networks, people tend to hire in their own image, and women may be considered unavailable for relocation. In addition, men tend to be perceived as having greater leadership potential, even when compared to women who have the same skill sets. A study of twenty-eight hundred high-potential managers examined ratings by supervisors and found that while women were rated somewhat higher than men on their current competencies, men were rated significantly higher in terms of their potential as leaders.

19. See Mnookin et al., "The Tension." This is somewhat akin to the empathy-assertiveness framework Mnookin and his colleagues propose. They suggest that effective negotiators are able to manage the tension between using empathy to consider the other person's concerns and perspective while at the same time being assertive to advocate for her own interests.

20. See Magee, Galinsky, and Gruenfeld, "Power, Propensity." The authors describe experiments using two different power primes to affect negotiating behavior. One way the researchers primed their subjects to be powerful was by asking them to "recall a particular incident in which you had power over another individual or individuals. By power, we mean a situation in which you controlled the ability of another person or persons to get something they wanted, or were in a position to evaluate those individuals. Please describe this situation in which you had power—what happened, how you felt, etc." Another power prime used similar language but referred specifically to negotiation, asking subjects to "recall a particular incident in which you had power in a negotiation. Please describe this situation in which you had power—what happened, how you felt, etc." In several experiments, those who had been primed for high power using these reflection exercises were more likely to initiate negotiations and achieve better results than those who had been primed for low power. These sorts of primes can be particularly helpful for those who are in a position of low power based on their place in an organization's hierarchy, and when used by women might help to address the propensity of women not to negotiate on their own behalf as much as men.

21. See Pfeffer, "You're Still the Same." Jeffrey Pfeffer explains that a sense of self-efficacy, a belief in your ability to succeed, can lead to an action orientation. This can become a self-fulfilling prophecy, because having an action orientation provides a greater chance of success. Thus, the more powerful people feel, the more likely they are to act and be successful, reinforcing their sense of power and control.

22. Carney, Cuddy and Yap, "Power Posing." The authors found that men and women who stood in high-power poses for two minutes changed their hormone levels and experienced an increase in testosterone and a decrease in cortisol. These changes led them to feel more powerful and more tolerant of taking a risk, allowing them to respond more effectively to stress. Those who used low-power poses experienced the opposite effects. Carney, Cuddy, and Yap suggest their findings can be particularly helpful for members of low-power social groups or those lower in an organizational hierarchy. They argue that people can indeed "fake it 'til they make it." By acting more confident, we can become more confident. For a quick introduction to power poses, see Amy Cuddy's TED talk: "Your Body Language Shapes Who You Are" (http://www.ted.com/talks/amy_cuddy_your_body_language_shapes _who_you_are.html).

23. See Forgas, "On Feeling Good."

24. Brooks and Schweitzer, "Can Nervous Nelly Negotiate?" Recent research by Alison Wood Brooks and Maurice Schweitzer has examined the role of stress and anxiety in negotiations and found that people who are anxious are more likely to reach a quick agreement, often by lowering their aspirations and making quick concessions. This isn't surprising. If we're worried about how our manager will react to our idea for a new project or request for a promotion, we might want to get the ask out of the way quickly and then get back out the door. Brooks and Schweitzer found that individuals who listened to relaxing music prior to a negotiation stayed in negotiations longer and obtained better results than those who were made anxious by listening to discordant music. Also see *Negotiation Newsletter*, "Manage Your Anxiety and Overconfidence."

25. Davis, Eshelman, and McKay, *Relaxation and Stress Reduction Handbook*. Diaphragmatic breathing—slow breathing that contracts the diaphragm—helps reduce tension and stress and normalizes the heart rate. However, as adults, we don't often breathe this way unless we are consciously making an effort to do so. To practice breathing from your diaphragm, place your hand on your abdomen and take a deep breath. You should feel your abdomen expand as you inhale. Also see Paul et al., "A Longitudinal Study." An interesting study of medical students found that students who practiced diaphragmatic breathing for five minutes before going to class experienced less test anxiety and self-doubt along with increased concentration. This would suggest that in similar situations such as negotiations, taking a few minutes to breathe deeply can help reduce stress and self-doubt so we can negotiate more confidently and assuredly.

26. See Bowles, Babcock, and Lai, "Social Incentives for Gender Differences"; Eagly and Carli, *Through the Labyrinth*; and Ely, Ibarra and Kolb, "Taking Gender into Account."

27. See Bell and Nkomo, *Our Separate Ways*.

28. Quindlen, "Say Goodbye to the Virago."

29. Ury, *Getting Past No.*

30. Bowles and Babcock. "How Can Women." Given the findings that women who negotiate for greater compensation can face a backlash, Hannah Bowles and Linda Babcock explored whether women could frame requests for higher compensation in a way that would not cause them to face social penalties. They found that when women demonstrated concern for organizational relationships and legitimized their requests (such as by saying their team leader suggested they ask for a pay increase), they had better social and economic outcomes. Bowles and Babcock suggest women can advocate for themselves without facing

backlash if they legitimize their requests in a way that shows concern for organizational relationships.

31. See Amanatullah and Morris, "Negotiating Gender Roles."

32. Ely and Rhode, "Women and Leadership." Robin Ely and Deborah Rhode suggest that women benefit from operating from an "ecosystem" rather than "egosystem" motivation. Within the ecosystem framework, one sees the self as part of a larger whole and realizes what is good for oneself might also be good for others. By operating out of a commitment to the organizational mission or broader purpose, one is motivated to take a learning stance rather than focus on her self-image.

33. See "Elizabeth Warren Interview," *Daily Show*. This is from an appearance on the *Daily Show* in which Jon Stewart had put together a series of news clips to illustrate the double bind, prompted by the announcement that Hillary Clinton would soon be a grandmother. Stewart's clips contrasted the responses to Clinton's announcement—"Will she still want to be president?" "How could she be president *and* a grandmother"—with images of male presidential candidates, such as Mitt Romney, surrounded by grandchildren. As Stewart pointed out, no one ever questioned whether a man could be a grandfather and president at the same time. Warren's response to Stewart's questioning nicely exemplifies the strategy researchers suggest. She legitimizes her actions and connects them to others and a purpose: she's advocating on behalf of others about important issues, as she was elected to do.

34. Brzezinski, *Knowing Your Value*.

35. See Ibarra, "Homophily and Differential Returns"; Ragins and Kram, *The Handbook of Mentoring*; and McPherson, Smith-Lovin, and Cook, "Birds of a Feather." Research has shown that men's and women's networks tend to vary in form and function. While men's networks tend to be homophilous (mostly men) and multipurpose, women are more likely to build multiple networks for different purposes. Women tend to build networks of men for instrumental support and to network with other women for social support.

36. There is a large body of research on the notion of social capital—that social structure is a form of capital that can create a competitive advantage for some individuals or groups. See Burt, "The Network Structure," 348. As Ronald Burt notes, "Better connected people enjoy higher returns." The value of sponsors is that they allow us to borrow social capital from someone who has it. Having a sponsor allows one to take on the sponsor's status as an insider rather than be viewed as an outsider. Thus for women, who are often viewed as outsiders in business settings (even when there are women in the business), sponsorship can very important in helping them access opportunities that would otherwise be limited for them.

37. See Hewlett et al., "The Sponsor Effect."

38. Lax and Sebenius, *3-D Negotiation*.

39. Fletcher, *Disappearing Acts*.

40. See Wells, "The Group as a Whole."

Chapter 5

1. See McGinn and Keros, "Improvisation and the Logic of Exchange." The authors studied eighty-seven two-party negotiation experiments and found negotiators quickly improvised cooperative or competitive processes for their negotiations, which had an impact on their outcomes overall. Also see Curhan and Pentland, "Thin Slices of Negotiation." Jared Curhan and Alex Pentland studied four conversational dynamics: activity level, engagement, emphasis (such as vocal stress), and mirroring (mimicking the other's speech patterns). They found that the outcome of a negotiation could be predicted by how the parties used these dynamics in the first five minutes of their negotiation. Also see Wheeler,

"Anxious Moments," 164. Mike Wheeler explains that openings are important because "they require us to commit to certain actions and foreclose others." For example, if we decide to begin a negotiation by haggling, it is hard to change the tone later to one of cooperation and mutual problem solving.

2. See Hammond, Keeney, and Raiffa, "The Hidden Traps"; Chertkoff and Conley, "Opening Offer"; Liebert et al., "The Effects of Information"; and Benton, Kelley, and Liebling, "Effects of Extremity." We made use of some of these insights in our discussion of anchoring around options in chapter 3.

3. See McGinn and Keros, "Improvisation and the Logic of Exchange."

4. See Walton and McKersie, *A Behavioral Theory of Labor Negotiations*.

5. See Taylor and Donahue, "Hostage Negotiation Opens Up."

6. See chapter 1 for a complete definition of *n-negotiations* and *N-negotiations*.

7. See chapter 3 for more on mindfulness.

8. Fisher and Shapiro, *Beyond Reason*.

9. Mika Brzezinski, *Knowing Your Value*, 75.

10. Though our focus is on negotiations with those who are above you in the organizational hierarchy, it's best practice to have regular check-ins with people you work closely with regardless of their position. Setting regular meetings with subordinates, your team, or peers can be helpful in building rapport and a sense of common purpose as a basis for productive negotiations when you need something from them in order to meet your objectives.

11. Wex, *Just Say Nu*, 10. While schmoozing has become associated with networking and more of a self-serving activity (as used in English), the original Yiddish use depended on an acknowledgment of the importance of the person you are conversing with. Wex writes: "Shmoozing is based on listening, on the idea of responding to what you hear and being answered in turn by someone who has listened to you." This original use nicely sums up the value of schmoozing in negotiations as a way to create connection, build trust, and set a pattern of mutual reciprocity.

12. See Nadler, "Build Rapport—and a Better Deal." Janice Nadler found that even a brief phone conversation could build enough rapport to have an impact on negotiation outcomes. She set up a negotiation simulation in which participants would e-mail strangers regarding the purchase of a new car. Half of the negotiating pairs were instructed to speak by phone for five minutes before e-mailing about any topic other than the negotiation at hand. The remaining participants went right to their e-mail negotiation. She found the small talk—even if just about the weather—had created rapport among the pairs who spoke first; they felt more cooperative, shared more information, and developed more trust. This increased rapport led to better outcomes: the negotiators who engaged in small talk were more than four times as likely to reach an agreement than those in the control group, who often walked away from the negotiation altogether. Also see Mislin et al., "Should We Chit-Chat?" Alexandra Mislin and her colleagues constructed an experiment to examine whether the benefits of small talk differed by gender. They found that men who made small talk prior to negotiations were perceived as significantly more communal and likeable than men who did not. In turn, men who engaged in chit-chat were granted significantly higher cash agreements. Perceptions of women's communality and likeability were not significantly affected by small talk, nor were their agreements. The researchers suggest that men benefit from making small talk because they are not expected to behave communally, whereas women are. This explains why the impact of making small talk can be beneficial for men but neutral for women. Of course, Nadler and Mislin's research probed the effect of small talk on negotiations between strangers. Within organizations, small talk can add to existing relationships in a way that might be just as beneficial for women as men.

13. Wheeler, *The Art of Negotiation*, 143.

14. See Lakin and Chartrand, "Using Nonconscious Behavioral Mimicry." Researchers found that participants who were attempting to create an affiliation with their interviewer (during a lab study) unconsciously mimicked the interviewer's shaking foot. The participants were unaware of their mimicry, leading the researchers to suggest that this might be something people do unconsciously when trying to increase affiliation. However, they caution us not to consciously mimic people in an attempt to build affiliation and trust. While the unconscious mimicry has a potential to increase people's liking for one another, obvious conformity can have the opposite effect.

15. See *Negotiation Newsletter*, "How Body Language Affects Negotiation." Research has shown that most of us trust others as a default. It's only when we have evidence to the contrary that we become suspicious. This article describes Max Bazerman's advice for testing another person's claims: ask specific questions, and repeat the questions several times with different wording. This will allow you to evaluate the consistency of responses; someone being dishonest is likely to give inconsistent answers. Also see, Kray, Kennedy, and Van Zant, "Not Competent Enough to Know the Difference." Laura Kray, Jessica Kennedy, and Alex Van Zant's research suggests women should be particularly attentive to the possibility that their counterpart might be lying to them. The researchers found that women are perceived as being easier to mislead than men and that both men and women are more likely to lie to women than they are to men in negotiations. In a real estate negotiation role-play by MBA students, women were more likely to be lured into agreements under false pretenses than men, who were given more honest information. Of course, this exercise simulated N-negotiations, in which the parties likely won't have to interact with each other again. There may be more incentive to be honest in n-negotiations, particularly among colleagues who work closely together.

16. See Bowles and Babcock, "How Can Women." As we discussed in chapter 4, this can be particularly helpful when women are asking for a promotion or something else that could be interpreted as self-serving. By connecting your request to the organization, you can avoid triggering a double bind.

17. We found this to be true in an experiment we conducted with Robin Ely and Elizabeth Bailey of Harvard Business School. Participants, all women, role-played a negotiation about an issue at work that was important to them. Afterward, they attended a leadership development session that focused on linking their work to a larger sense of purpose. The participants then repeated their negotiation role plays with the instruction that they do so in the context of their higher purpose: connecting their ask to organizational goals. Both role plays were videotaped and coded, and the results were fascinating. In the first set of role plays, women were more likely to undermine themselves and their goals with apologetic and accommodating language and a focus exclusively on what they needed and wanted. After incorporating purpose, they were more confident. They connected what they were asking for to what was good for the organization in a way that demonstrated their commitment to company goals and strategy. Participants reported that the more connected they felt to their larger purpose, the more satisfied they were with their performance. Connecting to their purpose helped them avoid knee-jerk reactions and made them less self-conscious, and their counterparts rated them as more effective. While there is likely some positive effect of repeating the role play, our hypothesis is that by creating a conscious goal of connecting to the organization's mission, negotiators felt more justified and confident while negotiating, which improved their outcomes as well as how they were perceived.

18. See Bowles and Babcock, "How Can Women." Amari also does a nice job of tying her ask to organizational relationships, which, according to Bowles and Babcock, should help her avoid social consequences for asking for more resources.

19. Sandberg, *Lean In*, 46.

20. See Cobb, "Empowerment and Mediation." Sara Cobb notes, in the context of mediation, that participants need to be empowered by both the agreement and the process of coming to agreement. This is true in n-negotiations as well: it's not in your best interest to get what you want at the expense of your boss's feeling resentful. When you have an ongoing working relationship, the way you get to an agreement can be as important as the agreement itself. Cobb argues that an ingredient for each person to be empowered by the process is to feel legitimate and "have their say," and have their "say" recognized and even elaborated on by the other party. By raising your counterpart's "good reasons," you demonstrate that they are legitimate and can create a positive rather than an adversarial negotiation.

21. See Cobb and Rifkin, "Practice and Paradox." An analysis of discourse processes in mediation found this to be true. Researchers found that the first story that was told in mediation ended up framing the agreement 75 percent of the time. Only 25 percent of the time was the final agreement constructed out of later issues that were raised. This suggests that by introducing the objection yourself, you are more likely to control the narrative and to determine which of your counterpart's objections will get the most discussion.

22. This example comes from a case written by Joyce Fletcher and Deborah Kolb.

23. See Farrell and Finkelstein, "Organizational Citizenship Behavior." Researchers studying "organizational citizenship behavior"—behavior that is not recognized by the formal reward system but helps the organization function—have found a greater expectation for women to take on these types of extra roles. The expectation that women will take on these tasks, and that men will not, means that men are more likely to be recognized and rewarded for them than women. Also see Mitchell and Hesli, "Women Don't Ask?"

24. See Vesterlund, Babcock, and Weingart, "Breaking the Glass Ceiling with 'No'."

Chapter 6

1. Sebenius and Hulse, "Charlene Barshefsky (B)."

2. See Kolb and Williams, *Everyday Negotiation*.

3. See Sebenius, "Are You Ready for the 'Hardest Question?'"

4. See Bowles, Thomason, and Bear, "Women's Career Negotiations."

5. See McGinn, Long Lingo, and Ciano, "Transitions through Out-of-Keeping Acts." Kathleen McGinn and her colleagues have analyzed hundreds of simulated and actual negotiations and established categories of out-of-keeping acts—statements or acts (such as emotional outbursts) that can take a negotiation off course, changing the topic and even the tone of the discussion. They note these acts can be abrupt or gradual, but when one occurs, there is a potential for transition. When faced with such an act, you can continue down the path of the new logic that has been introduced or use the act to transition in another (or the original) direction.

6. See Ifert and Roloff, "Overcoming Expressed Obstacles to Compliance." Danette Ifert and Michael Roloff study what they call obstacles to compliance, noting that a refusal usually takes at least one of three forms: someone may be unwilling to comply, may find the request an imposition (the cost of complying is too great), or may be unable to grant the request. Paying attention to cues about which of the obstacles is present can help negotiators adapt within the negotiation to be more effective.

7. See Ridgeway, "Gender, Status, and Leadership."

8. See Fisher, Ury, and Patton, *Getting to Yes*. Fisher, Ury, and Patton outline a number of dirty tricks, including the good guy/bad guy routine, threats, and outright deception. Being aware of the types of dynamics people can use to manipulate the negotiation can help us avoid becoming victims.

9. See Kolb and Williams, *Everyday Negotiation*.
10. Ibid.
11. Cobb, "A Developmental Approach to Turning Points." Sara Cobb consciously describes these as *moments* and stresses that the response by the person who has been delegitimized will determine the rest of the interaction.
12. Brzezinski, *Knowing Your Value*, 151.
13. See Gherardi, *Gender, Symbolism, and Organizational Cultures*.
14. Ibid. Also see Kolb and Williams, *Everyday Negotiation*.
15. See Sebenius, "Are You Ready for the 'Hardest Question?'"
16. See Barrett, "Critical Moments as 'Change' in Negotiation." Frank Barrett alerted us to this idea. He suggests that having a repertoire of possible turns could allow negotiators to act more confidently with the knowledge that they have ways to recover if critical moments occur.
17. See De Dreu, "Coercive Power." Carsten De Dreu designed an experiment to test how differing levels of power affected negotiators' patterns of communications and demands, with the finding that when negotiators had an equal amount of power, they communicated more cooperatively. De Dreu suggests there is a greater chance for reciprocity when the negotiators come from a position of parity, whereas in cases of power imbalance, they are more likely to become engaged in a competitive spiral.
18. See Druckman and Olekalns, "Punctuated Negotiations." In a review of the literature on turning points and interruptions in negotiations, Daniel Druckman and Mara Olekalns suggest that interruptions can lead to better outcomes. They suggest interruptions might provide parties with the motivation to break stalemates, particularly if they take a deliberate break to think about how to build cooperation.
19. See Newman, "The Sounds of Silence."
20. Gherardi, "Gendered Organizational Cultures."
21. Sebenius, "Are You Ready for the 'Hardest Question?'"
22. Meyerson, *Tempered Radicals*, 61.
23. Fisher, Ury, and Patton, *Getting to Yes*.
24. Wheeler, *The Art of Negotiation*, 176.

Chapter 7

1. See Rackham and Carlisle, "The Effective Negotiator." Researchers compared a group of expert negotiators (so designated by their colleagues and counterparts) with a control group of average negotiators. They found the experts spent twice as much time asking questions as the control group—which made up an average of 20 percent of the negotiating time. Interestingly, experts were also more likely to talk about their feelings and check their understanding by summarizing their counterparts' position.
2. See chapter 1 for a full discussion of *n-negotiations* and *N-negotiations*.
3. This case was written by Fleur Weigert under the direction of Deborah M. Kolb, Simmons Graduate School of Management, 2000. Revised 2012.
4. Stone, Patton, and Heen, *Difficult Conversations*.
5. Mnookin, Peppet, and Tulumello, *Beyond Winning*, 46.
6. See Cobb, "Negotiation Pedagogy."
7. I've adapted this exercise from one used commonly in the Program on Negotiation at Harvard Law School.
8. See Stephan and Finlay, "The Role of Empathy." Role-playing exercises have been widely used to build empathy in work on intergroup relations, including those designed to help members of different racial groups engage in dialogue and decrease racial divisiveness.

9. We highly recommend using this exercise, particularly in preparation for a major negotiation. Ask a friend to spend half an hour helping you to prepare for your negotiation. First, spend ten or fifteen minutes in the role of your counterpart while your friend interviews you. Then switch roles, and ask your friend to take the role of your counterpart while you negotiate as yourself. Doing the entire role-play exercise is best practice in preparation: it helps you understand your counterpart's concerns and perspective and work out your approach, even down to the language you want to use.

10. See Sebenius and Schneeman, "Lakhdar Brahimi."

11. *Negotiation Newsletter*, "Beyond Walking Away."

12. Miles, "Developing Strategies for Asking Questions in Negotiation."

13. Ibid. Edward Miles notes that it can be difficult to distinguish whether a question is posed for competitive or cooperative reasons, which makes it possible for people to misconstrue your motives, even when you are exploring the potential for mutual gains. People being questioned can feel threatened despite your best intentions. Miles suggests a part of one's questioning strategy should be the consideration of how to help your counterpart save face. This is why it's important to carefully consider the types of questions you begin the conversation with and to frame questions in an appreciative manner. For instance, asking, "Can you deliver this in two weeks?" has the potential to provoke defensiveness, whereas, "Is it feasible to deliver this in two weeks?" allows the respondent to save face. Also see Fisher and Shapiro, *Beyond Reason*.

14. Husted Medvec et al., "Choice and Achievement."

15. Ibid. Victoria Husted Medvec and her colleagues found that negotiators who received multiple equivalent simultaneous offers (MESOs) were more likely to accept an offer than those who received single offers. In another experiment, they found that making MESOs served to anchor the negotiation and resulted in better outcomes. Negotiators who made MESOs were perceived by their counterparts as being more flexible and cooperative than negotiators who made single offers. MESOs were also found to be helpful in dispute resolution, using a simulation that was based on a power imbalance with the potential to provoke strong emotional responses. Participants who were instructed to exchange MESOs reached a settlement 86 percent of the time, compared to only 63 percent of those who exchanged package offers. Husted Medved and her colleagues suggest that making multiple equivalent simultaneous offers can be an effective way to gather information about your counterpart's priorities, particularly if the equivalent offers are carefully constructed to do just that. They also note that since using MESOs is interpreted by the other party as a sign of flexibility, negotiators can in fact be more persistent without being perceived as stubborn.

16. See Cialdini, *Influence*. Also see Cliffe, "The Uses (and Abuses) of Influence." Robert Cialdini explains the rule of reciprocity this way: people will help you if you've done something to advance their goals. He recommends not only helping other people out, but being very deliberate in how you frame that help. Rather than brushing away a thank-you, Cialdini recommends harnessing the immediate influence you've earned by noting that of course you helped; that's what partners and colleagues do for each other.

17. See Bohnet, "Did You Give at the Office?" Iris Bohnet suggests that a key part of making reciprocity work is to make your counterpart feel indebted. One way to signal your willingness to cooperate is by making concessions early in the negotiations. Showing that you're willing to make concessions encourages your counterpart to do the same. If-then questions help establish a pattern of reciprocity by showing that you're willing to make some concessions to come to an agreement that works for both of you, provided your counterpart will do the same. Also see *Negotiation Newsletter*, "How to Build Trust," which describes Deepak Malhotra's advice that when you do make concessions like these to build trust, it's important to name them. We can't assume our counterpart knows that we're making

a concession. This is particularly important since unreciprocated concessions can lead to resentment and an erosion of trust. Thus, if we're trying to build reciprocity by making small concessions, it's important to be clear about two things: that our counterpart recognizes we're offering concessions and that we recognize our counterpart's concessions.

18. See Cobb, "Empowerment and Mediation" and "A Narrative Perspective on Mediation"; and Fleuridas, Nelson, and Rosenthal, "The Evolution of Circular Questions." Drawn from therapeutic discourse, circular questions are a series of queries that collectively create interdependence by stressing the experience of the individual actors to create deeper understanding and connection. This discourse moves from personal narratives and experiences to analysis of situations in ways that remove blame from the process.

19. See Putnam, "Transformation and Critical Moments in Negotiation." Linda Putnam describes this as transformation—a moment in the conflict when new understandings of the situation can redefine the nature of the conflict, the relationship, or the problems being faced. After a transformation, the negotiators' view of the problem can be fundamentally different from when they entered the negotiation; these are the "aha" moments that can occur with true dialogue and problem solving.

20. Woolf, Mrs. Dalloway.

21. We are not discussing another kind of bump in the road—the use of dirty tricks such as authority ploys, good guy/bad guy routines, escalation of commitment, last-minute nibbling, and so on. For a good discussion of such tricks, see Fisher, Ury, and Patton, Getting to Yes, chapter 8 ("What If They Use Dirty Tricks?"). Many of these tricks are more common in N-negotiations, but there are certainly some that could play out in n-negotiations as well. For instance, the person you're negotiating with may not have the authority to make a decision or take action. In that case, rather than treating it like a dirty trick, it is best to treat this as a problem that needs to be solved: How can you help that person get authority? Also see Negotiation Newsletter, "Are You Prepared for Dirty Tricks?" and Shell, Bargaining for Advantage.

22. Ury, Getting Past No.

23. See Stone, Patton, and Heen, Difficult Conversations.

24. Liljenquist and Galinsky, "Turn Your Adversary."

25. Bohnet, "Did You Give at the Office?"

26. See Forester, "Lawrence Susskind."

27. Kolb, "Women's Work."

28. Druckman and Olekalns, "Punctuated Negotiations."

29. See Ryan and Haslam, "The Glass Cliff." Michelle Ryan and Alexander Haslam suggest that while we generally have a tendency to "think manager—think male," this can vary in different contexts. In fact, researchers have found a tendency to "think crisis—think female" and associate women with the type of leadership that is useful in times of crisis. In one study, graduate business students were asked to choose among three candidates for a company's executive board. The candidates consisted of one man and one woman who were equally qualified and a man who was markedly less qualified. Some participants were told the company's performance had been improving; others were told the company was on the decline. Researchers found the business students were much more likely to hire the woman for the company on the decline than the company that was doing well. In practice, this can put women on the ledge of a "glass cliff"—placed in prominent, high-risk positions with a low chance of success. Of course, when women do fail in these types of roles, it reinforces perceptions that women are lacking in some way.

Negotiating in glass-cliff assignments is critical for support, for success criteria, for buy-in, and for contingency plans. That requires thinking through the different reasons you might go off that cliff and negotiating to mitigate them. An executive named Rachel told us a great story of negotiating for support when asked to take on a risky reorganization. "When the department heads come to you and complain about me, will you support me?" she asked the CEO. "Yes," he answered. "And when the SVPs come to you and complain they need all of their staff, will you still support me?" "Yes," he answered. "And when the division heads threaten to quit, will you still support me?" The CEO agreed, and he did in fact support her when those things happened. Knowing she had his support allowed her to be more effective in making the transition. And by spelling out the specific ways he would need to support her, Rachel earned his buy-in and helped him understand the gravity of his commitment. Also see Kolb, Williams, and Frohlinger, *Her Place at the Table*, chapter 2, "Mobilizing Backers."

Chapter 8

1. See Strauss, *Negotiations*; Barley, "Contextualizing Conflict"; and Kolb and McGinn, *Beyond Gender and Negotiation*.
2. See Meyerson and Tompkins, "Tempered Radicals as Institutional Change Agents," 303. Deb Meyerson and Megan Tompkins explain that "gender inequities persist in workplaces because the processes that produce them are part of the normal and legitimate workings of contemporary institutions." They use the example of tenure within academia to illustrate this point. Tenure is an "up-or-out" system in which professors are expected to be extremely productive fairly early in their careers. Yet that system was developed at a time when academics were mostly male with wives who took care of their families. Now, however, the tenure system creates inequities for women, for whom the timing of having children likely coincides with tenure expectations for increased productivity. Yet assumptions around the necessity for the tenure system are deeply rooted in academic institutions, making it resistant to change or even questioning.

    Also see Rapoport et al., *Beyond Work-Family Balance*. Rhona Rapoport and her colleagues identify the potential to create change by addressing a dual agenda that addresses work effectiveness and work- and personal-life integration. They argue that in order to improve gender equity or employees' work-life balance, we need to address the work issues that can be problematic, such as the example of tenure that Meyerson and Tompkins discuss. They suggest that when work-life or gender equity is brought in as a personal incentive, employees are more motivated to reflect on how the organization could work better and more likely to be successful in changing those practices that perpetuate inequality.
3. See Sturm, "Negotiating Workplace Equality." Susan Sturm suggests that individual negotiations can reveal norms and practices within the organization, leading to an opportunity for learning. These individual learnings have the potential to lead to reflection and institutional change, particularly in organizations that recognize the value of negotiation in helping to address inequality and rethink organizational effectiveness.
4. We give credit to Lori Nishiura MacKenzie at the Clayman Institute for giving us the idea for this chapter. She suggested to us that so many people write about how individuals can negotiate better, but we don't often think about what organizations can do. While we don't do that precisely in this chapter, we do hope to connect negotiation to change and highlight the potential for a virtuous cycle in which individual negotiations shape organizations such that it is easier for individuals to negotiate for changes that help them and help the organization.
5. See Bowles, Babcock, and McGinn, "Constraints and Triggers."
6. See Sturm, "Negotiating Workplace Equality." Sturm argues that access to knowledge is an area of systemic inequality, one that has an influence on individual negotiations. Individuals have different access to information needed to obtain resources, access

opportunities, and gain recognition. These are the kinds of tacit knowledge that women and people of color are less likely to know and less likely to have access to through their networks.

7. See Reskin and McBrier, "Why Not Ascription?" If Alicia's negotiation can help Bob shift from this sort of shoulder-tapping practice to more formal recruitment processes, she could help create substantive change in their company. In a review of data from 516 work establishments, Barbara Reskin and Debra McBrier found that hiring practices have a dramatic impact on the gender breakdown of managers within an organization. Specifically, they found that recruiting through informal networks results in the disproportionate hiring of male managers. By using formal personnel practices—not just policies—including open recruitment and specifying objective selection criteria, organizations increase the proportion of women managers. Though the researchers point out that this does not eliminate inequality altogether, even small differences in promotion and hiring practices can have a substantial effect when they are played out over time.

   Also see Martell, Lane, and Emrich, "Male-Female Differences: A Computer Simulation." Richard Martell and his colleagues used a computer simulation to examine how even very small levels of inequality and bias could play out in the context of one's career. They modeled an organization that had eight levels of hierarchy, with five hundred employees at the bottom and ten at the very top. They found that even when organizations start with gender equality at the lowest levels, a small bias can accumulate to dramatic inequality over time. Their model started with an even number of men and women at the most junior level. They then applied a random bias of 1 percent in favor of men, and after seven promotion cycles the percentage of women leaders at the top level dropped to only 35 percent. When they simulated a 5 percent bias in favor of men, the results were even more dramatic. The cohort that started as 50 percent women was down to 29 percent women at the end of seven promotion cycles.

8. See Reskin and McBrier, "Why Not Ascription?" Also see Roth, "The Social Psychology of Tokenism," and Purcell, MacArthur, and Samblanet, "Gender and the Glass Ceiling."

9. See Fletcher, *Disappearing Acts*. Joyce Fletcher argues that negotiation can be a useful strategy to make sure one's work is not "disappeared," particularly for women who are disproportionately asked to do tasks that contribute to the organization but do not contribute to their career capital. By negotiating to claim value for that work, Fletcher argues, women can get credit for their achievements while also revealing, at a larger level, how performance reviews and compensation can be biased against such tasks. Elena's story is a good example of this potential for an individual negotiation to help change the standards for how different tasks are valued. She found a way to assign a financial value to work that could easily be devalued or disappeared. By creating an alternate metric for compensating partners, she helps lay the groundwork for future partners who wish to take on internal roles without sacrificing their careers and salaries.

10. See Ryan and Haslam, "The Glass Cliff."

11. See Ibarra, "Homophily and Differential Returns"; Ibarra and Hunter, "How Leaders Create and Use Networks"; Sturm, "Negotiating Workplace Equality."

12. See Bennett and Gadlin, "Collaboration and Team Science." In their work for the National Institutes of Health, Michelle Bennett and Howard Gadlin outline processes to support scientific collaboration, including establishing channels in advance for mediation of disputes or even creating "governance committees" to resolve conflicts when the parties are not able to do so themselves. Also see Kolb, "Corporate Ombudsman," and Groysberg and Connolly, "Great Leaders."

13. See Sturm, "The Architecture of Inclusion." In her study of ADVANCE, a National Science Foundation program to increase the participation and advancement of women in

science and engineering as it has been implemented at the University of Michigan, Susan Sturm identifies the critical role of the "organizational catalyst"—an internal role in which leaders with knowledge and credibility are placed in positions to support institutional change. These catalysts might gather information about patterns of exclusion and link different groups together to strengthen networks as a way to address inequality.

14. While women's networks can be helpful for women to turn to for information prior to negotiations, it's worth noting that women's network programs alone do not have a dramatic impact on increasing diversity in organizations. See Kalev, Dobbin, and Kelly, "Best Practices or Best Guesses?" Alexandra Kalev, Frank Dobbin, and Erin Kelly found that while networking programs led to moderate increases in leadership for white women and mentoring efforts led to moderate increases in leadership for black women, those types of programs in isolation create only marginal benefits. They found the organizational efforts that had the most impact in improving diversity are those that assign responsibility for doing so, such as with affirmative action plans, diversity committees, and diversity staff positions.

15. See Institute for Women's Policy Research, "Pay Secrecy and Wage Discrimination." This is even truer in the private sector, where 62 percent of women and 60 percent of men report that their wage information is secret.

16. See White House, "Expanding Opportunity for All." This is an issue that affects women disproportionately given the potential for a gender pay gap within organizations. As a part of the same initiative, President Obama also issued an executive order requiring federal contractors to submit data on employee compensation by sex and race to the Department of Labor.

17. See Kay and Shipman, *The Confidence Code*, 21. A study done at Hewlett-Packard found men were willing to apply for a promotion if they met 60 percent of the requirements, whereas women would apply only if they met 100 percent of the qualifications. This is why Spencer's small win created a big gain—what ended up being a simple shift in how they wrote job requirements caused a dramatic shift in who applied and how many women were hired.

18. Meyerson, *Tempered Radicals*, xi.

19. As we noted earlier, we all hold forms of implicit bias that tend to go unexamined unless we're prompted to reflect on them. See Banaji and Greenwald, *Blindspot*. These unconscious associations can be reinforced by any number of factors, including our own family situations. See Desai, Chugh and Brief, "The Implications of Marriage Structure." Sreedhari Desai, Dolly Chugh, and Arthur Brief studied 232 married male managers from a US accounting firm. They found that married men in traditional marriages (with stay-at-home wives) were significantly less likely to recommend a woman for promotion than they were to recommend an identically qualified man. Men in modern marriages (with working wives) were less likely than those in traditional marriages to deny women opportunities for promotion. Also see Dahl, Dező, and Ross, "Like Daughter, Like Father." Michael Dahl and colleagues found that women's wages increased relative to men's when their CEO had a daughter, particularly if the daughter was the CEO's firstborn. Also see Davis and Greenstein, "Gender Ideology," in which Davis and Greenstein document that men and women who have been reared by working mothers are more likely to take more egalitarian attitudes in the workplace.

20. Rapoport et al., *Relinking Life and Work*.

21. See Castilla, "Bringing Managers Back In." Emilio Castilla analyzed personnel data, including thousands of performance reviews, at a large US private company. He found that managers who were structurally connected—within the same social system—tended to agree with each other more when it came to judging performance of employees, which

can have a substantial impact on employees' compensation and career progression. This has an interesting implication when it comes to spreading small wins. It's possible that by helping her boss to think about criteria, Charlotte has put her boss in the position to influence other managers to do so as well.

22. See Fleming, "Narrative Leadership." David Fleming describes storytelling as an effective tool for leaders, particularly during times of change. Narratives can be used to help create and reinforce organizational culture and transformation. He notes it's particularly useful when leaders can recognize a "narrative moment"—an opportunity to use storytelling to address a salient issue in the organization such as the "teachable moments" we've described.

23. See Rapoport et al., *Relinking Life and Work*; Kolb and Meyerson, "Keeping Gender in the Plot"; and Kolb et al., "Making Change."

24. Ely and Meyerson, "Theories of Gender in Organizations"; Kolb and Merrill-Sands, "Waiting for Outcomes."

25. Kolb and Merrill-Sands, "Waiting for Outcomes."

26. Ibid.

27. See Ibarra, Ely, and Kolb, "Women Rising," and Ely, Ibarra, and Kolb, "Taking Gender into Account." These "safe-identity workspaces" could be created through coaching relationships, peer affiliation groups, or women's leadership programs (WLPs), all of which provide space for women to support each other's learning and experimentation. These women-only spaces allow women to support and challenge each other in a safe environment and to discuss gender issues and leadership challenges more freely than in mixed-sex groups. Indeed, when women's leadership development efforts do not address the context of second-generation gender issues, programs are more likely to take a "fix the women" approach, in which women are counseled to behave more like the men in their organizations in order to be successful. WLPs that examine gender bias enable women to develop their leadership identities with awareness of how to navigate gender issues in their organizations.

28. See Ely, Ibarra, and Kolb, "Taking Gender into Account," and Ibarra, Ely, and Kolb, "Women Rising."

29. See Perlow and Porter, "Making Time Off Predictable." Also see Perlow, *Sleeping with Your Smartphone*.

30. See Perlow, *Sleeping with Your Smartphone*, 212–213.

REFERENCES

Adler, Nancy J. "Expecting International Success: Female Managers Overseas." *International Executive* 27, no. 2 (1985): 13–14.

Amanatullah, Emily T. "Negotiating Gender Role Stereotypes: The Influence of Gender Role Stereotypes on Perceivers' Evaluations and Targets' Behaviors in Value Claiming Negotiations and Situational Moderation by Representation Role." PhD diss., Columbia University, 2007.

Amanatullah, Emily T., and Michael W. Morris. "Negotiating Gender Roles: Gender Differences in Assertive Negotiating Are Mediated by Women's Fear of Backlash and Attenuated When Negotiating on Behalf of Others." *Journal of Personality and Social Psychology* 98, no. 2 (2010): 256–267.

Amanatullah, Emily T., and Catherine H. Tinsley. "Punishing Female Negotiators for Asserting Too Much … or Not Enough: Exploring Why Advocacy Moderates Backlash Against Assertive Female Negotiators." *Organizational Behavior and Human Decision Processes* 120, no. 1 (2013): 110–122.

American Association of University Women. "The Simple Truth about the Gender Pay Gap (2014)." Accessed May 6, 2014, http://www.aauw.org/research/the-simple-truth-about-the-gender-pay-gap/.

Andreoni, James, and Lise Vesterlund. "Which Is the Fair Sex? Gender Differences in Altruism." *Quarterly Journal of Economics* 116, no. 1 (2001): 293–312.

Anthony, Kathryn H., and Meghan Dufresne. "Potty Parity in Perspective: Gender and Family Issues in Planning and Designing Public Restrooms." *Journal of Planning Literature* 21, no. 3 (2007): 267–294.

Auletta, Ken. "A Woman's Place: Can Sheryl Sandberg Upend Silicon Valley's Male-Dominated Culture?" *New Yorker*, July 11, 2011, http://www.newyorker.com/reporting/2011/07/11/110711fa_fact_auletta?currentPage=all.

Babcock, Linda, and Sara Laschever. *Women Don't Ask: Negotiation and the Gender Divide.* Princeton, NJ: Princeton University Press, 2003.

Babcock, Linda, and Sara Laschever. *Ask for It: How Women Can Use the Power of Negotiation to Get What They Really Want.* New York: Bantam Dell, 2008.

Bacharach, Samuel B., and Edward J. Lawler. *Bargaining: Power, Tactics, and Outcomes.* San Francisco: Jossey-Bass, 1981.

Banaji, Mahzarin, and Anthony G. Greenwald. *Blindspot: Hidden Biases of Good People.* New York: Delacorte Press, 2013.

Barley, Stephen R. "Contextualizing Conflict: Notes on the Anthropology of Disputes and Negotiation." In *Research on Negotiation in Organizations*, edited by M. Bazerman, R. Lewicki, and B. Sheppard, 165–199. Greenwich, CT: JAI Press, 1991.

Barrett, Frank J. "Critical Moments as 'Change' in Negotiation." *Negotiation Journal* 20, no. 2 (2004): 213–219.

Barron, Lisa A. "Ask and You Shall Receive? Gender Differences in Negotiators' Beliefs about Requests for a Higher Salary." *Human Relations* 56, no. 6 (2003): 635–662.

Bazerman, Max H., and James J. Gillespie. "Betting on the Future: The Virtues of Contingent Contracts." *Harvard Business Review* 77, no. 5 (1998): 155–160.

Bazerman, Max H., and Margaret A. Neale. *Negotiating Rationally*. New York: Simon & Schuster, 1994.

Bear, Julia. "Passing the Buck: Incongruence between Gender Role and Topic Leads to Avoidance of Negotiation." *Negotiation and Conflict Management Research* 4, no. 1 (2011): 47–72.

Bear, Julia B., and Linda Babcock. "Negotiation Topic as a Moderator of Gender Differences in Negotiation." *Psychological Science* 23, no. 7 (2012): 743–744.

Bell, Ella L. J. Edmondson, and Stella M. Nkomo. *Our Separate Ways: Black and White Women and the Struggle for Professional Identity*. Boston: Harvard Business Press, 2003.

Belliveau, Maura A. "Blind Ambition? The Effects of Social Networks and Institutional Sex Composition on the Job Search Outcomes of Elite Coeducational and Women's College Graduates." *Organization Science* 16, no. 2 (2005): 134–150.

Bennett, L. Michelle, and Howard Gadlin. "Collaboration and Team Science: From Theory to Practice." *Journal of Investigative Medicine* 60, no. 5 (2012): 768–775.

Benton, Alan A., Harold H. Kelley, and Barry Liebling. "Effects of Extremity of Offers and Concession Rate on the Outcomes of Bargaining." *Journal of Personality and Social Psychology* 24, no. 1 (1972): 73–83.

Bergeron, Diane M. "The Potential Paradox of Organizational Citizenship Behavior: Good Citizens at What Cost?" *Academy of Management Review* 32, no. 4 (2007): 1078–1095.

Bertrand, Marianne, Claudia Goldin, and Lawrence F. Katz. "Dynamics of the Gender Gap for Young Professionals in the Financial and Corporate Sectors." *American Economic Journal: Applied Economics* 2, no. 3 (2010): 228–255.

Blau, Francine D., and Lawrence M. Kahn. "The Gender Pay Gap: Have Women Gone as Far as They Can?" *Academy of Management Perspectives* 21, no. 1 (2007): 7–23.

Bohnet, Iris. "Did You Give at the Office? Leveraging the Power of Reciprocity." *Negotiation Newsletter* 8, no 7 (July 2005): 7–9.

Bohnet, Iris, and Greig, Fiona. "Gender Matters in Workplace Negotiations." *Negotiation* 10 (2007): 4–6.

Bowles, Hannah Riley, and Linda Babcock. "How Can Women Escape the Compensation Negotiation Dilemma? Relational Accounts Are One Answer." *Psychology of Women Quarterly* 37, no. 1 (2013): 80–96.

Bowles, Hannah Riley, Linda Babcock, and Lei Lai. "Social Incentives for Gender Differences in the Propensity to Initiate Negotiations: Sometimes It Does Hurt to Ask." *Organizational Behavior and Human Decision Processes* 103, no. 1 (2007): 84–103.

Bowles, Hannah Riley, Linda Babcock, and Kathleen L. McGinn. "Constraints and Triggers: Situational Mechanics of Gender in Negotiation." *Journal of Personality and Social Psychology* 89, no. 6 (2005): 951–965.

Bowles, Hannah Riley, Julia Bear, and Bobbi Thomason. "Claiming Authority: Negotiating Career Challenges vs. Opportunities." Presentation delivered at the Academy of Management Annual Meeting, San Antonio, TX, 2011.

Bowles, Hannah Riley, Bobbi Thomason, and Julia Bear. "Women's Career Negotiations." Presentation delivered at the Academy of Management Annual Meeting, Lake Buena Vista, FL, August 2013.

Braiker, Harriet B. *The Disease to Please: Curing the People-Pleasing Syndrome.* New York: McGraw-Hill, 2001.

Brooks, Alison Wood, and Maurice E. Schweitzer. "Can Nervous Nelly Negotiate? How Anxiety Causes Negotiators to Make Low First Offers, Exit Early, and Earn Less Profit." *Organizational Behavior and Human Decision Processes* 115, no. 1 (2011): 43–54.

Brzezinski, Mika. *Knowing Your Value: Women, Money and Getting What You're Worth.* New York: Weinstein Books, 2010.

Burt, Ronald S. "The Network Structure of Social Capital." *Research in Organizational Behavior* 22 (2000): 345–423.

Buzzanell, Patrice M., and Melina Liu. "Struggling with Maternity Leave Policies and Practices: A Poststructuralist Feminist Analysis of Gendered Organizing." *Journal of Applied Communication Research* 33 (2005): 1–25.

Calhoun, Patrick S., and William P. Smith. "Integrative Bargaining: Does Gender Make a Difference?" *International Journal of Conflict Management* 10 (1999): 203–224.

Carney, Dana R., Amy J. C. Cuddy, and Andy J. Yap. "Power Posing: Brief Nonverbal Displays Affect Neuroendocrine Levels and Risk Tolerance." *Psychological Science* 21, no. 10 (2010): 1363–1368.

Castilla, Emilio J. "Bringing Managers Back In: Managerial Influences on Workplace Inequality." *American Sociological Review* 76, no. 5 (2011): 667–694.

Catalyst. "Historical List of Women CEOs of the Fortune Lists: 1972–2013." 2013.

Catalyst Knowledge Center, "US Women in Business," accessed March 3, 2014, http://www.catalyst.org/knowledge/us-women-business.

Chertkoff, Jerome M., and Melinda Conley. "Opening Offer and Frequency of Concession as Bargaining Strategies." *Journal of Personality and Social Psychology* 7 (1967): 181–185.

Cialdini, Robert B. *Influence: How and Why People Agree to Things.* New York: Quill, 1984.

Cliffe, Sarah. "The Uses (and Abuses) of Influence: An Interview with Robert Cialdini." *Harvard Business Review* 91, no. 7/8 (July/August 2013): 76–81.

Cobb, Sara. "A Developmental Approach to Turning Points: Irony as an Ethics for Negotiation Pragmatics." *Harvard Negotiation Law Review* 11 (2006): 147–197.

Cobb, Sara. "Empowerment and Mediation: A Narrative Perspective." *Negotiation Journal* 9, no. 3 (1993): 245–259.

Cobb, Sara. "A Narrative Perspective on Mediation: Toward the Materialization of the 'Storytelling' Metaphor." In *New Directions in Mediation: Communication Research and Perspectives,* edited by Joseph P. Folger and Tricia S. Jones, 48–63. Thousand Oaks, CA: SAGE, 1994.

Cobb, Sara. "Negotiation Pedagogy: Learning to Learn." *Negotiation Journal* 16, no. 4 (2000): 315–319.

Cobb, Sara, and Janet Rifkin. "Practice and Paradox: Deconstructing Neutrality in Mediation." *Law and Social Inquiry* 16, no. 1 (1991): 35–62.

Correll, Shelley, with Stephen Benard and In Paik. "Getting a Job: Is There a Motherhood Penalty?" *American Journal of Sociology* 112 (2007): 1297–1338.

Coughlin, Linda. "The Time Is Now: A Leader's Personal Journey." In *Enlightened Power: How Women Are Transforming the Practice of Leadership,* edited by Linda Coughlin, Ellen Wingard, and Keith Hollihan. Hoboken, NJ: Wiley, 2005.

Curhan, Jared R., and Alex Pentland. "Thin Slices of Negotiation: Predicting Outcomes from Conversational Dynamics within the First Five Minutes." *Journal of Applied Psychology* 92, no. 3 (2007): 802–811.

Dahl, Michael S., Cristian L. Dezső, and David Gaddis Ross. "Like Daughter, Like Father: How Women's Wages Change When CEOs Have Daughters" (Working Paper), 2011. *SSRN 1774434.*

Davies, Bronwyn, and Rom Harré. "Positioning: The Discursive Production of Selves." *Journal for the Theory of Social Behaviour* 20, no. 1 (1990): 43–63.

Davis, Martha, Elizabeth Robbins Eshelman, and Matthew McKay. *The Relaxation and Stress Reduction Workbook.* Oakland, CA: New Harbinger Publications, 2008.

Davis, Shannon N., and Theodore N. Greenstein. "Gender Ideology: Components, Predictors, and Consequences." *Annual Review of Sociology* 35 (2009): 87–105.

De Dreu, Carsten K. W. "Coercive Power and Concession Making in Bilateral Negotiation." *Journal of Conflict Resolution* 39, no. 4 (1995): 646–670.

Deaux, Kay, and Brenda Major. "A Social-Psychological Model of Gender." In *Theoretical Perspectives on Sexual Difference*, edited by Deborah L. Rhode, 89–99. New Haven, CT: Yale University Press, 1990.

DeGroot, Christine, Aditi Mohapatra, and Jamie Lippman. "Examining the Cracks in the Ceiling: A Survey of Corporate Diversity Practices of the S&P 100." 2003. http://www.calvert.com/NRC/literature/documents/BR10063.pdf.

Desai, Sreedhari D., Dolly Chugh, and Arthur P. Brief. "The Implications of Marriage Structure for Men's Workplace Attitudes, Beliefs, and Behaviors toward Women." *Administrative Science Quarterly* 59, no. 2 (2014): 330–365.

Desmaris, Serge, and James Curtis. "Gender and Perceived Pay Entitlement: Testing for the Effects of Experience with Income." *Journal of Personality and Social Psychology* 72, no. 1 (1997): 141–150.

Diamond, Irene, and Lee Quinby. *Feminism & Foucault: Reflections on Resistance.* Boston: Northeastern University Press, 1988.

Donohue, William A., and Anthony J. Roberto. "Relational Development as Negotiated Order in Hostage Negotiation." *Human Communication Research* 20, no. 2 (1993): 175–198.

Druckman, Daniel, and Mara Olekalns. "Punctuated Negotiations: Transitions, Interruptions, and Turning Points." In *Handbook of Negotiation*, edited by Mara Olekalns and Wendi Adair. Cheltenham UK: Edward Elgar, 2013.

Eagly, Alice Hendrickson. *Sex Difference and Social Behavior: A Social Role Interpretation.* Hillsdale, NJ: Erlbaum, 1987.

Eagly, Alice Hendrickson, and Linda Lorene Carli. *Through the Labyrinth: The Truth about How Women Become Leaders.* Boston: Harvard Business Press, 2007.

Eckert, Penelope. "Cooperative Competition in Adolescent 'Girl Talk.'" In *Gender and Conversational Interaction*, edited by Deborah Tannen, 32–61. New York: Oxford University Press, 1993.

"Elizabeth Warren Interview." *Daily Show with Jon Stewart*, Comedy Central, New York, April 22, 2014.

Ely, Robin J., Herminia Ibarra, and Deborah M. Kolb. "Taking Gender into Account: Theory and Design for Women's Leadership Development Programs." *Academy of Management Learning and Education* 10, no. 3 (2011): 474–493.

Ely, Robin J., and Debra E. Meyerson. "Theories of Gender in Organizations: A New Approach to Organizational Analysis and Change." *Research in Organizational Behavior* 22 (2000): 103–151.

Ely, Robin, and Irene Padavic. "A Feminist Analysis of Organizational Research on Sex Differences." *Academy of Management Review* 32, no. 4 (2007): 1121–1143.

Ely, Robin J., and Deborah L. Rhode. "Women and Leadership: Defining the Challenges." In *Handbook of Leadership Theory and Practice*, edited by Nitin Nohria and Rakesh Khurana. Boston: Harvard Business Press, 2010.

Emerson, Richard M. "Power-Dependence Relations." *American Sociological Review* 27, no. 1 (1962): 31–41.

Equality and Human Rights Commission, UK. "Sex and Power 2011," accessed May 18, 2014, http://www.equalityhumanrights.com/key-projects/sexandpower/.

Farrell, Sara K., and Lisa M. Finkelstein. "Organizational Citizenship Behavior and Gender: Expectations and Attributions for Performance." *North American Journal of Psychology* 9, no. 1 (2007): 81–95.

Fast, Nathanael J., Deborah H. Gruenfeld, Niro Sivanathan, and Adam D. Galinsky. "Illusory Control a Generative Force behind Power's Far-Reaching Effects." *Psychological Science* 20, no. 4 (2009): 502–508.

Felstiner, William L. F., Richard L. Abel, and Austin Sarat. "The Emergence and Transformation of Disputes: Naming, Blaming, Claiming…" *Law and Society Review* 15 (1980): 631–654.

Fernandez, Roberto M., and Weinberg, Nancy. "Sifting and Sorting: Personal Contacts and Hiring in a Retail Bank." *American Sociological Review* 62, no. 2 (1997): 883–902.

Fisher, Roger, and Daniel Shapiro. *Beyond Reason: Using Emotions as You Negotiate*. New York: Penguin, 2005.

Fisher, Roger, William L. Ury, and Bruce Patton. *Getting to Yes: Negotiating Agreement without Giving In*. New York: Penguin, 2011.

Fleming, David. "Narrative Leadership: Using the Power of Stories." *Strategy and Leadership* 29, no. 4 (2001): 34–36.

Fletcher, Joyce K. "Leadership as Relational Practice." In *Extraordinary Leadership: Addressing the Gaps in Senior Executive Development*, edited by Kerry Bunker, Douglas T. Hall, and Kathy E. Kram, 123–135. San Francisco: Jossey-Bass, 2010.

Fletcher, Joyce K. *Disappearing Acts: Gender, Power, and Relational Practice at Work*. Cambridge, MA: MIT Press, 2001.

Fletcher, Joyce K. "Relational Practice: A Feminist Reconstruction of Work." *Journal of Management Inquiry* 7, no. 2 (1998): 163–186.

Fleuridas, Colette, Thorana S. Nelson, and David M. Rosenthal. "The Evolution of Circular Questions." *Journal of Marriage and Family Therapy* 12, no. 2 (1986): 113–127.

Follett, Mary Parker. "Constructive Conflict." In *Prophet of Management*, edited by Pauline Graham. Boston: Harvard Business School Press, 1996.

Follett, Mary Parker. *Creative Experience*. New York: Peter Smith, 1951.

Forgas, Joseph P. "On Feeling Good and Getting Your Way: Mood Effects on Negotiator Cognition and Bargaining Strategies." *Journal of Personality and Social Psychology* 74, no. 3 (1998): 565–577.

Forester, John. "Lawrence Susskind: Activist Mediation and Public Disputes." In *When Talk Works: Profiles of Mediators*, edited by Deborah M. Kolb, 309–354. San Francisco: Jossey-Bass, 1994.

Frankel, Lois P. *Nice Girls Don't Get the Corner Office: 101 Unconscious Mistakes Women Make That Sabotage Their Careers*. New York: Warner, 2004.

Galinsky, Adam D., Joe C. Magee, M. Ena Inesi, and Deborah H. Gruenfeld. "Power and Perspectives Not Taken." *Psychological Science* 17, no. 12 (2006): 1068–1074.

Galinsky, Adam D., Thomas Mussweiler, and Victoria Husted Medvec. "Disconnecting Outcomes and Evaluations: The Role of Negotiator Focus." *Journal of Personality and Social Psychology* 83, no. 5 (2002): 1131–1140.

Gerson, Judith M., and Kathy Peiss. "Boundaries, Negotiation, Consciousness: Reconceptualizing Gender Relations." *Social Problems* 32, no. 4 (1985): 317–331.

Gherardi, Silvia. *Gender, Symbolism, and Organizational Culture*. Thousand Oaks, CA: SAGE, 1996.

Gherardi, Silvia. "Gendered Organizational Cultures: Narratives of Women Travellers in a Male World." *Gender, Work and Organization* 3, no. 4 (1996): 187–201.

Goffman, Erving. *Interaction Ritual: Essays in Face-to-Face Behavior*. New York: Doubleday/ Anchor, 1967.

Greenberg, Danna, Jamie Ladge, and Judy Clair. "Negotiating Pregnancy at Work: Public and Private Conflicts." *Negotiation and Conflict Management Research* 2, no. 1 (2009): 42–56.

Groysberg, Boris. "How Star Women Build Portable Skills." *Harvard Business Review* 86, no. 2 (2008): 74–81.

Groysberg, Boris, and Robin Abrahams. "Manage Your Work, Manage Your Life." *Harvard Business Review* 92, no. 3 (March 2014): 58–66.

Groysberg, Boris, and Katherine Connolly. "Great Leaders Who Make the Mix Work." *Harvard Business Review* (September 2013): 68–76.

Groysberg, Boris, Andrew N. McLean, and Nitin Nohria. "Are Leaders Portable?" *Harvard Business Review* 84, no. 5 (May 2006): 92–100.

Hammond, John S., Ralph L. Keeney, and Howard Raiffa. "The Hidden Traps in Decision Making." *Harvard Business Review* 76, no. 5 (May 1998): 47–58.

Heil, Emily. "Senate Women's Restroom Expanding to Accommodate Historic Numbers." *Washington Post*, June 11, 2013. http://www.washingtonpost.com/blogs/in-the-loop/post/ senate-womens-restroom-expanding-to-accommodate-historic-numbers/2013/06/11/ e0ebc1b0-d29b-11e2-a73e-826d299ff459_blog.html?wprss=rss_national.

Heilman, Madeline E., and Tyler G. Okimoto. "Why Are Women Penalized for Success at Male Tasks? The Implied Communality Deficit." *Journal of Applied Psychology* 92, no. 1 (2007): 81–92.

Hewlett, Sylvia Ann, and Carolyn Buck Luce. "Extreme Jobs: The Dangerous Allure of the 70-Hour Workweek." *Harvard Business Review* 84, no. 12 (December 2006): 49–59.

Hewlett, Sylvia Ann, with Kerrie Peraino, Laura Sherbin, and Karen Sumberg. "The Sponsor Effect: Breaking Through the Last Glass Ceiling." *Harvard Business Review Research Report*, December 2010.

Higgins, Monica C., and Kathy E. Kram. "Reconceptualizing Mentoring at Work: A Developmental Network Perspective." *Academy of Management Review* 26, no. 2 (2001): 264–288.

Holvino, Evangelina. "Intersections: The Simultaneity of Race, Gender and Class in Organization Studies." *Gender, Work and Organization* 17, no. 3 (2010): 248–277.

Holvino, Evangelina. "Complicating Gender: The Simultaneity of Race, Gender, and Class in Organization Change(ing)" (Working Paper 14). Boston: Center for Gender in Organizations, 2001. Accessed May 18, 2014, http://www.simmons.edu/som/docs/cgo_wp14_DNC .pdf.

Husted Medvec, Victoria, Geoffrey J. Leonardelli, Adam D. Galinsky, and Aletha Claussen-Schulz. "Choice and Achievement at the Bargaining Table: The Distributive, Integrative, and Interpersonal Advantages of Making Multiple Equivalent Simultaneous Offers," International Association of Conflict Management 18th Annual Conference, Seville, Spain, 2005.

Ibarra, Herminia. "Homophily and Differential Returns: Sex Differences in Network Structure and Access in an Advertising Firm." *Administrative Science Quarterly* 37 (1992): 422–447.

Ibarra, Herminia. "Personal Networks of Women and Minorities in Management: A Conceptual Framework." *Academy of Management Review* 18, no. 1 (1993): 56–87.

Ibarra, Herminia, Robin Ely, and Deborah Kolb. "Women Rising: The Unseen Barriers." *Harvard Business Review* 91, no. 9 (September 2013): 60–66.

Ibarra, Herminia, and Mark Hunter. "How Leaders Create and Use Networks." *Harvard Business Review* 85, no. 1 (January 2007): 40–47.

Ifert, Danette E., and Michael E. Roloff. "Overcoming Expressed Obstacles to Compliance: The Role of Sensitivity to the Expressions of Others and Ability to Modify Self-Presentation." *Communication Quarterly* 45, no. 1 (1997): 55–67.

Institute for Women's Policy Research. "Pay Secrecy and Wage Discrimination," Washington, DC, January 2014.

Jackson, Linda A., Philip D. Gardner, and Linda A. Sullivan. "Explaining Gender Differences in Self-Pay Expectations: Social Comparison Standards and Perceptions of Fair Pay." *Journal of Applied Psychology* 77 (1992): 651–663.

Jost, John T. "An Experimental Replication of the Depressed-Entitlement Effect among Women." *Psychology of Women Quarterly* 21, no. 3 (1997): 387–393.

Joy, Lois, Nancy M. Carter, Harvery M. Wagner, and Sriram Narayanan. "The Bottom Line: Corporate Performance and Women's Representation on Boards." *Catalyst* (October 2007).

Kalev, Alexandra, Frank Dobbin, and Erin Kelly. "Best Practices or Best Guesses? Assessing the Efficacy of Corporate Affirmative Action and Diversity Policies." *American Sociological Review* 71, no. 4 (2006): 589–617.

Kamen, Vicki S., and Charmine E. J. Härtel. "Gender Differences in Anticipated Pay Negotiation Strategies and Outcomes." *Journal of Business and Psychology* 9 (1994): 183–197.

Kanter, Rosabeth Moss. *Men and Women of the Corporation.* New York: Basic Books, 1977.

Kawakami, Christine, Judith B. White, and Ellen J. Langer. "Mindful and Masculine: Freeing Women Leaders from the Constraints of Gender Roles." *Journal of Social Issues* 56, no. 1 (2000): 49–63.

Kay, Katty, and Claire Shipman. *The Confidence Code: The Science and Art of Self-Assurance— What Women Should Know.* New York: HarperCollins, 2014.

Klos, Diana Mitsu. "The Status of Women in the US Media 2013." Women's Media Center, 2013. Accessed May 18, 2014, https://s3.amazonaws.com/wmc.3cdn.net/51113ed5df3e0d 0b79_zzzm6go0b.pdf.

Kolb, Deborah M. "Are We Becoming Part of the Problem? Gender Stereotypes in Negotiation Research." *Negotiation and Conflict Management Research* 5, no. 2 (2012): 127–135.

Kolb, Deborah M. "Corporate Ombudsman and Organization Conflict Resolution." *Journal of Conflict Resolution* 31, no. 4 (1987): 673–691.

Kolb, Deborah M. "Women's Work: Peacemaking in Organizations." In *Hidden Conflict in Organizations: Uncovering Behind-the-Scenes Disputes,* edited by Deborah M. Kolb and Jean Bartunek. Thousand Oaks, CA: SAGE, 1992.

Kolb, Deborah M., and Gloria Coolidge. "Her Place at the Table." In *Negotiation Theory and Practice,* edited by J. W. Breslin and J. Z. Rubin, 261–277. Cambridge, MA: PON Books, 1991.

Kolb, Deborah, Joyce Fletcher, Debra Meyerson, Deborah Merrill-Sands, and Robin J. Ely. "Making Change: A Framework for Promoting Gender Equity in Organizations." In *Reader in Gender, Work, and Organization,* edited by Robin J. Ely, Erica Gabrielle Foldy, and Maureen A. Scully, 10–15. Oxford: Blackwell Publishing, 1998.

Kolb, Deborah M., Lisa Jensen, and Vonda L. Shannon. "She Said It All Before, or What Did We Miss about Ms. Follett in the Library?" *Organization* 3, no. 1 (1996): 153–160.

Kolb, Deborah M., and Kathleen L. McGinn. "Beyond Gender and Negotiation to Gendered Negotiations" (Working Paper). Boston: Harvard Business School, 2008.

Kolb, Deborah M., and Deborah Merrill-Sands. "Waiting for Outcomes: Anchoring a Dual Agenda for Change to Cultural Assumptions." *Women in Management Review* 14, no. 5 (1999): 194–203.

Kolb, Deborah M., and Debra Meyerson. "Keeping Gender in the Plot: A Case Study of the Body Shop." *Gender at Work: Organizational Change for Equality,* edited by Aruna Rao, Rieky Stuart, and David Kelleher, 129–155. Boulder, CO: Kumarian Press, 1999.

Kolb, Deborah M., and Judith Williams. *Everyday Negotiation: Navigating the Hidden Agendas in Bargaining.* San Francisco: Jossey-Bass, 2003.

Kolb, Deborah M., Judith Williams, and Carol Frohlinger. *Her Place at the Table: A Woman's Guide to Negotiating Five Key Challenges to Leadership Success.* San Francisco: Jossey-Bass, 2010.

Kray, Laura J., and Michele J. Gelfand. "Relief versus Regret: The Effect of Gender and Negotiating Norm Ambiguity on Reactions to Having One's First Offer Accepted." *Social Cognition* 27, no. 3 (2009): 418–436.

Kray, Laura J., Jessica A. Kennedy, and Alex B. Van Zant. "Not Competent Enough to Know the Difference? Gender Stereotypes about Women's Ease of Being Misled Predict Negotiator Deception." *Organizational Behavior and Human Decision Processes*, 2014. http://dx.doi.org/10.1016/j.obhdp.2014.06.002.

Kray, Laura J., and Thompson, L. "Gender Stereotypes and Negotiation Performance: A Review of Theory and Research." *Research in Organizational Behavior* 26 (2005): 103–182.

Kulik, Carol T., and Mara Olekalns. "Negotiating the Gender Divide Lessons from the Negotiation and Organizational Behavior Literatures." *Journal of Management* 38, no. 4 (2012): 1387–1415.

Lakin, Jessica L., and Tanya L. Chartrand. "Using Nonconscious Behavioral Mimicry to Create Affiliation and Rapport." *Psychological Science* 14, no. 4 (2003): 334–339.

Langer, Ellen. *Mindfulness.* Boston: Da Capo Press, 1990.

Lax, David A., and James K. Sebenius. *The Manager as Negotiator: Bargaining for Cooperation and Competitive Gain.* New York: Free Press, 1986.

Lax, David A., and James K. Sebenius. *3-D Negotiation: Powerful Tools to Change the Game in Your Most Important Deals.* Boston: Harvard Business Review Press, 2006.

Liebert, Robert M., William P. Smith, J. H. Hill, and Miriam Keiffer. "The Effects of Information and Magnitude of Initial Offer on Interpersonal Negotiation." *Journal of Experimental Social Psychology* 4, no. 4 (1968): 431–441.

Liljenquist, Katie A., and Adam D. Galinsky. "Turn Your Adversary into Your Advocate." *Negotiation Newsletter* 10, no. 6 (June 2007): 4–6.

Lyness, Karen S., and Donna E. Thompson. "Climbing the Corporate Ladder: Do Female and Male Executives Follow the Same Route?" *Journal of Applied Psychology* 85, no. 1 (2000): 86–101.

Magee, Joe C., Adam D. Galinsky, and Deborah H. Gruenfeld. "Power, Propensity to Negotiate, and Moving First in Competitive Interactions." *Personality and Social Psychology Bulletin* 33, no. 2 (2007): 200–212.

Major, Brenda, and Ellen Konar. "An Investigation of Sex Differences in Pay Expectations and Their Possible Causes." *Academy of Management Journal* 27, no. 4 (1984): 777–792.

Malhotra, Deepak, and Max Bazerman. *Negotiation Genius: How to Overcome Obstacles and Achieve Brilliant Results at the Bargaining Table and Beyond.* New York: Random House, 2007.

Martell, Richard F., David M. Lane, and Cynthia Emrich. "Male-Female Differences: A Computer Simulation." *American Psychologist* 51(1996): 157–158.

Martin, Beth Ann. "Gender Differences in Salary Expectations When Current Salary Information Is Provided." *Psychology of Women Quarterly* 13, no. 1 (1989): 87–96.

McGinn, Kathleen L., and Angela T. Keros. "Improvisation and the Logic of Exchange in Socially Embedded Transactions." *Administrative Science Quarterly* 47, no. 3 (2002): 442–473.

McGinn, Kathleen L., Elizabeth Long Lingo, and Karin Ciano. "Transitions through Out of Keeping Acts." *Negotiation Journal* 20, no. 2 (2004): 171–184.

McGuire, Gail M. "Gender, Race, and the Shadow Structure: A Study of Informal Networks and Inequality in a Work Organization." *Gender and Society* 16, no. 3 (2002): 303–322.

McKeon, Nancy, "Women in the House Get a Restroom." *Washington Post,* July 28, 2008. http://www.washingtonpost.com/lifestyle/style/women-in-the-house-get-a-restroom/2011/07/28/gIQAFgdwfl_story.html.

McPherson, M., Smith-Lovin, L., and Cook, J. "Birds of a Feather: Homophily in Social Networks." *Annual Review of Sociology* 27 (2001): 415–444.

Meyerson, Debra. *Tempered Radicals: How Everyday Leaders Inspire Change at Work*. Boston: Harvard Business Press, 2003.

Meyerson, Debra, and Megan Tompkins. "Tempered Radicals as Institutional Change Agents: The Case of Advancing Gender Equity at the University of Michigan." *Harvard Journal of Law and Gender* 30 (2007): 303–322.

Miles, Edward W. "Developing Strategies for Asking Questions in Negotiation." *Negotiation Journal* 29 (2013): 383–412.

Miles, Edward W. "Gender Differences in Distributive Negotiation: When in the Negotiation Process Do the Differences Occur?" *European Journal of Social Psychology* 40, no. 7 (2010): 1200–1211.

Miller, Claire Cain. "The Motherhood Penalty versus the Fatherhood Bonus: A Child Helps Your Career, if You're a Man." Accessed March 3, 2014, http://www.nytimes.com/2014/09/07/upshot/a-child-helps-your-career-if-youre-a-man.html?ref=business&_r=0&abt=0002&abg=1.

Miller, Jean Baker. *Toward a New Psychology of Women*. Boston: Beacon Press, 1976.

Mislin, Alexandra A., Brooke A. Shaughnessy, Tanja Hentschel, and Claudia Peus. "Should We Chit-Chat? Benefits of Small Talk for Male but not Female Negotiators." Presentation at the Academy of Management Annual Meeting, Philadelphia, PA, August 2014.

Mitchell, Sara McLaughlin, and Vicki L. Hesli. "Women Don't Ask? Women Don't Say No? Bargaining and Service in the Political Science Profession." *PS: Political Science and Politics* 46, no. 2 (2013): 355–369.

Mizruchi, Mark S., and Linda Brewster Stearns. "Getting Deals Done: The Use of Social Networks in Bank Decision-Making." *American Sociological Review* 66 (2001): 647–671.

Mnookin, Robert H. "Why Negotiations Fail: An Exploration of Barriers to the Resolution of Conflict." *Ohio State Journal on Dispute Resolution* 8, no. 2 (1993): 235–249.

Mnookin, Robert H., Scott R. Peppet, and Andrew S. Tulumello. *Beyond Winning: Negotiating to Create Value in Deals and Disputes*. Cambridge, MA: Harvard University Press, 2000.

Mnookin, Robert H., Scott R. Peppet, and Andrew S. Tulumello. "The Tension between Empathy and Assertiveness." *Negotiation Journal* 12, no. 3 (1996): 217–230.

Murphy, Evelyn, with E. J. Graff. *Getting Even: Why Women Don't Get Paid Like Men—and What to Do about It*. New York: Touchstone, 2005.

Nadler, Janice. "Build Rapport—and a Better Deal." *Negotiation Newsletter* 10, no. 3 (March 2007): 9–11.

Neale, Margaret A., and Max H. Bazerman. "The Effects of Framing and Negotiator Overconfidence on Bargaining Behaviors and Outcomes." *Academy of Management Journal* 28, no. 1 (1985): 34–49.

Negotiation Newsletter. "Are You Prepared for Dirty Tricks?" Program on Negotiation, Harvard Law School, vol. 13, no. 8 (August 2010): 1–4.

Negotiation Newsletter. "Beyond Walking Away: Facing Difficult Negotiation Tactics Head-On." Program on Negotiation, Harvard Law School, vol. 17, no. 5 (May 2014): 1–4.

Negotiation Newsletter. "How Body Language Affects Negotiation." Program on Negotiation, Harvard Law School, vol. 11, no. 11 (November 2008): 4–7.

Negotiation Newsletter. "How to Build Trust at the Bargaining Table." Program on Negotiation, Harvard Law School, vol. 12, no. 1 (January 2009): 1–3.

Negotiation Newsletter. "Lessons from the New Wave of High-Stakes Deals." Program on Negotiation, Harvard Law School, vol. 16, no 5 (May 2013): 1–3.

Negotiation Newsletter. "Manage Your Anxiety and Overconfidence." Program on Negotiation, Harvard Law School, vol. 14, no. 12 (December 2011): 1–4.

Negotiation Newsletter. "To Capture the Force, Be Patient." Program on Negotiation, Harvard Law School, vol. 16, no. 6 (June 2013): 1–4.

Newman, Helen M. "The Sounds of Silence in Communicative Encounters." *Communication Quarterly* 30, no. 2 (1982): 142–149.

O'Donnell, Liz. *Mogul, Mom and Maid: The Balancing Act of the Modern Woman.* Brookline, MA: Bibliomotion, 2014.

Paul, Gina, Barb Elam, and Steven J. Verhulst. "A Longitudinal Study of Students' Perceptions of Using Deep-Breathing Meditation to Reduce Testing Stresses." *Teaching and Learning in Medicine* 19, no. 3 (2007): 287–292.

Perlow, Leslie. *Sleeping with Your Smartphone: How to Break the 24/7 Habit and Change the Way You Work.* Cambridge, MA: Harvard Business Press, 2012.

Perlow, Leslie A., and Jessica L. Porter. "Making Time Off Predictable—and Required." *Harvard Business Review* 87, no. 10 (2009): 102–109.

Pfeffer, Jeffrey. "You're Still the Same: Why Theories of Power Hold over Time and across Contexts." *Academy of Management Perspectives* 27, no. 4 (November 2013): 269–280.

Podolny, Joel M., and James N. Baron. "Resources and Relationships: Social Networks and Mobility in the Workplace." *American Sociological Review* 62 (1997): 673–693.

Pruitt, Dean. *Negotiation Behavior.* New York: Academic Press, 1981.

Purcell, David, Kelly Rhea MacArthur, and Sarah Samblanet. "Gender and the Glass Ceiling at Work." *Sociology Compass* 4, no. 9 (2010): 705–717.

Putnam, Linda L. "Transformations and Critical Moments in Negotiations." *Negotiation Journal* 20, no. 2 (2004): 275–295.

Quindlen, Anna. "Say Goodbye to the Virago." *Newsweek,* June 16, 2003.

Rackham, Neil, and John Carlisle. "The Effective Negotiator—Part I: The Behaviour of Successful Negotiators." *Journal of European Industrial Training* 2, no. 6 (1978): 6–11.

Ragins, Belle Rose, and Kathy E. Kram, eds. *The Handbook of Mentoring at Work: Theory, Research and Practice.* Thousand Oaks, CA: SAGE, 2007.

Raiffa, Howard. *The Art and Science of Negotiation.* Cambridge, MA: Belknap Press, 1985.

Ramarajan, Lakshmi, Kathleen L. McGinn, and Deborah Kolb. "An Outside-Inside Evolution in Gender and Professional Work" (Working Paper). Boston: Harvard Business School, 2012.

Rapoport, Rhona, Lotte Bailyn, Joyce K. Fletcher, and Bettye H. Pruitt. *Beyond Work-Family Balance: Advancing Gender Equity and Workplace Performance.* San Francisco: Jossey-Bass, 2001.

Rapoport, Rhona, Lotte Bailyn, Deborah Kolb and Joyce K. Fletcher. *Relinking Life and Work: Toward a Better Future.* Pegasus Communications, 1998.

Reskin, Barbara F., and Debra Branch McBrier. "Why Not Ascription? Organizations' Employment of Male and Female Managers." *American Sociological Review* 65, no. 2 (2000): 210–233.

Ridgeway, Cecelia L. "Gender, Status, and Leadership." *Journal of Social Issues* 57, no. 4 (2001): 637–655.

Roth, Louise Marie. *Selling Women Short: Gender and Money on Wall Street.* Princeton, NJ: Princeton University Press, 2006.

Roth, Louise Marie. "The Social Psychology of Tokenism: Status and Homophily Processes on Wall Street." *Sociological Perspectives* 42, no. 2 (2004): 189–214.

Rubin, Jeffrey Z. "Negotiation: An Introduction to Some Issues and Themes." *American Behavioral Scientist* 27, no. 2 (1983): 135–147.

Ryan, Michelle K., and S. Alexander Haslam. "The Glass Cliff: Exploring the Dynamics Surrounding the Appointment of Women to Precarious Leadership Positions." *Academy of Management Review* 32, no. 2 (2007): 549–572.

Salmon, Elizabeth, Laura Severance, Juliet Aiken, Michele Gelfand, Hannah Bowles, and Linda Babcock. "Negotiating to No: Gender and Resistance to Undesirable Requests." Paper presented at the Academy of Management Annual Meeting, San Antonio, TX, August 2011.

Sandberg, Sheryl. *Lean In: Women, Work, and the Will to Lead.* New York: Random House, 2013.

Schneider, Andrea Kupfer. "Aspirations in Negotiation." *Marquette Law Review* 87, no. 4 (2004): 675–680.

Sebenius, James K. "Are You Ready for the 'Hardest Question?'" *Negotiation Newsletter* 15, no. 11 (November 2012): 4–5.

Sebenius, James K., and Rebecca Hulse. "Charlene Barshefsky (B)." Harvard Business School Case, March 2001, 801–922.

Sebenius, James K., and Kristin Schneeman. "Lakhdar Bramimi—Negotiating a New Government for Afghanistan." Harvard Law School Program on Negotiation. Accessed May 18, 2014, http://www.pon.harvard.edu/shop/great-negotiator-case-study-series-lakhdar-brahimi -negotiating-a-new-government-for-afghanistan/.

Seidel, Marc-David L., Jeffrey T. Polzer, and Katherine J. Stewart. "Friends in High Places: The Effects of Social Networks on Discrimination in Salary Negotiations." *Administrative Science Quarterly* 45, no. 1 (2000): 1–24.

Shell, G. Richard. *Bargaining for Advantage: Negotiation Strategies for Reasonable People.* New York: Penguin, 2006.

Small, Deborah A., Linda Babcock, Michele Gelfand, and Hilary Gettman. "Who Goes to the Bargaining Table? The Influence of Gender and Framing on the Initiation of a Negotiation." *Journal of Personality and Social Psychology* 93, no. 4 (2007): 600–613.

Solnick, Sara J. "Gender Differences in the Ultimatum Game." *Economic Inquiry* 39, no. 2 (2001): 189–200.

Stein, Janice Gross, ed. *Getting to the Table: Process of International Prenegotiation.* Baltimore, MD: Johns Hopkins University Press, 1989.

Stephan, Walter G., and Krystina Finlay. "The Role of Empathy in Improving Intergroup Relations." *Journal of Social Issues* 55, no. 4 (1999): 729–743.

Stevens, Carl M. *Strategy and Collective Bargaining Negotiation.* Westport, CT: Greenwood Press, 1978.

Stevens, Cynthia Kay, Anna G. Bavetta, and Marilyn E. Gist. "Gender Differences in the Acquisition of Salary Negotiation Skills: The Role of Goals, Self-Efficacy, and Perceived Control." *Journal of Applied Psychology* 78, no. 5 (1993): 722–735.

Stone, Douglas, Bruce Patton, and Sheila Heen. *Difficult Conversations: How to Discuss What Matters Most.* New York: Penguin, 2010.

Stuhlmacher, Alice F., and Amy E. Walters. "Gender Differences in Negotiation Outcome: A Meta Analysis." *Personnel Psychology* 52, no. 3 (1999): 653–677.

Sturm, Susan. "The Architecture of Inclusion: Advancing Workplace Equity in Higher Education." *Harvard Journal of Law and Gender* 29 (2006): 247–334.

Sturm, Susan. "Negotiating Workplace Equality: A Systemic Approach." *Negotiation and Conflict Management Research* 2, no. 1 (2009): 92–106.

Strauss, Anselm. *Negotiations: Varieties, Contexts, Processes, and Social Order.* San Francisco: Jossey-Bass, 1978.

Susskind, Lawrence. *Good for You, Great for Me: Finding the Trading Zone and Winning at Win-Win Negotiation.* New York: Public Affairs, 2014.

Taylor, Paul, and William Donohue. "Hostage Negotiation Opens Up." In *The Negotiator's Fieldbook,* edited by Andrea Kupfer Schneider and Christopher Honeyman, 667–674. Washington, DC: American Bar Association, 2006.

Thompson, Leigh L. *The Mind and Heart of the Negotiator,* 5th ed. Upper Saddle River, NJ: Prentice Hall, 2011.

Ury, William. *Getting Past No: Negotiating in Difficult Situations.* New York: Bantam, 1993.

Ury, William. *The Power of a Positive No: How to Say No and Still Get to Yes.* New York: Random House, 2007.

Ury, William L., Jeanne M. Brett, and Stephen B. Goldberg. *Getting Disputes Resolved: Designing Systems to Cut the Costs of Conflict.* San Francisco: Jossey-Bass, 1988.

Vesterlund, Lise, Linda Babcock, and Laurie Weingart. "Breaking the Glass Ceiling with 'No': Gender Differences in Declining Requests for Non-Promotable Tasks." Carnegie Mellon Working Paper, Pittsburgh, PA, 2013.

Walton, Richard E., and Robert B. McKersie. *A Behavioral Theory of Labor Negotiations: An Analysis of a Social Interaction System.* New York: McGraw-Hill, 1965.

Walters, Amy E., Alice F. Stuhlmacher, and Lia L. Meyer. "Gender and Negotiator Competitiveness: A Meta Analysis." *Organizational Behavior and Human Decision Processes,* 76 (1998): 1–29.

Watson, Carol. "Gender versus Power as a Predictor of Negotiation Behavior and Outcomes." *Negotiation Journal* 10, no. 2 (1994): 117–127.

Watson, Carol, and L. Richard Hoffman. "Managers as Negotiators: A Test of Power vs. Gender as Predictors of Feelings, Behaviors and Outcomes." *Leadership Quarterly* 7, no. 1 (1996): 63–86.

Weick, Karl E. "Small Wins: Redefining the Scale of Social Problems." *American Psychologist* 39, no. 1 (1984): 40–49.

Weirup, Amanda Plummer. "Favors Feel Different for Females: Gender Differences in the Cognition and Emotion of Favor Deliberation." PhD diss., Carnegie Mellon University, Pittsburgh, PA, 2008.

Wells, Leroy, Jr. "The Group as a Whole: A Systematic Socioanalytic Perspective on Interpersonal and Group Relations." In *Groups in Context: A New Perspective on Group Dynamics,* edited by Jonathon Gillette and Marion McCollom. Lanham, MD: University Press of America, 1995.

Wex, Michael. *Just Say Nu: Yiddish for Every Occasion (When English Just Won't Do).* New York: Macmillan, 2007.

Wharton, Amy S. *The Sociology of Gender: An Introduction to Theory and Research.* Malden, MA: Blackwell, 2005.

Wheeler, Michael. "Anxious Moments: Openings in Negotiation." *Negotiation Journal* 20, no. 2 (2004): 153–169.

Wheeler, Michael. *The Art of Negotiation: How to Improvise Agreement in a Chaotic World.* New York: Simon & Schuster, 2013.

White, Sally Blount, and Margaret A. Neale. "Reservation Prices, Resistance Points, and BATNAs: Determining the Parameters of Acceptable Negotiated Outcomes." *Negotiation Journal* 7, no. 4 (1991): 379–388.

White House. "Expanding Opportunity for All: Ensuring Equal Pay for Women and Promoting the Women's Economic Agenda" (Fact Sheet). Washington, DC, April 1, 2014.

Williams, Joan C., and Amy J. C. Cuddy. "Will Working Mothers Take Your Company to Court?" *Harvard Business Review* 90, no. 9 (September 2012): 94–100.

Williams, Joan C., and Rachel Dempsey. *What Works for Women at Work: Four Patterns Working Women Need to Know.* New York: New York University Press, 2014.

Woolf, Virginia. *Mrs. Dalloway.* Tonawanda, NY: Broadview Press, 2012.

Zartman, William. "Prenegotiation: Phases and Functions." In *Getting to the Table: The Processes of International Prenegotiation,* edited by Janice Gross Stein. Baltimore, MD: Johns Hopkins University Press, 1989.

INDEX

Bring Deborah Kolb in to Work with You and Your Organization

Negotiating at Work author Deborah M. Kolb is a foremost authority on leadership, negotiation, and gender.

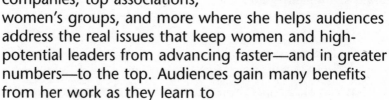

Deborah—a globally recognized advisor to many of today's most senior women and organizations—is a revered professor, acclaimed author, and media commentator.

Deborah is also an in-demand speaker to Fortune 1000 companies, top associations, women's groups, and more where she helps audiences address the real issues that keep women and high-potential leaders from advancing faster—and in greater numbers—to the top. Audiences gain many benefits from her work as they learn to

- Understand the hidden barriers that often go unrecognized in organizations
- Develop new concrete strategies and skills required to navigate these barriers
- Secure wins for high potential leaders and those around them that become big gains for the organization as a whole

For more, including details on Deborah's latest keynotes and availability, contact her directly at DMK@DeborahMKolb.com.

Bring Jessica L. Porter
to Your Organization

Negotiating at Work coauthor Jessica L. Porter is an expert on gender and leadership.

Jessica consults with companies and organizations to create change and advance women by connecting research with practice. She works with clients to develop customized programs and strategies to help ensure talented women make it to the top. Her clients range from Fortune 500 companies to international NGOs.

Jessica is a dynamic speaker available to women's groups, corporate audiences, and local women's networks. Her focus is on helping women navigate often-invisible barriers to leadership. She emphasizes practical strategies and tools to negotiate for success so women can advance their own careers while creating value for their organizations.

For more information on Jessica's availability, visit her website at www.JessicaLPorter.com or contact her directly at jp@JessicaLPorter.com.